About Island Press

ISLAND PRESS, a nonprofit organization, publishes, markets, and distributes the most advanced thinking on the conservation of our natural resources—books about soil, land, water, wildlife, and hazardous and toxic wastes. These books are practical tools used by public officials, business and industry leaders, natural resource managers, and concerned citizens working to solve both local and global resource problems.

Founded in 1978, Island Press reorganized in 1984 to meet the increasing demand for substantive books on all resource-related issues. Island Press publishes and distributes under its own imprint and offers these services to other nonprofit organizations.

Support for Island Press is provided by Apple Computer, Inc., Geraldine R. Dodge Foundation, The Energy Foundation, The George Gund Foundation, William and Flora Hewlett Foundation, The Joyce Foundation, The John D. and Catherine MacArthur Foundation, The Andrew W. Mellon Foundation, The Joyce Mertz-Gilmore Foundation, The New-Land Foundation, The J. N. Pew, Jr. Charitable Trust, Alida Rockefeller, The Rockefeller Brothers Fund, The Rockefeller Foundation, The Florence and John Schumann Foundation, The Tides Foundation, and individual donors.

Understanding Environmental Administration and Law

UNDERSTANDING
ENVIRONMENTAL
ADMINISTRATION
AND LAW

Susan J. Buck

Foreword by R. W. Behan

ISLAND PRESS

Washington, D.C. • *Covelo, California*

Library of Congress Cataloging-in-Publication Data

Buck, Susan J.
    Understanding environmental administration and law/Susan J. Buck.
        p.   cm.
    Includes bibliographical references and index.
    ISBN 1-55963-020-5 (cloth).—ISBN 1-55963-021-3 (paper)
    1. Environmental law—United States. I. Title.
KF3775.B83 1991
344.73'046—dc20
[347.30446]

                                                                91-15608
                                                                CIP

Printed on recycled, acid-free paper

Manufactured in the United States of America
10 9 8 7 6 5 4 3 2 1

To Albert K. Chase, Jr.

CONTENTS

FOREWORD

This book will be an invaluable resource for people who take an active interest in the status, the inevitable stressing, and the professional nurture of the biophysical environment. Natural-resource managers, environmental administrators, officials and executives, members and leaders of environmental organizations, students in undergraduate environmental programs, and concerned citizens will find in Susan Buck's book an accessible, intelligent clarification of the nature and substance of environmental law, and of the processes of making and executing it.

Many readers are anxious about environmental lawsuits—anxious to enter them, to avoid them, or to support one side or the other. Lawsuits seem to be the endgame of jurisprudence.

All will be well served by Professor Buck's conscientious work in assembling the relevant laws and discussing their administration and their several purposes. Citizens, affiliated with effective environmental organizations and inclined to litigate, will find here the statutory bases for litigation.

The importance of these bases is often overlooked by the legally naive. Outraged by the Reagan administration's gleeful and wholesale transfer of public wealth, in the form of energy resources, to equally gleeful private, largely corporate, recipients, I once indulged in such naiveté. I phoned a Washington acquaintance, an attorney of demonstrated competence in environmental litigation. "Why don't you sue James Watt?" I demanded.

"Why? Has he done something illegal?" my friend inquired.

The Mineral Leasing Act of 1920, I knew, did not encourage—but neither did it prohibit—Mr. Watt's massive leasing of coal, offshore oil, and shale resources to the energy companies at shamelessly discounted prices.

"No," I replied.

"Then we can't sue him, can we?"

Had I understood then the *nature* of law as well as I understood some of its substance—had I absorbed the knowledge contained in this book, for example—I might have avoided the embarrassing reply I was forced to make to my friend: "No, if he hasn't broken the law, we can't sue him." *Understanding Environmental*

Administration and Law can be seen as a handbook for those intent on litigation but uncertain as to the fundamental questions of why and how.

The book's value to prospective defendants, of course, will be equally great. Administrators of environmental laws and managers of environmental resources will find here much of what they need to know to avoid legal complaints or, failing that, to deal with the plaintiffs who file the complaints.

I suppose it would be courteous, at this point, to explicate my own biases. As an educator of professional foresters, my appreciation and sympathies for the task of resource management remain strong, though I maintain some firm convictions respecting the limits of expertise. And I am moderately predisposed to endorse Shakespeare's dictum about killing all the lawyers.

One can hardly avoid, in 1991, the discomforting feeling that environmental management has crossed some sort of threshold into an era of juridical gridlock. If resource managers hew strictly to the entire corpus of procedural law, they will not have time, energy, staff, or budget for the execution of substantive law. Doing things right—the focus of procedural law—will probably always compromise to some degree the doing of right things, which is arguably the purpose of substantive law. Lawyers defend the one while managers pursue the other; and the antipathy I share with the managers is easily understood.

Complaining about jurisprudence to those schooled in its practice is not productive, I have concluded, even at the margin. Litigation is a zero-sum game, I would argue, in which the benefits accorded the winner equal the costs borne by the loser. Both sides have incurred substantial legal fees (it is well known that "the lawyers never lose"), an exchange has taken place—but Pareto optimality is unchanged: society at large enjoys no net increase in welfare. Whereupon my attorney friends challenge me to design a better system for the conduct of social affairs. Whereupon the argument ends; I cannot.

In the honored and honorable custom of settling out of court, however, I believe there lies an appealing escape. When compromises are bargained or negotiated between the competing parties, the game is transformed into one with a positive-sum outcome. Everyone wins something. Settling out of court is guaranteed, of course, if managers can stay out of court; and the way to do that is simple in principle, though perhaps difficult in practice.

In order to do right things, managers must do things right enough to avoid litigation. And that will call for extraordinarily good judgment; sufficiency calls are difficult to make. A careful reading and retention of *Understanding Environmental Administration and Law* will aid immensely in the birth and nurture of that judgment.

Among other themes, Professor Buck argues persuasively that environmental administration is not merely a technical matter but also, perhaps preeminently, an activity that is intensely political. Professional resource managers will grudgingly agree, since they frequently complain about "politics," going along with the stereotypical view that their science and technique will inevitably have to yield to a politician's compulsive pursuit of job security.

Counteracting the stereotype is not the least of this book's virtues. In proclaiming the political nature of environmental administration, Dr. Buck invites the manager to embrace and refine the political skills of negotiating, bargaining, and compromise, in order to engineer settlements without litigation—settlements that are, by definition, out of court. And she invites constituent groups to expect that behavior from managers and to participate in what is, after all, a parapolitical process.

Failure in this process—that is to say, a rush to litigation—is more likely if managers are timid. Many actions taken by environmental administrators (and many deliberate inactions, for that matter) can be challenged as illegal, I believe. If administrators merely seek passively and in isolation to execute laws, they will be intimidated indeed. If instead they seek creatively and proactively to solve problems and seize opportunities to enhance the common weal, they will inevitably stimulate the participation of affected publics, and negotiated settlements can be constructed. And that is not a bad description of a political process.

Paul Appleby, a student of public administration whose name only scholars of my vintage will recognize, asserted nearly fifty years ago that administration *is* political. Susan Buck has said it again, in a time with perhaps a great deal more at stake—if the survivability of the environment (or survivability in the environment) is more than an ephemeral issue. It is an important message for environmental managers and concerned citizens to hear, to heed, and to exploit. *Understanding Environmental Administration and Law* is timely and provocative. It deserves to be carefully read.

R. W. Behan
Professor of Forest Policy
School of Forestry
Northern Arizona University

PREFACE

This book springs from two basic premises. The first is that environmental managers need to understand the legal context of their work, and the second is that existing books are inadequate to the task.

Of course, most environmental managers understand the laws and regulations affecting their own jobs. However, they usually view these as constraints on their own autonomy. As the Boatman in *A Man for All Seasons* says, lamenting that the fee is the same for rowing upstream as down: "Whoever makes the regulations doesn't row a boat." Most managers are taught their professional and scientific disciplines first, and their training for administration is on-the-job training. Thus they learn the "right" way to measure floodways or to harvest trees, and when state budgetary constraints preserve inaccurate maps or leave a prime stand of trees uncut, managers are outraged—they have not been taught that political factors are as valid a basis for decision making as scientific measurements are.

Setting aside the question of whether political issues *ought* to be considered, the fact remains that they *are* considered. Good managers need to understand how the legal and political process operates, in order to anticipate political changes and perhaps to channel their impacts in ways that are helpful to their own professional goals.

Environmental managers deal with the law every day. At the very highest level, statutes and executive orders define the boundaries of job responsibilities. At the lowest level, rules and regulations provide guidance and at times restrictions on bureaucratic activities. Somewhere in between is the middle manager, that fabled creature who must translate the larger commands into operations. At the middle manager's level, the law is both friend and master. The law is *flexible*, and a good manager learns how to use it to achieve the organization's policy goals.

Typically the middle manager has come up through the technical ranks and, as a reward for good technical skills, has become an administrator. At this point the infamous Peter Principle may come into play: employees rise to their level of incompetence. Administration is a skill, as much art as science, and it has its own special tools. One of the most important tools for an environmental manager is the law.

My second premise was that existing books do not provide an adequate explanation of the legal process for environmental managers. Of course, there are many excellent books on environmental law.* These are, however, casebooks suitable for law students; they do not provide insights into the practical application of law for managers. For example, in the case of *National Audubon Society v. Department of Water and Power of the City of Los Angeles* (1983), a California court held that a public trust protected the waters of Mono Lake. Los Angeles was required, under this decision, to reconsider its use of water from the lake. To a lawyer, this case is of great legal interest. To an employee of the Los Angeles water department, the case is a nightmare, providing no useful guidelines as to whether, when, or how water may still be diverted from Mono Lake for the urgent water supply needs of the city.

The purpose of this book is to show how the policy process is infused with the legal process. I hope to demystify the law, to translate it from the law books, and to make it accessible to the non-lawyer. The law is like chess: a finite number of pieces, each with its own moves, resulting in infinite combinations and strategies. Here I hope the readers will find the pieces pictured and the moves defined. They must play their own game.

---

*Especially noteworthy are *Environmental Law*, vols. 1 and 2 by Jackson Battle, and vol. 3 by Mark Squillace (Cincinnati: Anderson Publishing Co., 1986 and 1988), and *Environmental Policy Law* by Thomas Schoenbaum (Mineola, N.Y.: Foundation Press, 1985).

ACKNOWLEDGMENTS

Several students helped with the research for this book. David Cushing's work was essential; without his efforts with interlibrary loan, the manuscript would have been years late. Dana Dooley prepared the bibliography and list of cases, saving me much time and trouble. Megan Schmid provided the full citations for the statutes. Three other students, Jeff Bimmer, Paul Bivens, and Joe Morgan, chose to write annotated bibliographies for this book in lieu of research papers; their excellent research eased my own task considerably.

I am especially grateful to two colleagues, Marlene Gaither and Harley Hiett, who wrote about actual cases to help present the practitioner's view of environmental law.

Understanding Environmental Administration and Law

CHAPTER ONE

THE AMERICAN LEGAL SYSTEM

Legal scholars over the centuries have offered many definitions of law. A definition that meets with the approval of most Americans is that of the nineteenth-century jurist John Austin: the law is the command of the sovereign backed by a sanction. In other words, the law is whatever the government says it is, and if we choose not to comply, the government will punish us. For citizens whose encounters with the law are largely limited to traffic police or the IRS, such a definition is adequate. But citizens whose daily work is bounded by a governmental structure of rules and regulations see more to the law than simply commands. Who gives the sovereign the right to issue commands? Are there areas of public or private endeavor in which the sovereign has no right to issue commands? What is the range of penalties for noncompliance? Does it matter if the noncompliance is accidental, or unavoidable? How does a citizen *discover* the latest governmental command?

All of these questions are pertinent to environmental managers. The scope of their administrative authority and the intent of the legislature in giving them that authority are important parameters. Managers in regulatory enforcement must know when they may or should compromise and when they must bring their full enforcement powers to bear on a violator. Resource managers must maintain the delicate balance between resource protection and resource use. Their arsenal is not restricted to the "sanctions" of the sovereign. They have persuasion, political pressure, and incentives on their side as well. To understand these managerial tools, managers must also understand the system in which they wield them.

This chapter explores the legal system in which American environmental managers must operate. The first section discusses the English roots of the American common law and how this body of law became accepted in the new United States. It also discusses the other sources of law: statutes, rules and regulations, and the Constitution. How judges apply the law is discussed in the second section. The impact of our complex federal system on environmental administration and law is discussed in the third section.

SOURCES OF LAW

In Western countries the law is based on one of two systems: the English common law or the European civil law. The simplest way to distinguish between these two systems is to look at the judicial decision-making process. In the civil-law system, the law is always spelled out in statutes. In deciding a case, the judge locates the appropriate statute and then applies it to the situation at hand. In the common-law system, by contrast, the judge bases his or her decision not only on the applicable statute but also on how appellate courts have interpreted the statute. In some areas of the common law there are no statutes, only rules set forth by appellate courts. The common-law system is based on the idea of precedent: a lower court must follow the decisions of an appellate court.

THE COMMON LAW

The common-law system developed in the thirteenth century. When the English feudal system began to weaken and the cities to develop, the kings appointed royal judges to decide controversies. This was done primarily to increase the king's power and authority as the power of the feudal lords waned. Each manor had its own customs, and the judges would weigh their own perceptions of fairness, the existing customs, and the political repercussions in reaching decisions. As we might expect, the decisions were often based on unclear reasoning, and similar cases might be decided differently. The clerks accompanying the judges began to record the decisions and the reasoning. Back at the palace the clerks compared notes, and gradually the judges started to refer to the decisions of their colleagues for guidance. Eventually the recording of decisions became regularized, and the judges were required to set out their reasoning for the formal record. Any deviation from precedent had to be justified. In this way the common law—the system of law common to the entire country—was established.

In the American colonies the judges based their decisions on the English common law.[1] At the time of the Revolution, there was debate about whether the new country would follow the English tradition; in some quarters the feelings were very strong that a complete break from England was the only correct approach. It was suggested that the common-law tradition be replaced by the civil-law system used by allies such as the French. Despite the radical proposals to change the law, the English system prevailed (except in Louisiana, a former French possession, which is still governed by a civil-law system). Colonial lawyers and judges had been trained in the common law, and contracts, property transfers, and all forms of legal transactions were already in the English style. Besides, despite the outpourings of anti-English sentiment immediately following the Revolution, most colonists still thought of themselves as English in spirit. Edmund Burke, the English statesman and philosopher, excused the American Revolution on the grounds that good Englishmen *should* rebel when treated unfairly. Common sense and common law prevailed, and the American legal system was based upon the English one.

One of the earliest environmental cases resting on common-law traditions was decided by the United States Supreme Court in 1842. *Martin v. Waddell* originated with the contention by a New Jersey riparian landowner, Waddell, that he had the exclusive right to take oysters from the Raritan River. He based his assertion on a grant made by King Charles in 1664 to the Duke of York, which gave the Duke "all the powers of government." Waddell claimed that his rights to the mudflats were directly descended from the property rights granted to the Duke of York. Waddell's opponent, Martin, argued that the king held certain resources (among them, mudflats) in trust for the people, and that the king's grant to the Duke of York required the duke to hold these resources in trust as well. Thus, despite language that might be interpreted otherwise, the duke did not have the power to transfer the mudflats to private ownership any more than the king did. The Supreme Court agreed with Martin that the original grant did not include the *exclusive* right to fish the adjacent waters.

Following the Revolution, the state of New Jersey had of course formed a new government. The Court therefore had to decide whether New Jersey was similarly prohibited from granting private, exclusive rights to lands that under common law were public-trust lands. Justice Taney held that the public-trust doctrine had survived the Revolution:

> [W]hen the people of New Jersey took possession of the reins of government, and took into their own hands the powers of sovereignty, the prerogatives and regalities which before belonged either to the

crown or the Parliament, became immediately and rightfully vested in the State.[2]

Although *Martin v. Waddell* is not the only case where the court articulated the continuance of English traditions, it is one of the clearest. Of course, the changing social and economic situation in the United States led to many diversions from the English law, but the basis was firmly established.

OTHER SOURCES OF AMERICAN LAW

In addition to the common law, which continues to develop, the sources of American law are statutes and ordinances, rules and regulations, and federal and state constitutions.

STATUTES AND ORDINANCES The formal acts of legislation passed by Congress or the state legislatures are known as statutes; similar enactments by county and city governments are known as ordinances. Sometimes statutes are very specific, setting, for example, the maximum permissible automobile emission levels. At other times, however, the legislatures establish broad guidelines and leave the details to the executive branch. This is done for several reasons. First, the legislators have neither the time nor the expertise to hammer out the details of implementation. Second, the legislative process is slow and cumbersome; it is designed that way so that the decisions are as free from circumstantial pressure as possible. Administrative actions are comparatively speedy, as will be seen in chapter 5. Finally, by passing the responsibility for detailed implementation to the executive branch, the legislature avoids some of the political repercussions of unpopular decisions. When the Bureau of Land Management (BLM) proposed raising the cost of federal-land grazing permits to market levels, the resulting firestorm engulfed the BLM bureaucrats and not the legislature that had given them the authority to raise fees.

RULES AND REGULATIONS Technically, under the U.S. Constitution only the Congress has the authority to make federal laws. However, the Congress has delegated some of its law-making authority to the executive agencies. From the late nineteenth century until the New Deal, the constitutionality of this legislative delegation of authority was questioned, and even today some commentators argue that the Congress in particular cannot give rule-making powers to the executive branch without very clear and restrictive guidelines. The federal agencies—and their state counterparts—thus have the power to make rules and regulations that have the force of law. These rules must meet two constitutional standards: *procedural due process* (Did the agency follow proper procedures in deciding the rules or regulations?) and *substantive due process* (Is the agency operating within the policy boundaries designated by the legislature?). These constitutional requirements will be discussed more fully in chapter 4. Any rule or regulation that is formulated with the proper procedures and is within the authority delegated to an agency has the same status as any piece of legislation passed by the legislature and signed by the executive.

THE CONSTITUTION The U.S. Constitution plays a vital part in environmental regulation. For example, the common urban practice of zoning raises the constitutional question of the "taking" of an individual's property. We are accustomed to thinking of zoning as a way to regulate and to protect the welfare and orderly development of a community. However, the Fifth Amendment clearly states: "No person shall . . . be deprived of life, liberty, or property, without due process of law; nor shall private property be taken for public use, without just compensation." Is zoning the equivalent of taking a person's property "for public use"? If the zoning significantly reduces the value of the property or makes it unusable, must the owner be compensated? Or does the act of zoning consitute "due process of law," so that no compensation need be paid? Until recent years, zoning has been consistently interpreted by the courts as a legitimate exercise of a state's police power: the obligation to protect public health, safety, and welfare. But court decisions in the 1980s have begun to find some forms of zoning to be a taking; this is partially a result of the increasing number of conservative justices now in the legal system following the Reagan years.

Another constitutional issue in environmental law is the legitimacy of agency rule making. The issue seemed to be settled with the passage of the Administrative Procedure Act in 1946. However, as the Supreme Court becomes more conservative, it may return to the position that Congress is neglecting its duties in delegating its legislative authority. Dissenting from the court's opinion in *American Textile Manufacturers v. Donovan* (1981), Justice William Rehnquist wrote that in delegating rule-making responsibility for cotton-dust standards to the Occupational Safety and Health Administration (OSHA),

> Congress simply abdicated its responsibility for the making of a fundamental and most difficult policy choice. . . . That is a "quintessential legislative" choice and must be made by the elected representative of the people, not by nonelected officials in the Executive Branch. . . . [I]n so doing Congress unconstitutionally delegated its legislative responsibility to the Executive Branch.[3]

Justice Antonin Scalia, while not ruling out such delegation of responsibility, is inclined to encourage Congress to give more precise policy directions to the agencies. The issue of delegation, far from having been settled in the middle of the twentieth century, seems likely to be contentious well into the twenty-first century.

Other constitutional issues arise with respect to agencies' procedures for appeals, investigations, and hearing procedures. These will be looked at again in the discussion of the Administrative Procedure Act in chapter 5.

JUDICIAL DECISION MAKING

In deciding the cases brought before them, judges are required to interpret the relevant statutes and regulations, to follow common-law precedents, and to apply constitutional principles. One of the more difficult areas for judicial review is statutory interpretation.

STATUTORY INTERPRETATION

When a citizen challenges official behavior with an accusation that the official has violated a statute, the first task is to determine just what the statute means. The court can do this by several techniques.

The court may examine the intent of the lawmakers as it is spelled out in the statute itself and as it is shown in the legislative history. The legislative history is the formal record of the evolution of the statute: testimony offered in support of or opposition to the statute, or to parts of the statute; the debates on the legislation; and the amendment sequence. This sounds relatively simple, but it may be a judicial morass. First, the testimony is often conflicting. Second, the debates are *real* debates, during which legislators may become convinced that the position of the opposition has merit. A legislator may express one opinion on one day and a different opinion on the next. The legislative history may thus record intentions that were ultimately abandoned. Third, the *Congressional Record*, which is the official record of these testimonies and debates, is given to the members for correction prior to publication. This was originally intended to allow members to correct slips of the tongue; but there is a temptation to edit with the home constituents in mind, and what is printed in the *Record* may bear only a superficial resemblance to what was said on the floor of the Congress.

In interpreting statutes, the courts also look at contemporary administrative interpretations. The courts presume that if an agency were very far off the mark in its application of the statute, the legislature would have corrected the mistake. In theory this is so, but in fact only those aberrations that are brought to the attention of an elected representative with both the interest to do something and the position within the legislature to accomplish it are likely to be corrected. The legislators are far too busy with new legislation, constituent services, and reelection to exercise constant oversight over all the administrative agencies.

The courts will consider nonlegislative changes that have taken place since the statute was enacted. For example, the Federal Communication Commission (FCC) was established long before cable television existed, but courts are required to determine the cable industry's compliance with the regulatory apparatus put in place by the FCC. The courts must look beyond the direct language of both the statute and the legislative history to find the *intent* of the legislature. Again, when the Forest Reserve Act was enacted in 1891, the legal concept of "endangered species" had not been imagined. In 1989 and 1990, the spotted owl controversy forced legislators, judges, and Forest Service administrators to reconcile the 1891 act with the requirements of the Endangered Species Act of 1973 in adjudicating the demands of the troubled logging industry and environmentalists.

The courts also examine past judicial opinions on the statute, partly to search out the reasoning of other courts (in obedience to the dictates of the common-law system) and partly again on the assumption that the legislature would move to correct any misplaced judicial opinions.

JUDICIAL PRECEDENTS

The theory underlying common-law interpretation is deceptively simple: judges determine the facts and then, finding previous cases with similar facts, reason from analogy to reach their conclusions. In practice, of course, this may be an amazingly complex process. Astute attorneys will find cases that parallel their client's position, while the opposing attorneys, working from the same set of facts, will offer cases which support an opposite conclusion. The judge must use discretion to choose between the competing precedents. If there are no applicable precedents, the judge may create a new rule to decide the case. This is why common-law decisions are often referred to as "judge-made" law.

APPLICATION OF CONSTITUTIONAL PRINCIPLES

In applying constitutional principles, the court must first consider the language of the Constitution itself. For example, the First Amendment states: "Congress shall make *no law* respecting an establishment of religion, or prohibiting the free exercise thereof; or abridging the freedom of speech, or of the press; or the right of the people peaceably to assemble, and to petition the Government for a redress of grievances" (emphasis added). The Supreme Court justices Hugo Black and William Douglas were known as absolutists because they insisted that "*no law* means *no law.*" Their colleagues on the bench disagreed, relying on another facet of constitutional interpretation: the intent of the Framers, as reflected in documents from the Constitutional Convention and the private and public papers of the men who wrote the Constitution. From these documents and papers it is clear that the Framers intended to protect only political speech and printed matter such as broadsheets and pamphlets. Probably the Framers would be surprised to find their amendment protecting obscene photographs and the *National Enquirer*.

Most judges and legal scholars agree that the Constitution is a living document whose interpretation must be allowed to change with changing conditions. For example, there is no right to privacy written into the Constitution, yet the Supreme Court has held that the Constitution confers such a right on all citizens. This right to privacy was first announced by Justice Douglas in *Griswold v. Connecticut* (1965), when he concluded that the guarantees in the Bill of Rights imply a right to privacy because they could not be achieved without it.

FEDERALISM

One of the most important characteristics of our political system often gets lost in our focus on national government activities. The United States is a federal system: an interlocking system of local governments, state governments, and the national or federal government. Each level has some degree of autonomy, although the national government has been increasing in power for the last century. Federalism is especially important in environmental law because typically the federal agencies rely upon the states to enforce environmental regulations. Even in nonregulatory areas, the federal presence of such agencies as the Bureau of Land Management, the Forest Service, and the National Park Service affects the states. These agencies manage most federally owned land, and in some states (especially in the West) large tracts of undeveloped land are owned by the national government. In Alaska, Colorado, Oregon, and Utah over half the land belongs to the federal government; in Nevada, 86 percent of the land is federally owned.[4] This has a substantial impact on economic development, tourism, recreation, and the tax base of the state and local governments.

Another reason that federalism is so important in environmental issues is that so many environmental problems cross political boundaries. For example, the Chesapeake Bay's shorelines are in the states of Maryland and Virginia; history suggests that the two states would not readily cooperate to solve the bay's environmental problems by themselves. However, the Constitution provides a vehicle for state cooperation in many environmental areas: interstate compacts, which are subject to Senate ratification. For example, the Potomac River Compact was agreed between Maryland and Virginia in 1958. Under the compact, the river fisheries are managed in accordance with Maryland laws, unless the Potomac River Fisheries Commission (a regulatory body formed in 1963) decides otherwise. Commission regulations may be challenged in court, but the commission has never lost a court challenge. Regulations may be changed or revoked by a joint resolution of the Maryland and Virginia legislatures, but this process has never been used. Although the commission must rely on the states for enforcement, the power to issue fishing licenses is so well accepted by the fisheries community that effective regulation is easily achieved. Many other jurisdictions across the country that must deal with transboundary issues of water quality, air quality, wildlife management, bridges, harbors, and conservation choose to use such interstate compacts.

Federalism has other, less obvious effects on environmental law. Lobby groups can take advantage of the multiple points of access provided by multiple levels of government. State policymakers may be more vulnerable to lobbying than their federal counterparts because their state economies are more fragile. One western state, for example, has decided not to comply with the state natural resource trustee requirement of the Superfund Amendment and Reauthorization Act (SARA) for fear of alienating one of the major businesses in the state; that particular business would be a likely candidate for state-resource damage suits were a trustee to be appointed.[5] Another factor that increases the access points for lobbyists is the staggered campaigns in a federal system. With national elections held every two years for the House of Representatives, every four years for the presidency, and every six years for the Senate, plus the various gubernatorial and state house elections, a busy lobbyist can be permanently involved with helping or hindering candidates' election prospects at all levels of government. The lobbyist can then pick and choose the races and the candidates that will be the most helpful to the lobbying organization's goals.

It is no accident that the national terms of office are so staggered. The Constitution is designed around a federal system. The House, allocated by population—the larger a state's population, the more representatives it has—is balanced by the Senate, which has two senators per state regardless of the state's land mass or population. Until 1913, senators were not even popularly elected but were chosen by their state legislatures. The structure of the Senate, agreed on during the Constitutional Convention, was intended to accommodate the concerns of the states that each be fairly represented. One unanticipated result was that at times the states were sufficiently balanced to cancel each other, leaving a clear field for the president and his own policies.

The federal government has grown in power since its founding in 1787, and the states no longer have the same independence they once had. This can be attributed to several factors.[6] First, for the past century presidential candidates have believed in and campaigned for a strong national government; members of Congress—often inadvertently—contribute to this strengthening when they provide services to their constituents in order to earn reelection. Second, there has been a widespread disillusionment with the state governments. Many eastern states are dominated by rural interests, and the cities suffer in legislative allocations; as a result, the cities seek federal relief and further enlarge the national power. Third, the United States has had a series of national crises that were clearly beyond the abilities of the state governments to handle: World War I, the Great Depression, World War II, and the several "police actions" since. The expansion of federal social programs to cope with the Depression and the increase in defense spending from both active military engagements and the cold war have increased the power of the national government at the expense of the states.

The national culture has changed from the predominately agrarian times of Thomas Jefferson. The increased urbanization and industrialization, the development of national transportation networks and international communications, and the increasing social problems such as homelessness, drug abuse, and AIDS are beyond the states' capacities to manage or even to coordinate. The civil rights movement, which could never have succeeded without federal involvement, has also changed the relationship between the states and the national government. Finally, in the past century, state politicians have found it easier to get money from the federal government than to raise state and local taxes, thus endangering their own chances for reelection. And in intergovernmental relations (as well as practically everywhere else), those who pay the piper call the tune.

The *Tangier Sound* case, discussed below, provides a good illustration of the complexities of intergovernmental involvement in resource management. This case also illustrates some of the points to be discussed in chapter 4: the doctrine of state ownership of wildlife, conflicts with federal law, and limitations on state and federal authority to regulate.

THE TANGIER SOUND CASE

Tangier Sound is an area of the Chesapeake Bay that is especially rich in crab habitat. Unfortunately, the Virginia-Maryland state line runs through Tangier Sound; the crabs tend to live in Virginia, while the crabbers live in Maryland.

Prior to 1982, Virginia imposed a residency requirement on anyone seeking a license to fish in Virginia waters. This meant that the Maryland crabbers could not legally follow the crab supply out of their state jurisdiction. An association of Maryland watermen sued the state of Virginia; the Watermen's Association argued that the residency requirement created an improper barrier to interstate commerce, thereby violating article I, section 8, of the U.S. Constitution: "Congress shall have Power . . . to regulate Commerce with foreign Nations, and among the several States." The association further argued that the only justification for such an interference with interstate commerce would be a legitimate and compelling state interest such as conservation—and Virginia clearly had no conservation interest, since there was no limit on the number of Virginia residents allowed to have crabbing licenses. The watermen also argued that article 4, section 2, of the Constitution ("The Citizens of each State shall be entitled to all Privileges and Immunities of Citizens of the several States") and the equal protection clause of the Fourteenth Amendment ("No state shall . . . deny to any person within its jurisdiction the equal protection of the laws") protected their rights to work in Virginia water. Finally, the watermen noted that many of their fishing vessels were federally licensed and were therefore exempt from state restrictions.

Virginia argued that the state had a compelling state interest to allow the residency requirement to stand. First, effective enforcement of regulations required that only residents be allowed to crab. That enabled Virginia inspectors to check boats unloading in Virginia and to ensure court appearances of violators who otherwise must be either arrested or extradited. Second, the requirement was essential for conservation measures. By limiting crabbing to residents, each resident could use the most efficient possible gear, thus maximizing his catch. If nonresident crabbers were permitted, restrictions on gear would be required to protect the crab resource from stress. This in turn would reduce each crabber's catch, and a state may legitimately protect an internal industry. As an aside, Virginia offered the federalism defense: by restricting a state's control of its resources, the state is restrained from trying "novel social and economic experiments without risk to the rest of the country."[7]

Virginia dismissed the constitutional claims advanced by the watermen. The commerce clause was not violated because the residency requirement was not a barrier to *trade*; nonresidents were allowed to buy or sell crabs and to transport them into, out of, or through the state. The only prohibition was against catching crabs in the state. The privileges and immunities clause was not violated because the watermen were not restricted from pursuing their lawful trade, only from pursuing a trade that was not lawful. In a desperate attempt to stave off the inevitable, Virginia advanced the trespass argument: since crabbing necessarily disturbs the bottom, any taking of crabs is a trespass on state-owned land. (The states do own the submerged lands; it is navigation on the water above that is given into federal jurisdiction.)

Of course, what was truly at issue here was Virginia's desire to prevent out-of-state crabbers (and in particular, Maryland crabbers, with whom Virginia crabbers had a centuries-old feud) profiting from Virginia wildlife. Virginia was really asserting state independence from federal interference in natural-resource management. Such federal interference in fisheries management in the Chesapeake Bay takes two forms: legal constraints like those at issue in *Tangier Sound*, and certain species-specific (for example, striped bass) management plans.

Neither state was particularly eager to enter into cooperative management plans (although in the late eighties those positions softened). Maryland was so reluctant that she entered the *Tangier Sound* case on the side of Virginia and against her own citizens. The arguments raised against cooperative management had four bases. First was the difference in political philosophy between the two states. Virginia legislators were more reluctant to impose fisheries regulations than was Maryland, but once regulatory authority was delegated, the Virginia legislature was willing to rely upon the administrative expertise of the Virginia Marine Fisheries Commission. Second, Maryland's economic and political base was more dependent on fisheries than was that of Virginia. This dependence reduced Maryland's willingness to negotiate and to compromise. If Maryland and Virginia were to formalize a cooperative agreement through, for example, an interstate compact, some state control would be lost and a new center of power developed. Both states were understandably reluctant to risk this. Third, the regulatory structures in place and the implementation strategies that were used varied greatly between the two states; they did not agree on season, catch limits, size limits, or even legal gear. Finally, the portion of the Bay under Maryland jurisdiction is to a great extent biologically homogeneous. In contrast, Virginia has a separate ecosystem in each major river; in addition there is a great difference between the mouth of the Chesapeake Bay and the areas closer to the Virginia-Maryland state line. The Bay is a marine environment in its lower reaches, becoming a brackish one as it approaches the Susquehanna River. Even if the Chesapeake were within only one political jurisdiction, its size and variability would make management difficult.

In 1982, the federal district court in Richmond decided in favor of the Watermen's Association. One more area of state autonomy was reduced in favor of broader resource-management objectives.

Suggested Reading

Carter, Lief. *Reason in Law.* 2nd ed. Boston: Little, Brown and Co., 1984. An elegant and pithy explanation of how judges think and how they *ought* to think.

Cox, Susan J. B[uck]. "Interjurisdictional Management in Chesapeake Bay Fisheries." *Coastal Management* 16 (1988): pp. 151–166. This article elaborates on the issues raised in the *Tangier Sound* case.

Garraty, John, ed. *Quarrels That Have Shaped the Constitution.* New York: Harper and Row (Torchbook), 1964. Sixteen landmark Supreme Court cases are presented in a "we were there" format. They are highly readable and give a clear understanding of the cases. Especially relevant for environmental law are the Dartmouth College case, the Steamboat case, and the Charles River Bridge case.

Nice, David. *Federalism: The Politics of Intergovernmental Relations.* New York: St. Martin's Press, 1987. Academic but thorough.

CHAPTER TWO

ENVIRONMENTALISM IN THE UNITED STATES

American environmentalism is rooted in the works of philosophers such as Henry David Thoreau, preservationists like John Muir, and politically active conservationists like Theodore Roosevelt and Gifford Pinchot, but the contemporary emphasis on environmentalism as regulatory policy is of fairly recent origin. This chapter traces the growth of the environmental movement in the United States, from its beginnings in the 1960s. The keystone legislation of the thirty-year period from the sixties to the nineties is the 1969 National Environmental Policy Act (NEPA). The forces leading up to NEPA's passage and the intentions of Congress in passing it are discussed in the second section of the chapter. The third section discusses the *Calvert Cliffs* case, which set the stage for the powerful application of NEPA's environmental impact statement (EIS) provision. The fourth section takes a brief look at the Environmental Protection Agency set up in 1970. The last two sections discuss the "environmental decade" of the seventies, and the developments of the eighties.

BEGINNINGS OF THE ENVIRONMENTAL MOVEMENT

In the fall of 1962, Rachel Carson's book *Silent Spring* was published, with little fanfare. Formerly a biologist with the U.S. Fish and Wildlife Service, Carson had written wonderful, lyrical books about nature; this book took on the chemical industry in much the same way as Ralph Nader's *Unsafe at Any Speed* would take on the auto industry in 1965. The chemical industry predicted an early demise for the book: "It is fair to hope that by March or April *Silent Spring* no longer will be an interesting conversational topic."[1] The title was an act of genius, and the American imagination was caught by the vision of a spring devoid of birdsong or katydids or bullfrogs bellowing in the night. Carson's book is still an interesting conversational topic a quarter of a century later. Its effects were larger than reducing the use of pesticides or saving the bald eagle. The book was a triggering event for the entire environmental movement because it mobilized the average American. Biocide was in everyone's back yard.

There were other forces at work as well in the sixties. The Vietnam War was provoking intense controversy and conflict in American society, and the counterculture movement was prompting a romantic, back-to-nature perspective. The financial prosperity of the fifties, coupled with increasing mobility and leisure time, regenerated interest in outdoor activities. Causes were "in," and the environment, with its appeal to health and aesthetics and its underlying antibusiness philosophy, was a prime candidate to become a cause. This cause was embraced so thoroughly by the American people that it has now become one of our enduring American values, as Ronald Reagan discovered to his dismay when he misinterpreted his electoral mandate to include reduced environmental protection.

Looking back through the sixties, we can see the inexorable building of American consciousness toward the first Earth Day, in 1970. In 1963 the amended Clean Air Act authorized federal hearings on *potential* air pollution problems; in 1964 the Wilderness Act set aside tracts of land and barred them permanently from development. In 1966 the Endangered Species Preservation Act was passed. In 1968 the spectacular American Apollo space flight that circled the globe produced moving photographs of a fragile planet.

Early in 1969, a major trigger event shocked the American public into demanding immediate action to protect the environment. On January 28, Union Oil Company's Platform A began to disgorge oil. Over eleven days, 235,000 gallons of crude oil spread out, ruining forty miles of Santa Barbara's beautiful Pacific beaches. Thousands of birds and mammals died; one dramatic photograph shows an oil-soaked bird surrounded by debris and gazing in a doomed stupor over the surf. The spill became a national event, searing the public conscience with images of ruined water and pathetic, dying animals. Five months later the Cuyahoga River in Ohio caught fire. One of President Nixon's aides wrote that the political mood in Washington engendered by the public outcry could only be captured by the word *hysteria*. On January 1, 1970, President Nixon signed the National Environmental Policy Act, arguably the most important piece of environmental legislation in the century.

THE NATIONAL ENVIRONMENTAL POLICY ACT

Congress had five major objectives in passing the National Environmental Policy Act (NEPA) of 1969. These objectives were spelled out in section 2 of the act:

> To declare a national policy which will encourage productive and enjoyable harmony between man and his environment; to promote efforts which will prevent or eliminate damage to the environment and biosphere and stimulate the health and welfare of man; to enrich the understanding of the ecological systems and natural resources important to the Nation; and to establish a Council on Environmental Quality.[2]

NATIONAL POLICY

The first purpose of NEPA was to provide a clear mandate for all federal agencies, regardless of their mission or position within the government, "to create and maintain conditions under which man and nature can exist in productive harmony." [3] There were no exemptions for any federal agency; all were expected to comply and to cooperate with other agencies.

ACTION-FORCING REQUIREMENTS

The second objective of the act was to establish action-forcing procedures for the federal agencies. It was not enough to contemplate environmental concerns; the agencies were now required to write an Environmental Impact Statement (EIS) for all federal projects and to circulate the statements to local, state, and other federal agencies for their comments. This provision was to explode into a powerful weapon for the citizen lobbies to delay or to halt numerous projects.

The act stipulated that the social sciences were to be integrated into the decision processes; no longer were the relatively simple physical data sufficient. This provision has not been fully utilized. For example, a model social impact assessment was performed on the proposed Chief Joseph Dam. In considering the impact that an influx of several hundred unmarried construction workers would have on the recreation demands and social patterns in a rural town with a population of less than two thousand, the Army Corps of Engineers analysts wrote that "patterns of adult entertainment of new citizens may be somewhat different" from those of the original residents.[4] This is certainly an understatement.

Other action-forcing requirements were that agencies must consider qualitative information, must protect the global environment where consistent with the foreign policy of the United States, and must deliberately seek the least damaging alternatives. This latter provision was to cause some difficulties during the first Reagan administration. One of Reagan's first acts as president was to issue Executive Order 12291, which mandates cost-benefit analyses on all proposed federal regulations, in effect giving the Office of Management and Budget the authority to delay implementation of regulations that were not the most cost-effective. Since this raises conflicts with clear Congressional expectations of environmental protection, which is often *not* the least costly way to accomplish goals, Reagan's Executive Order faced a rare legal challenge, and the question of its validity was still before the courts in 1990.

COUNCIL ON ENVIRONMENTAL QUALITY

Another objective of NEPA was to create the Council on Environmental Quality (CEQ). This council, consisting of three members appointed by the president subject to Senate confirmation, has statutory obligations to collect data and to make an annual report to the president. Reagan tried to abolish the CEQ early in his first administration but was thwarted by the statutory requirement that a council must be appointed. He contented himself with cutting the council's budget by 62 percent, thus reducing both its staff and its reports.

ENVIRONMENTAL QUALITY REPORT

Just as the CEQ must report annually to the president, the president must send to the Congress an annual Environmental Quality Report which sets out:

> (1) the status and condition of the major natural, manmade, or altered environmental classes of the Nation, including, but not limited to, the air, the aquatic, including marine, estuarine, and fresh water,

and the terrestrial environment, including, but not limited to, the forest, dryland, wetland, range, urban, suburban, and rural environment; (2) current and foreseeable trends in the quality, management and utilization of such environments and the effects of those trends on the social, economic, and other requirements of the Nation; (3) the adequacy of available natural resources for fulfilling human and economic requirements of the Nation in the light of expected population pressure; (4) a review of the programs and activities (including regulatory activities) of the Federal Government, the State and local government, and nongovernmental entities or individuals, with particular reference to their effect on the environment and on the conservation, development and utilization of natural resources; and (5) a program for remedying the deficiencies of existing programs and activities, together with recommendations for legislation.[5]

Clearly, the Council on Environmental Quality has a substantial role to play in providing the substance of this report.

DEVELOPMENT OF INFORMATION

The federal government, and especially the CEQ, is to foster the development of information on and indices of environmental quality. This is not as simple as it might sound. For example, Maryland and Virginia have shorelines on the Chesapeake Bay. Several fisheries stocks migrate between the two states (and sometimes into federal waters). Both states have sophisticated biological data collection systems, but the two systems are not statistically compatible. The data collected in Virginia measures slightly different variables at different times in the life cycles or in the calendar than does the data collected in Maryland. However, statistical packages are being developed to integrate the data sets. The Chesapeake Bay problem is relatively simple, involving only one (admittedly large and varied) body of water and two state governments. Other problems are more complex. Some are simply not amenable to even the most cooperative of efforts. For example, the ecological systems associated with water supplies vary so extensively across several thousand miles of territory that no single data set can adequately describe them.

Of the five objectives of NEPA, the most impact has come from the first two: the universal federal mandate to be concerned for the environment, and the action-forcing procedures exemplified by the EIS requirement. The first court decision to examine the underlying intent of NEPA was the *Calvert Cliffs* case.

THE CALVERT CLIFFS CASE

The case of *Calvert Cliffs Coordinating Committee, Inc. v. United States Atomic Energy Commission* (1971) arose when the Atomic Energy Commission (AEC) issued rules governing the granting of construction and licensing permits for nuclear power plants. The AEC claimed that its rules complied with the procedural requirements of NEPA. However, the Calvert Cliffs Coordinating Committee, a Maryland public-interest group trying to halt the licensing of a partially constructed nuclear plant on the Chesapeake Bay, sued on the basis that the AEC did not adequately consider environmental issues when the rules were promulgated. The Calvert Cliffs group had four specific complaints. First, the hearing board within the AEC that made the final determinations on permits and licenses was not required to consider environmental factors unless an outside party or the regulatory staff raised the issue during the review. Second, nonradiological environmental issues were not allowed to be raised in cases where the hearing notice was published in the *Federal Register* prior to March 4, 1971. This was seen as an attempt to "grandfather" some facilities, that is, to exempt them from the new rules on the grounds that they preexisted the rules. Third, if other federal agencies certified to the AEC that their environmental standards were satisfied by the construction project, the hearing board was prohibited from itself considering the same environmental factors. Finally, any facility with a construction permit issued before NEPA compliance was required could not be formally reevaluated until the contractors applied for an operating license.

One of the most important aspects of Judge Skelly Wright's decision was the distinction he drew between the substantive requirements of NEPA's section 101 and the procedural requirements of section 102, which contains the EIS provision. Section 101, he wrote, provided a broad, substantive mandate to all federal agencies to "use all practicable means and measures" to protect the environment. Environmental values were to become part of a pantheon of values that must be considered before any federal agency acted. Judge Wright found this mandate to be flexible, giving wide discretionary powers to the agencies. In contrast, he found the procedural requirements of section 102 to be very strict. Unlike section 101, with its "practicable means and measures" language, section 102 compels the agencies to consider environmental factors "to the fullest extent possible":

We must stress as forcefully as possible that this language does not provide an escape hatch for footdragging agencies; it does not make NEPA's procedural requirements somehow "discretionary." Congress did not intend the Act to be such a paper tiger. Indeed, the requirement of environmental consideration "to the fullest extent possible" sets a high standard for the agencies, a standard which must be rigorously enforced by the reviewing courts.[6]

The importance of this ruling can hardly be overestimated. By the time the EIS issue reached the Supreme Court, Judge Wright's opinion had been cited as precedent over two hundred times. The legal sophistication of the environmental lobbies is rooted in their response to the power of the EIS. NEPA changed from a bill viewed by most of its proponents as a "motherhood and apple pie" measure to an act that delayed the B-1 bomber and the Alaska oil pipeline. The courts have used NEPA and the EIS requirement to force federal agencies to consider seriously all environmental factors when any federal action, however loosely defined, is contemplated.

FORMATION OF THE ENVIRONMENTAL PROTECTION AGENCY

The Environmental Protection Agency (EPA) is the federal agency with the primary responsibility for regulating the national environment. The EPA was created by President Nixon's executive order in 1970. It is probably the most powerful regulatory agency in the government, with jurisdiction over air pollution, water pollution, drinking water contamination, hazardous waste disposal, pesticides, radiation, and toxic substances.[7] The EPA is unique in its organization. All other regulatory agencies (as opposed to regulatory commissions, which are not headed by a single political appointee) are housed administratively in some executive-branch department such as the Department of the Interior or the Department of Agriculture. But the head of the EPA reports directly to the president. The EPA conducts its own research, and "by recruiting employees who value environmental protection, EPA has also developed a high level of cohesion."[8] This gives the EPA political independence and control over its own information sources—both major factors in wielding political power in the federal government.

THE ENVIRONMENTAL DECADE

The seventies have been called the environmental decade. Major pieces of legislation were put into place during the ten-year period between NEPA and the first Reagan administration. In 1970 the Resource Recovery Act (Solid Waste Disposal Act) was passed, the Clean Air Act Amendment was enacted, and the EPA was established. April 22, 1970, was Earth Day, celebrated by millions of Americans, who were also celebrating the apparent end to our involvement in Vietnam. In 1971 Barry Commoner published *The Closing Circle*, and the Alaska Native Claims Settlement Act authorized federal nomination of "national interest lands." In 1972 the Federal Water Pollution Control Act, the Federal Environmental Pesticide Control Act, the Ocean Dumping Act, and the Coastal Zone Management Act were all passed. After this, legislation was refined rather than initiated; the most impressive legislative achievement was the 1980 Comprehensive Environmental Response, Compensation, and Liability Act (CERCLA or Superfund).

Nonlegislative landmarks included the United Nations Conference on the Human Environment, which led to the United Nations Environmental Programme, and the publication of *The Limits to Growth* by the Club of Rome and *Small Is Beautiful* by the English economist E. F. Schumacher. However, the environmental accomplishments of the seventies were overshadowed by the tragedies of Love Canal and Three Mile Island.

In October 1973, the Organization of Petroleum Exporting Countries (OPEC) voted to cut its oil production by 5 percent; the Saudis halted their oil exports to the United States, threatening to maintain their embargo until the Nixon administration changed its pro-Israeli stance. Fuel prices at the gas pump shot up, and Americans old enough to be driving in 1973 remember long lines and quotas on gasoline. The "crisis" continued in one form or another through the Ford and Carter administrations; even when petroleum products were reasonably plentiful, the fear of a recurrence drove federal energy policy. Reagan was committed to deregulation even in energy policy, believing that a free market and regulatory relief would be most beneficial for the beleaguered energy industry. This brought his administration in direct conflict with environmentalists as federal lands and the outer continental shelf were opened, or proposed for opening, for exploration.

ENVIRONMENTAL ACTION IN THE EIGHTIES

With many of Reagan's policies, what was perhaps bad for the environment was good for the environmental movement. During the seventies, environmental concerns became routinized, and the dramatic events of the sixties faded from public memory. The scandals of the Reagan administration in the EPA, and the lightning-rod activities of Reagan's secretary of the interior, James Watt, reignited general public concern.

Arguably the best thing that could have happened to the environmental movement was Reagan's appointment of Anne Gorsuch (later Burford) to head the EPA and of James Watt to be Secretary of Interior. Brilliant in their own ways, neither Gorsuch nor Watt was sympathetic to the conservation, preservation, and regulation ideologies of the environmental establishment. Warning bells were sounded when Reagan discovered killer trees robbing us of our oxygen. Watt explained during his Senate confirmation hearings that conservation was necessary only for one more generation, until the Second Coming, and he changed the buffalo on the Interior Department stationery to face right instead of left. "Good science" was the excuse used to delay environmental decisions. Even in the mid-eighties the Reagan administration was refusing to acknowledge the damage done on this continent by acid rain, pending further scientific investigations. During Burford's administration the EPA became politicized, or at least it was perceived to be politicized, causing damage to its effectiveness with both the regulated industries and the Congress, neither of which now trusted its findings or accepted its decisions.

Despite these problems, several important pieces of legislation were passed or renewed during Reagan's tenure. In 1986, Superfund was reauthorized in the Superfund Amendment and Reauthorization Act (SARA). SARA did more than simply continue the 1980 Superfund legislation. It added, among other provisions, a community right to know, which has caught the attention—and conscience—not only of communities but also of the businesses within the communities. Now local communities must be informed of the location, nature, and volume of all hazardous materials within their jurisdiction. Many corporations had simply never bothered to assemble this information, and at least one, DuPont, was so horrified at its aggregate data that it initiated a nationwide chemical reduction program. The focus of SARA expanded from simply cleanup to include the protection and management of natural resources. The new requirements for natural-resource trustees included, for the first time, payment for habitat destruction and for indirect damage to natural resources. This expanded focus requires unprecedented cooperation between the regulatory agencies and the resource-management agencies at both the federal and the state level.

Reagan's heir in the White House, George Bush, promised to be the environmental president. The early signs were encouraging. He appointed William Reilly, president of the World Wildlife Fund and Conservation Foundation, to be head of the EPA. Bush's choice of Michael Deland, former director of EPA's Region I office in Boston, as chairman of the CEQ was widely supported in the environmental communities. However, Bush's other nominations to environmental positions were less well received. For example, James Cason, Bush's nominee to head the Forest Service, was not confirmed by the Senate because of charges he was biased toward mining and oil interests.

In his efforts to promote environmentalism, Bush was partly hampered by budget concerns; perhaps for this reason he has so far done little to prove that his proenvironment campaign position was more than just rhetoric. With the federal deficit perceived by the majority of Americans as the most severe problem facing the country, and with energy sources increasingly uncertain, generous environmental budgets are unlikely. Only modest budget increases have been projected for the Bush administration, and the machinations of the "Hundred and Worst" Congress in resolving the budget crisis of 1990 were not encouraging. The federal government responded slowly to the *Exxon Valdez* spill off the coast of Alaska in March 1989, and the administration was obstructive during the initial phases of setting up an international conference on global warming. The old Reagan specter of "good science" reappeared during discussions of global warming, the depletion of the ozone layer, and acid rain.

Reagan's New Federalism continued the policy of federal environmental decisions being implemented by the states, and as the states face economic disasters, environmental enforcement may suffer as well. As a good conservative, Bush favored market solutions to environmental problems, and thus encountered opposition to new programs from the largely Democratic Congress. Although he seemed to prefer regulatory reform over deregulation (one might argue that not much remained to deregulate, leaving only reform as an alternative anyway), budgetary constraints inhibited the flexibility of either the president or the Congress to commit needed resources even if desired.

Suggested Reading

Anderson, Frederick. *NEPA in the Courts: A Legal Analysis of the National Environmental Policy Act.* Baltimore: Johns Hopkins University Press for Resources for the Future, 1973. An excellent discussion of the purposes behind NEPA and of its impact in the first three years after passage.

Lash, Jonathan, Katherine Gillman, and David Sheridan. *A Season of Spoils.* New York: Pantheon, 1984. Subtitled *The Reagan Administration's Attack on the Environment,* this book exposes the excesses of the first Reagan administration. While it is certainly biased in its interpretations of the facts, the research is solid. The book is entertaining as well as informative.

Nash, Roderick. *American Environmentalism: Readings in Conservation History.* 3rd ed. New York: McGraw-Hill, 1990. A superb collection of original documents in American conservation history, with clear introductory comments. Be sure to get the third edition, as the first two are not edited as crisply.

Vogel, David. "The Politics of the Environment, 1970–1987: A Big Agenda." *Wilson Quarterly* 11 (no. 4, Autumn 1987): pp. 51–68. A graceful summary of the political influences on major environmental actions during the seventies and eighties.

CHAPTER THREE

THE PUBLIC POLICY PROCESS

Beloved by social scientists, models of how the world works are at best only approximations. Models of the public policy process are no better—and no worse. The process described in this chapter appears to be an elegant and linear process, but be forewarned that public policy is in reality a complex, confused, and confusing Rube Goldberg device into which an infinite variety of ingredients are poured, and out of which comes . . . a surprise. Still, as a heuristic device, a linear description of public policy can be helpful.

There are four basic types of public policy—distributive, competitive regulatory, protective regulatory, and redistributive—each with its own set of policy actors and characteristics. These four types and their relationship to environmental policy are discussed in the first section of this chapter. The remaining sections discuss the mechanics of the public policy process. First, the governmental reactions to the 1969 Santa Barbara oil spill provide an overview of the policy process. The next sections describe the four stages of the policy process: agenda setting, policy formation, implementation and evaluation.

TYPES OF PUBLIC POLICY

Domestic public policy can be divided into four major categories: distributive, competitive regulatory, protective regulatory, and redistributive.[1] Many policies have some characteristics of more than one of these policy types; nevertheless, the categorization is useful because it highlights the different policy actors and policy process associated with each type.

DISTRIBUTIVE POLICY

Distributive policy uses public resources to support private activities that are beneficial to society but that would not usually be undertaken by the private sector. For example, certain kinds of medical research are expensive and have little, if any, financial reward for the companies involved; the government may subsidize such research. Farmers need support through the bad times if they are to be able to produce agricultural products on a regular basis; the federal government instituted price supports. In the nineteenth century, settlement of the American West was physically dangerous and economically risky; the government, eager to encourage western expansion, gave away land and leased federally owned lands at below-market prices. This subsidy of western cattle ranchers continues today.

Distributive policies usually have low visibility. The people involved (e.g., the ranchers and the officials of the Bureau of Land Management) maintain cordial relations, and unless some unexpected event triggers media interest, the decisions governing this sort of policy are made by *subgovernments*. A subgovernment—also known as an iron triangle—is a coalition of three groups of actors: the affected interest group, the relevant agency in the executive branch, and the appropriate congressional committees or subcommittees. Such a coalition is a quiet and stable network of policy actors with similar interests and goals.

In distributive policy, which is not often the focus of public controversy, the subgovernments are king. When controversy does arise, the subgovernments disintegrate, only to re-form when the dust settles. The first Reagan administration saw an effort by some western states to obtain control of the federal lands within their state boundaries. This "Sagebrush Rebellion" pitted the Bureau of Land Management (BLM) against its normal allies, the cattlemen. In previous times, the environmentalists and the BLM had been bitter enemies, the environmentalists claiming that poor management and overgrazing were ruining the public lands of the West. One BLM official told me that a year before the Sagebrush Rebellion started he would never have believed he would be leaking advance information to the environmental lobby. However, the environmentalists were, for once, on the same side as the BLM as they both fought to keep the federal lands out of the control of what they perceived as rapacious state developers. Once the controversy subsided, the environmentalists and the BLM found themselves again on opposite sides of the fence.[2]

COMPETITIVE REGULATORY POLICY

The control of radio broadcasting by the Federal Communications Commission (FCC) is an example of competitive regulatory policy. Several parties compete for the right to broadcast on a certain frequency; the successful applicant is then regulated by the agency. Thus competitive regulatory policy limits the provision of specific goods and services to a few who are chosen from a group of competitors, and then regulates the selected companies. Other examples are television stations and, before Reagan deregulated them, airlines and trucking companies. The regulation of trucking companies was so extensive at one time that trucking lines were told specifically which goods could be carried between two points and in what direction. Airlines had to agree to service feeder lines in order to be awarded major, profitable runs. Since deregulation, the importance of competitive regulatory policy has diminished considerably.

These are usually low visibility policies. Decisions are made at the bureau level, or by independent regulatory commissions such as the FCC or the Securities and Exchange Commission, or by the courts. Often the regulated industries have a great deal of input into the regulatory decisions. This leads to the problem of the captured agency, an agency that identifies so closely with the interests of the regulated industry that it forgets its responsibilities to society. For several years after the commercial development of cable television, the FCC was accused of being a captured agency in thrall to the Big Three of broadcasting: ABC, CBS, and NBC. Critics of the agency attribute the slow acceptance of cable television to the networks' ability to influence FCC decisions.

PROTECTIVE REGULATORY POLICY

Many governmental bodies protect the public by regulating private activities. Unlike the other types of policy, protective regulatory policy may be an active policy, not only prohibiting certain actions (such as emitting sulfur dioxide into the atmosphere) but also requiring some activities (building tall smokestacks or inspecting automobiles or recycling waste). When bankers tell their loan customers the total price of a car *including* interest, they do so in obedience to a protective regulatory policy, not because they have big hearts.

The main actors in protective regulatory policies are the committees and subcommittees of the Congress, the full House and Senate, executive agencies, and business interest groups. Many of these policies cannot be relegated to a subgovernment level; for example, an announcement by the Surgeon General of the United States about the medical dangers of second-hand smoke is front-page news. Usually, however, these policies have only moderate visibility, and the parties involved work out their decisions through bargaining and compromise.

Most environmental policy falls into the protective regulatory category. Some observers of the environmental scene blame the slow improvement of the nation's environment on the federal choice of protective regulatory policy as a vehicle for compliance, rather than distributive policies. By defining pollution control as punitive, allowing certain amounts of pollutants to be released or generated and stored, and then punishing any excess, the federal government provides corporate America with little incentive to develop waste reduction policies or to look for alternate production methods. Critics suggest that more progress would be made by rewarding recycling, material conservation, and waste reduction than by continuing an adversarial, litigious approach.

REDISTRIBUTIVE POLICY

The most controversial type of policy is redistributive, which seeks to change the allocation of valued goods or services—money, property, or rights—between social classes or racial groups or genders. In this policy, unlike the others, there are usually clearly defined winners and losers. Most often the winners are from disadvantaged groups in society; for example, affirmative action is a redistributive policy. Because of the high visibility of this type of policy, the political actors also have high visibility: the president, the congressional leaders, and large interest groups.

ENVIRONMENTAL POLICY

Most environmental policy fits into either the protective regulatory category (for example, air and water pollution policies) or the distributive category (for example, national parks). Sometimes a policy may overlap categories. For example, the burros at Grand Canyon

National Park were a nuisance and also destroyed habitat needed for native species. Unfortunately for the Park Service, burros are cute; one in particular, Brighty, had been the subject of a very popular children's book, and a statue of him had been erected on the South Rim. To preserve the canyon ecosystem, the Park Service decided to shoot the wild burros, prompting an avalanche of protest. The Park Service ultimately compromised, allowing animal protection groups to rescue many of the burros before the rest were shot. Clearly the Park Service was not engaged in distributive policy when it decided to destroy wild burros to protect native species. Another example of crossover is the federal food stamp program. Federal food stamps are often pointed out as an example of a redistributive program, but they actually originated in a distributive program to buy surplus food during the New Deal.

Sometimes astute politicians can sell a program as a politically acceptable type of policy, knowing all the while that the real impact will be otherwise. Urban renewal is such a program. It was advertised as a redistributive program to help the poor of the inner cities; in practice the poor were pushed out, and high-rise offices and expensive condominiums replaced the slums. The poor simply shifted to more crowded and less convenient tenements. Instead of being redistributive, the program was distributive, subsidizing urban real estate speculators.

OVERVIEW OF THE PUBLIC POLICY PROCESS

One of the unfortunate truths about the depth of our political concerns is that we care most about those incidents that are closest to us. When an airplane crashes on an international flight, the media reports the number of *American* dead or injured, and if the plane is filled entirely by foreign nationals, the crash has only the briefest mention on the national media and is then forgotten. Just so do environmental issues come into the national consciousness. The January 1969 Santa Barbara spill was just such an event. For most Americans this was the first really big oil spill. However, on March 18, 1967, the *Torrey Canyon*, a 970-foot tanker with 117,000 tons of crude oil in its storage tanks, ran aground fifteen miles west of Land's End in Cornwall, northeast of the Isles of Scilly. Initially about 40,000 tons of oil were released by the ruptured tanks, but salvage efforts were futile, and all 117,000 tons of oil spilled into the western end of the English Channel. Eventually the oil washed up on the holiday coasts of England and France.

American environmentalists were a small but hardy band in the late sixties, and they watched the *Torrey Canyon* incident with horror. Oil experts, however, noted the narrowness of the Channel and peculiarities of the prevailing winds and currents, and they assured the American public that such an accident would not happen in American waters. Environmentalists received similar assurances about oil wells off the Pacific coast. The general public was not very worried, but the environmental activists were; when the Santa Barbara well blew, they were quick to take advantage.

Rapidly an interest group called GOO (Get Oil Out) was formed. The American media were much more concerned with the destruction of forty miles of Southern California beaches than they had been with the holiday sites of France and England. Within three days, GOO had collected more than fifty thousand signatures on petitions asking the president to stop deep-sea coastal oil drilling. Attention focused on the Outer Continental Shelf (OCS) oil leasing program administered by the Bureau of Land Management (BLM), although two other federal agencies—the U.S. Geological Survey and the Federal Water Pollution Control Administration—were also involved. The leasing program was temporarily halted by Interior Secretary Walter Hickel.

The incident also drew attention to the growing problem of other forms of marine oil pollution. Twenty percent of oil in the world's water comes from shipping, including accidents, bilge water dumping, and the emptying of ballast tanks. Natural oil seepage from the ocean floor contributes 15 percent, while offshore production is responsible for only 5 percent.[3] In the North Sea and North Atlantic alone, scientists estimate that as many as 450,000 marine birds die each year from chronic oil pollution.[4]

The public uproar over the Santa Barbara spill led to the passage of the National Environmental Policy Act in December of the same year; it was signed into law on January 1, 1970. It also had long-term repercussions on the federal oil leasing programs. Despite the oil crisis in the early seventies, OCS leasing goals were never met. The coastal states and communities were reluctant to have oil rigs drilling off their coastlines, and the political pressures caused by a constant stream of small spills and a few major disasters like the *Exxon Valdez* incident (which poured eleven million gallons of oil into Prince William Sound in Alaska) kept the public interested in the impact of oil development in the marine environment. In 1978 the Outer Continental Shelf Lands Act Amendments incorporated the coastal states into the planning process for OCS development. Since then, although the OCS oil production exceeds that of the dry lands, political pressures have prevented massive exploitation of the OCS.

Here we have a microcosm of the policy process. A trigger event (the Santa Barbara spill) is used by policy initiators or policy entrepreneurs (environmental lobbyists) to induce policy formation and legitimation (passage of NEPA) to achieve policy goals (de-emphasis on OCS wells and re-emphasis on environmental protection) that are implemented throughout the country (EPA regulations and state involvement in OCS planning). The next three sections discuss in more detail the various stages in this process, beginning with the setting of the public policy agenda.

AGENDA SETTING

Why do citizens strive to get their issues on the public agenda? Why not be satisfied with convincing their own circle of friends and colleagues of the correctness of their position? There are three reasons. First, public policy is legitimate. Government policies are usually regarded as legal obligations which citizens have a duty to uphold. The big exceptions—speed limits, Prohibition—are notable because they are exceptions. Nongovernmental groups and institutions may generate important policies (for example, corporate investment decisions or church rules on female clergy), and those policies may be regarded as binding on the members of the organization; but they have no authority for people who are not members. Only government policies are *legally* binding, and only government policies are legitimate almost automatically.

Second, government policies are universal. Membership in other policy-generating groups is voluntary, and these groups make policy only for their own members. But government policy applies—or may apply—to everyone.

Third, only the government has the power to force compliance with its policy decisions. Government has a monopoly on coercion in society; other organizations can legally exercise only limited sanctions. Only government can imprison (or even execute) individuals for refusing to obey its directives—though we do have laws that protect us from arbitrary coercion by the government; for example, the Fifth Amendment states that no person (not *citizen* but *person*) "shall be . . . deprived of life, liberty, or property without due process of law."

So, because government actions are legitimate, enact society-wide policies, and enforce these policies, people work to have their policy preferences become public policies. The rest of this section discusses the different types of agendas, initiators (people who initiate the agenda-setting process), and publics (groups of people whose political pressure helps to set the public policy agenda).

SYSTEMIC AND INSTITUTIONAL AGENDAS

In public policy there are two basic types of agendas: systemic and institutional.[5] The *systemic agenda* consists of all the issues that a political community agrees need to be resolved and that they also agree are within governmental authority. These are the issues that wax and wane in the public attention until finally an issue recurs often enough or becomes sufficiently problematic that it can no longer be ignored. When the public can convince its government that a problem exists *and* it is the government's business, the policy makers place the issue on their *institutional agenda*—the list of issues they plan to consider actively and seriously.

Systemic agendas are fairly abstract and fluid. Issues may appear on the systemic agenda for years before actually reaching the institutional agenda; some issues never do make it. Systemic agendas identify problem areas but rarely propose concrete alternatives and solutions.

Institutional agendas are specific, concrete, and limited. They identify the problem and its alternative solutions; often institutional agendas work within strict time constraints. Although an issue is usually placed on the systemic agenda before moving to the institutional agenda, some issues originate at the institutional level and others bypass the systemic agenda altogether.

The Congress (and indeed, most legislatures) deals with four kinds of problems: chronic problems, such as the federal budget, which recur annually; sporadic problems, such as reauthorizing environmental legislation; crisis problems, such as the savings and loan bailout that plagued the Congress in the early nineties; and discretionary problems.[6] The discretionary agenda is chosen by legislators for many reasons. Perhaps they have an ideological commitment to the issue, like Paul Rogers of Florida, who struggled for strong emission standards during the fight over the 1977 Clean Air Act amendments; or there are rewards to be gained in the political fray (paying old debts or creating new ones) or in subsequent elections (Rogers, for example, represented a south Florida constituency desperately concerned with respiratory problems of the elderly).

INITIATORS

There are four ways to create issues and four corresponding categories of initiators—people who use situations to place issues on the agenda. Often these categories overlap. *Readjustors* may perceive an inequality that affects them; they then strive to have the inequality reduced. For example, rural residents, who do not themselves generate low-level nuclear waste, fight to stop waste disposal sites being sited in their communities. *Exploiters* manufacture issues for their own gain. For example, when George Bush made an issue of the pollution in Boston Harbor during the 1988 presidential campaign, he was probably acting as an exploiter. *Circumstantial reactors* take advantage of unanticipated trigger events to create or to magnify issues. For example, the Santa Barbara oil spill was used to halt OCS development; the crash of an aircraft filled with tourists led to regulations prohibiting below-rim sightseeing flights in the Grand Canyon; the terrible forest fires that ravaged Yellowstone National Park in 1988 led to a reevaluation of the controlled burn policies of the federal resource-management agencies. Finally, *do-gooders* use events to publicize issues but gain no personal benefit from the issue. They may use inequalities or unanticipated events, but their motivation differs from that of the readjusters or circumstantial reactors.

PUBLICS

To move an issue even to the systemic agenda requires that the issue be of concern to as wide a range of the population as possible. There are four types of publics that an issue may reach. The smallest is the *identification group*, people with a detailed awareness of specific issues. For example, a local group concerned to stop a nuclear reactor in its neighborhood is an identification group. *Attention groups* focus on the broader implications of the issues that identification groups are concerned with. For example, an anti-nuclear power group is an attention group; unlike the identification group, which is interested only in the reactor threatening its own community, the attention group opposes nuclear reactors everywhere. The *attentive public* is the generally informed and educated layer of society. These are the people who, once they are convinced that an issue is important, inform the wider public. They may not have a passionate opposition to nuclear power, for example, but Three Mile Island and Chernobyl have convinced them that nuclear power is a danger. They will write articles, make speeches, join protests, influence their representatives in Congress, and discuss the issue at church suppers; the combined effect will be to bring the issue to the attention of the general public. The general or *mass public* is the last segment of the public to become involved in placing an issue on the systemic agenda. These people are less active, interested, and informed than any of the other kinds of public. Getting their attention requires highly generalized and symbolic issues, and keeping their attention for any length of time is difficult. However, without their concurrence, reaching the institutional agenda is virtually impossible.

Some issues never reach the mass public and yet manage to be placed on the institutional agenda as a result of desperate measures by the identification and attention groups. Issues that are confined to an identification group may gain the formal agenda when the group members threaten to disrupt the system; an example of such disruption is the monkeywrenching carried out by radical environmental groups that despair of the traditional political process. Issues that are confined to attention groups are brought to the formal agenda by threatening elected officeholders with legitimate sanctions such as recalls or the withholding of contributions or votes. When an issue reaches the attentive public, access is easier. The attentive public tends to have political power by virtue of its social and economic status. Here political brokerage techniques or controlling the media will bring an issue to the institutional agenda. The media are, of course, available to and used by identification and attention groups, but the attentive public has much more control of the media.

The key to getting an issue on the institutional agenda is issue expansion: placing the issue before as wide an audience as possible. The attention of the mass public is gained most easily by issues that are fairly ambiguous and have wider social significance. For example, defining an issue such as water pollution to incorporate "public health" (a fairly ambiguous concept) and "infant mortality" (an issue of social significance for all segments of the voting population) will increase the issue's chances of reaching the general public. Issues with long-term impacts and low technical complexity are also more successful; one reason fluoridation of public drinking water is difficult to expand to a larger public is that the technical information is confusing and experts contradict each other on its accuracy. Problems that cannot be solved by familiar remedies are interesting to the general public. While most issues have a built-in lifespan, some issues become perennial. Once the Three Mile

Island disaster was over, it became a symbol for the anti-nuclear lobbyists, but the reactor itself was no longer a national issue. Environmental quality, in contrast, has become an issue that is permanently on the institutional agenda.

POLICY FORMULATION

Deciding how an issue will be defined and which aspects of the issue problem will be addressed is part of the formulation process. While the entire policy process is political, the formulation and legitimation phases are the most intensely political. Many actors are involved. The bureaucracy, although most involved in the implementation phase of public policy, also has a role in suggesting policies to the legislature and providing information on the strengths and weaknesses of proposed solutions. The bureaus are given this role because they have, or are perceived to have, technical expertise that the elected officials and their staff lack; however, the bureaus often have their own organizational needs to be satisfied by the policy process (such as budgetary constraints, personnel demands, or program protection and expansion). The bureaucracy usually, but not always, reflects the president's policy position. Many times during the first Reagan administration, for example, the staff at EPA were at odds with the goals and initiatives of the political appointees and of the president. In fact, the accusation that the bureaucracy could not be trusted with the conservative agenda was a constant plaint of the administration. It took powerful and clear messages from the mass public to convince the president that the commitment to a protected and healthy environment was now a fixture in American values.

The media are also involved in formulation and legitimation as well. While they may create issues, as they did in the Watergate scandal and often do in such programs as "Sixty Minutes," the media are most often used by other actors to influence public or political opinion. Special interest groups watch the process carefully and intervene in those issues that affect their own concerns.

FORMULATION

One of the first difficulties in policy formulation is problem definition: legislators must first agree on the parameters of the problem before they can begin to formulate solutions. An example of the difficulties in problem definition may be found in the issue of tropical rain forest destruction. This destruction occurs in four main stages: road building and lumbering; colonization (made easier by the development of roads and the clearing of timber tracts) and crop planting (since the new settlers cannot live off the forested areas); soil exhaustion (because there is no dormant season); and grass planting and cattle grazing (which is inefficient, marginally profitable, and a factor contributing to soil erosion). Assuming that the governments having jurisdiction over the rain forests want to halt the destruction (or that other governments are convinced that this issue is important enough to justify interference in the activities of a sovereign nation), how might this problem be defined? The problem definition will guide the solutions to be attempted.

As a start, this might be defined as a timber problem. Obviously, one incentive to reduce rain forest destruction would be to reduce the world market for rain forest lumber. In a world where even eyeglass frames are made from mahogany, reducing the demand for fine furniture seems unlikely. A second definition might be as a problem of population pressures. If the developing countries with rain forests could house, feed, and employ their own populations within the urban or already existing rural environments, these people would not need to move into the rain forest areas denuded by the lumber companies. Unfortunately, there seems to be little political will to reduce populations; the developing countries sometimes perceive pressure to reduce their birth rates as hidden genocide.

Perhaps the rain forest destruction is a problem of agricultural techniques. The indigenous people of the forest survive very nicely without destroying the trees; the new settlers might be taught the indigenous farming practices. However, unlike the new settlers, the native peoples are unaccustomed to luxuries of urban life such as soft drinks, blue jeans, and boom boxes. Their farming methods are labor intensive and generate little cash crop. The food they do produce is neither familiar nor appealing to the settlers' palates. What about replenishing the soil so it does not become exhausted? Fertilizers are expensive and bring their own potentially harmful environmental effects.

Finally, the problem might be defined again as a market problem. By reducing world beef consumption (although hogs or sheep would do equally well—or poorly—on deforested land) or banning beef grown on deforested land (much as the EEC banned American beef from cattle fed growth hormones), the final stages of deforestation might be avoided.

None of these problem definitions or problem solutions seem useful. As the issue of the rain forest becomes expanded to wider publics, policy makers are going to be forced to find some way to address and to define the issue. "Stop the destruction of the rain forest" is an agenda-setting strategy with emotional appeal; *how* to stop the destruction is the formulation problem.

Once a problem has been defined, the solution that emerges is the result of bargaining and compromise by various factions within government, each of which believes it has the answer to the _problem. Various strategies may be used to delay the process. One such strategy is the "good science" strategy employed so effectively by the Reagan administration. When a problem appears intractable, the appointment of a study commission is a sure way to delay, and perhaps ultimately to avoid, a decision. Another strategy is to pass resolutions condemning the undesirable activity, while actually doing nothing.

An example of negotiation and bargaining is the process of formulating amendments to existing environmental legislation. In 1977, Congress considered amendments to the 1970 Clean Air Act. At issue was the auto industry's attempt to delay by five years its compliance with the auto emission standards imposed by the original act. There had already been three one-year extensions. Democrats led both sides of the battle in the House: Paul Rogers of Florida, chairman of the House Subcommittee on Health and the Environment, pushed for compliance within the extended time limits already agreed upon. John Dingall, representing Detroit with its blue-collar autoworkers and their threatened jobs, was joined by a majority of the Republicans in asking for the extension. Dingall usually was on the side of environmental legislation, but in this case his constituents' needs were paramount.

Rogers defined the issue in terms of health: respiratory problems in the elderly and the developing respiratory problems of children. Dingall defined it as jobs and the protection of an essential American industry. The issue that emerged from the subcommittee was defined as: "How can we clean up the air at the lowest possible cost?" This was a substantial victory for the auto industry; Rogers really didn't care how much it cost, but in order to get the opposing forces to compromise, he accepted their definition of the problem. By the time the final vote came on the floor of the House, Rogers had been forced to give even more ground. President Carter's energy policy had fueled Dingall's allies, and the automakers and sellers had exerted great lobbying pressure on all members of the

House. Dingall's forces carried the day, although their victory was somewhat diminished by the subsequent changes made in the conference with the Senate.

By defining the problem and then using negotiation and compromise to agree on a solution, the policy was formulated. It was legitimated by the same process. Although no one member of either the House or the Senate was truly satisfied with the outcome, all accepted it as legitimate because in the American political system the public generally accepts as legitimate the decisions made by the government.

LEGITIMATION

Legitimate policies have the authority of the state (in the American system, the authority of the people) attached.[7] Legitimacy is "a belief on the part of citizens that the current government represents a proper form of government and a willingness of the part of those citizens to accept the decrees of that government as legal and authoritative."[8]

Legitimacy is largely psychological. There is nothing that the government can do to force citizens to accept its policies as legitimate. Also, legitimacy is substantive as well as procedural; there are certain areas in which the citizens feel the government should not meddle. For example, a legislative decision to privatize municipal water supplies, as has been done in England, would not be perceived as legitimate in the United States, regardless of how scrupulous the legislature was to observe the correct procedures for enacting the legislation. Under American law, the states are responsible for public health and cannot abrogate that responsibility to a private concern. Finally, legitimacy is variable. Governments that are either consistently outside the areas of public acceptance or that violate the public trust may become illegitimate; this loss of legitimacy was a major factor in the resignation of President Nixon.

In the American system, legitimacy is achieved through the legislative process, the administrative process, the courts, and—rarely—direct democracy. The legislature is the source of primary legislation. Elected by the people, the legislators are expected to represent their constituencies.[9] As long as they collectively do not violate the wishes and expectations of the electorate, and they follow the procedural guidelines for their own legislative body, the laws they pass are legitimate to the voters.

The administrative process, being of fairly recent origin and handicapped by not being in the Constitution, has been subject to criticisms of its legitimacy from the earliest days of the administrative state. However, the rulemaking process or "secondary legislation" is generally accepted as legitimate. If the agencies follow the correct procedures, usually as laid down in the Administrative Procedure Act, their rules have the force and effect of legislative law. There is frequent opportunity for public input and influence in the administrative decision process, and while citizens may complain about a "fourth branch of government," administrative decisions are usually accorded legitimacy.

Court decisions, although subject to appeals or changes due to changing circumstances, are also legitimate. Court decisions are especially powerful because they have a direct constitutional connection and judges are, at most levels, less vulnerable to political pressures—they rarely need to compromise. A court may rule on the constitutionality of the actions of another branch of government. The decisions of the United States Supreme Court are particularly influential in legitimating government decisions because they are not subject to appeal. Only Congress can nullify a Supreme Court decision, either through legislation or by removing a disputed issue from the Court's jurisdiction.

The final source of legitimacy is direct democracy, most often expressed in referenda or initiatives. In recent years, stringent demands have been placed on state budgets by taxpayer initiatives, and these have had an inevitable effect on state environmental programs. Nuclear power issues have occasionally been taken directly to the people, but the use of direct democracy to make a policy decision or to legitimate a policy is unusual.

IMPLEMENTATION

Implementation occurs when the policy goals are translated into governmental actions which affect other branches of government or the citizens. Although implementation may be hampered by poor policy design or a lack of commitment by policymakers, once responsibility for the policy passes to the hands of the administrators, other factors come into play. The most important of these are bureaucratic resources.

BUREAUCRATIC RESOURCES

It is in implementation that bureaucracy shows its greatest influence.[10] The resources available to bureaucracies are considerable. The initial source of their power comes from their legal authority to implement legislation. Congress delegates its legislative authority to agencies, thus providing the legal justification for administrative rules and regulations. Bureaucratic power is also enhanced by the indispensable nature of the bureaucratic activity; modern government would be impossible without the agencies. The agencies are empowered by three other factors: technical expertise, constituencies, and discretionary actions.

TECHNICAL EXPERTISE Especially in the environmental agencies, the administrators are first trained in their substantive fields and then promoted to increasingly important administrative posts. In the Park Service, for example, the interpretation and historic preservation employees are trained in history, journalism, and related fields; the management employees have degrees in forestry, marine biology, environmental science, and similar technical areas. Superfund site administrators must be knowledgeable about chemical, physical, and biological processes. Many of the environmental agency staff have graduate degrees in their professional areas. Although rarely trained in administrative skills, the technical expertise of the bureaucrats and the intimate knowledge of their own policy areas far outreaches the knowledge base of even the most well-informed congressional staff. Despite the information available from the Congressional Research Service and the Office of Technology Assessment, the Congress is almost forced to rely upon information and analyses provided to them by the bureaucracy.

There is a negative side to the issue of technical expertise. Because agency personnel rarely have professional administrative experience, they often view the interjection of political ideas or values as a corruption of the decision-making process. This rejection of political influence is not limited to the agencies. Environmentalists deplore the position of lumber companies in the Pacific Northwest that bring political pressure to bear on the Congress and the Forest Service to allow them to clear-cut. Timber companies ridicule the claims of the Native Americans and the environmentalists to protect rare animals with no apparent commercial value. And government specialists, trained in the sciences, are outraged that Superfund sites take years to clean because the state and local governments insist on approving all EPA and responsible-party agreements. This is one area in which professional socialization is needed for the administrators. Political factors are a reality, and in a representative democracy, political factors are needed to balance the technical side of the decision process.

CONSTITUENCIES   Each agency develops its own constituencies; this is the obverse side of the "captured agency" coin. Any regulatory or management agency works closely with interest groups. These groups become accustomed to the working habits of the agency and learn effective patterns of negotiation and compromise. "Better the devil you know than the devil you don't" is their operating theory. They are reluctant to upset the stable relationships they have developed, and so a threatened agency may rely on its interest groups to protect it in times of budgetary crisis or changing political leadership. These client groups often have prestige and political influence, and they are a powerful factor in consolidating the position of the agencies. While they are not often called upon to defend the agency or to exercise influence on the agency's behalf, their very existence increases the authority of the agencies.

DISCRETIONARY POWER   The discretionary power of the agencies cannot be underestimated. Some commentators would like to limit discretion as much as possible, or even to eliminate it entirely, but it is essential for an effective administration. Legislatures cannot possibly draft legislation in the detail that is necessary for implementation. They lack the technical expertise that is such a powerful resource for the bureaucracy. And even if they had the necessary staff and expertise, the cumbersome legislative process of negotiation and compromise would bog down the governing process.

Discretion also gives administrators leeway to fit policy decisions to individual cases, to humanize the governmental process. It enhances their flexibility, allowing administrative law to evolve incrementally and to be checked or changed without the fanfare that accompanies legislative activity. Finally—and this is especially true in environmental administration—discretion compensates for changing technology. As scientific data accumulates, or drought endangers national forests, or new species are discovered, the discretionary powers of administrators can accommodate the changes.

This is not to say that governing necessarily continues to improve as discretionary powers increase. Too much discretion, which can lead to corruption, favoritism, or simple confusion, can be as harmful as too little discretion. The advantages of bureaucratic government rest in part on the regularity and predictability of government activity. A good administrator is able to strike a balance.

Administrators make three kinds of discretionary decisions: substantive, procedural, and complex. *Substantive* discretionary decisions are those in which an administrator makes a decision or promulgates a rule on a policy issue. These substantive decisions are one method for agencies to distribute benefits to their client groups. Agencies exercise this discretion in several ways. They decide, for example, where to locate research stations or unit headquarters which are frequently major sources of employment in small communities. In the late eighties, the Forest Service proposed consolidating the administrative offices of the Prescott and Coconino national forests in northern Arizona. The impact on the town of Williams, a very small community already endangered by an interstate bypass, was enormous, and the political fallout was great enough that the Forest Service shelved its plans, at least temporarily. A more subtle use of discretionary power is the wording of rules and regulations either to create client groups or to shape the benefits for which they are eligible. Sometimes discretion is at the "street level." In granting wetland permits, for example, state investigators have a wide latitude in interpreting potential soil erosion or habitat destruction.

Procedural discretionary decisions relate to the selection of the processes used to gather information or to make substantive decisions. A procedural discretionary decision might be whether to hire consultants or to use in-house personnel to develop a forest plan.

Complex discretionary decisions combine the features of both substantive and procedural decisions; for example: will the forest plan be based on timber-industry data, on agency data, or on a combination of both?

VARIABLES AFFECTING IMPLEMENTATION

Successful implementation is difficult, partly because it involves a number of interdependent actions which must be accomplished almost simultaneously.[11] These actions include acquiring resources (such as money, land, personnel, or equipment); interpreting directives, rules, and regulations; planning programs; organizing activities; and extending benefits and applying restrictions.

The implementation process is characterized by many complicating factors. First is the multiplicity of actors. At a minimum, bureaucrats are responsible to two masters: the president or his political appointee, and the Congress—which has authorized the agency's existence and which continues to hold the purse strings. The bureaucrats must also satisfy their client groups or, failing that, be able to defend their actions to the elected officials who receive the client groups' complaints. Some agencies have advisory groups with varying degrees of impact on the agency activities. There is always the possibility of judicial review, which even for the victorious agency is a process that consumes time and resources and perhaps even political goodwill.

Another complicating factor is the interstate context of environmental administration, mentioned in the discussion of the Chesapeake Bay environment in chapter 2. Each of the fifty states has its own bureaucratic organization to cope with environmental policy. In some states, there are as many as eight state agencies with some environmental responsibilities; no state has less than three.[12] This obviously complicates efforts by the states or the federal government to encourage interstate coordination in environmental administration. In addition, the state bureaucracies, although often given some responsibility for implementing federal programs, must also respond to the political pressures of their own state legislatures.

Because of the numerous agencies and policy-making bodies involved, the goals of any one policy may be diffuse, multiple, and competing. For example, the Forest Service is often frustrated by its multiple use mandate. Trained as silvaculturists, foresters view trees as a crop, to be nurtured and then harvested when mature. The Forest Service was established partially to ensure a steady, affordable, flexibly priced source of timber for the American construction industry. Being forced to allow old stands of timber to decay for habitat protection, when by forestry standards they should have been cut years ago, goes against the grain of responsible foresters. Equally dismayed is the entrepreneur who invests in patents for a new biological form of pest control only to find that, while one federal agency grants a patent, another refuses to let the entrepreneur sell the product. Or take the case of power plant operators forced to change reactor design long after approved construction has taken place. This "ratcheting" afflicts many industries subjected to EPA regulations.

Finally, there are unforeseen circumstances—hurricanes and floods, broken dams, decreasing ozone layers, economic recessions, the fall of the Berlin Wall—which can skew the best-designed and best-intentioned implementation strategies. Flexibility is key to effective implementation, but too much flexibility can result in improper waivers or weak enforcement.

FORMS OF IMPLEMENTATION

Each policy type generates its own set of issues during implementation. This subsection discusses the implementation of the two most environmentally important types of policies: distributive policy and protective regulatory policy.

DISTRIBUTIVE POLICY Although generally stable and dominated by subgovernments, distributive policy may erupt into conflict and difficulties for the implementing agencies. One problem arises when new responsibilities are added to existing, well-established policies. From the agenda setters' perspective, new issues may often be resolved by tacking them onto existing remedies. From the implementors' perspective, this shakes the comfortable coalitions, bringing in new client groups and usually necessitating a redistribution of resources. Another problem may occur when the elected officials change priorities. In theory, bureaucrats should be responsive to the political will of the electorate, which is expressed to them by the political appointees. However, responsive changes are difficult to accomplish after years of sunk costs and interest-group expectations.[13] This becomes especially complicated when the will of the executive differs from the will of the legislature. Finally, changes in society, either through technological advances or resulting from socioeconomic differences, may force bureaus to rethink their allocations of distributive benefits.

PROTECTIVE REGULATORY POLICY Inherently controversial and highly visible, protective regulatory policy is a tinderbox for the bureaucrat implementing it. As technology and economic conditions change, routines for enforcement must change too. Congress is closely involved in implementing protective regulatory policy, because its members hear so frequently from their regulated constituents. The president is also likely to become involved, as President Carter did during the passage of the 1977 Clean Air Act amendments which extended the automakers' deadline to comply with emission standards. Bureaucrats find themselves under pressure from industry and businesses to cut back on enforcement, whereas the environmentalists push for enforcement that often seems punitive.

An example of the enforcement of a protective regulatory policy is a county government's revocation of a restaurant license to protect the public health. The following discussion shows how the administrative process may be used by environmental managers to achieve their policy goals. The case demonstrates the importance of record keeping as part of good administration, and also the necessity of creating a good record during administrative enforcement proceedings.

In October 1987 the Mandarin Restaurant was inspected by two agents of the Coconino County (Arizona) Health Department. The restaurant received a low score, 45 out of a possible 100, which reflected numerous violations, including improper food and facility temperatures, tainted ground beef, and damaged canned goods. The restaurant was found to be keeping leftovers such as tea, rice, and fried wontons to re-serve to customers.

The two health inspectors closed the restaurant immediately because of the many serious violations and its overall poor condition which posed an imminent health hazard to the public. The officers discussed the inspection report with the owners, reviewing all the marked violations. During the inspection, food found at improper temperatures was discarded, and damaged canned goods were impounded as evidence. The operator signed the inspection reports, and the restaurant was closed until further notice.

After review and evaluation of the file, the Health Department decided to suspend the Mandarin Restaurant's health permit, and revocation proceedings were begun. The decision to move for revocation came about in part because the file showed that the restaurant had been closed twice before for imminent health hazards and repeated violations.

To revoke the operator's permit, the department had a choice between a judicial proceeding or an administrative hearing. An administrative hearing was chosen, partly to save money but primarily because it was the fastest way to proceed.

Organizing an administrative hearing was a real challenge for the staff, since this was the first time that the department had taken steps to revoke a food operator's permit. Everything had to be researched, from the sending of a revocation notice to the hiring of an administrative hearing officer. Each detail had to be carefully considered in order to prevent the case from being thrown out on a technicality.

In preparation for the hearing, department staff painstakingly reviewed the regulations for compliance procedures from the County Food Codes and the chapter on Administrative Procedure from the Arizona Revised Statutes. The County Food Code provided for an administrative hearing, outlining violations and the length of time an operator was given to correct them. The state statutes outlined the parameters for notice and hearing, including the

admissibility of evidence, due process, fairness of the hearing, the
appointment of a hearing officer, counsel, and witnesses.

The revocation notice was sent and the hearing date was set
for the end of October. The department then had the task of select-
ing a hearing officer. A judge from the City of Flagstaff was chosen
because of his experience with city court cases, and because he was
neither employed by the county nor personally or financially involved with the restaurant.

Another important element in the preparation for the hearing
was the meetings held with the County Attorney's Office. These
were crucial in the department's interpretation of the law governing the procedures for holding an administrative hearing. It was
equally important to familiarize the Attorney's Office with the Food
Code, so that the department could be effectively represented at
the hearing.

One of the most important aspects of the department's preparation for the hearing was establishing the findings of fact and
organizing the evidence to be presented, since the outcome of the
hearing would rest on these facts. The department's successful prosecution of this case may in large part be due to its extensive efforts
to make the written evidence as clear and concise as possible. This
was especially challenging, since eight handwritten inspection reports had to be reviewed for each repeated violation. This experience emphasized the importance of the clear and accurate
documentation of violations recorded by the health inspectors.

The representative from the County Attorney's office came
well prepared for the hearing. He was knowledgeable about the
Food Code and had reviewed the findings of fact thoroughly. The
department had provided the hearing officer with a copy of the
Food Codes well in advance of the hearing.

The food operators' testimony was weak and ill prepared; they
came to the hearing with an incomplete record of the inspection reports on their restaurant. They had been told they could be represented by an attorney, but they elected not to have one; and their
problems with the English language interfered with their understanding of the proceedings.

The hearing officer ruled in favor of the Health Department.

If the department is ever faced again with a license revocation
hearing, more emphasis will be placed on the collection of evidence, such as photographs of the facility. Additional preparation
would include the acquisition of more food samples, damaged food
equipment, and even insects or rodents (if present). While all this
evidence was not necessary in this revocation hearing, it might have

been needed if the operators had been represented by an attorney. Despite the difficulties the department encountered in this case, the experience was valuable because it revealed the basic steps required to organize and to hold an administrative hearing. These procedures were documented for future reference. While it is recognized that each situation with a food operation will differ in its particulars, the essential steps of collecting evidence, documenting the findings of fact, and presenting the case within the parameters of a hearing remain the same.

EVALUATION

Evaluation occurs at two stages of the policy process.[14] *Formative evaluation* takes place while the policy is being formed and implemented. It allows midcourse corrections if the policy goals are being bypassed or if new and unintended consequences seem imminent. It is flexible and encourages policy outcomes that fit policy intentions. *Summative evaluation* is used when a policy or program is completed. Analysts isolate the goals of the program and then observe how closely the program achieved the goals.

As complicated as implementation may be, evaluation is even more problematic. It is difficult to isolate the precise goals of many policies. Perhaps the legislation was vague, or the goals were impossible to attain given existing technology. The action-forcing provisions of NEPA raised just such problems: how should progress toward goals be evaluated? Policy goals may change between the time the policy reaches the systemic or institutional agendas and the time it is evaluated. Even if achieved, goals may have unintended consequences; for example, did Congress really intend the Endangered Species Act to be used to halt a federal project such as the Tellico Dam? Finally, stated goals may not be the true goals of a policy. For example, in 1984 the state of Maryland declared a moratorium on taking striped bass. One possible explanation for the controversial moratorium was a new state initiative, which had recently been implemented by the governor, to reduce pollution in the Chesapeake Bay. The moratorium would increase striped bass populations; the size of these populations is an indicator in the public mind of water quality, regardless of the effectiveness of the clean-up program. Thus the state program (and the governor) would appear effective even if the clean-up effort were unsuccessful.[15]

A second set of problems involves the measurement of outcomes. Some environmental activities have no direct market value, and various techniques of shadow pricing must be used to derive their monetary value. How, for example, does an evaluator put a price on a day at Yellowstone National Park? Most people would agree that there are some values that cannot be measured, such as the utility of a life or the preservation of the last dusky seaside sparrow, but the demands of regulatory analysis may require that some market value be assigned. Other management programs and directives may have competitive or synergistic effects.

Bureaucrats must also deal with a third set of problems: the dynamic between efficiency and effectiveness. It is often easier to measure efficiency in delivery than effectiveness in achieving goals. A park may increase its total visitor-days and claim legislative applause for serving more citizens per dollar spent. However, if the purpose of the park—or even its partial purpose—was to provide a certain level of satisfaction, information simply on the number of citizens served is not adequate.

Coping with the values of individuals and organizations involved in the policy process is the last problem in evaluation and is perhaps the least amenable to solution. Organizations have values (for example, the Park Service traditionally supports preservation values, while the Forest Service advocates conservation and use); professions within organizations have values (such as the silaculturists' desire to cut old timber); and clients and the general public have values (such as the preservation of wilderness and simultaneous access to the wilderness). Even the evaluator has his or her own values and expectations.

The environmental policy process is exceedingly complex. What appears as a relatively straightforward process is actually an iterative process. Evaluation, or predicting impacts and outcomes, begins with the agenda-setting process, and interest groups dissatisfied with the predicted outcomes begin immediately to reforge the agendas. Formulation and legitimation are shaped in a fluid system that reflects the constant activities of interest groups and the bureaucracies, all the while conscious of the possibility of judicial intervention. Evaluation strategies are chosen and rejected on the basis of their projected political outcomes.

What is necessary to negotiate the political process successfully? Political experience, flexibility, an acceptance of the validity of political decision making, and above all, the realization that nothing is ever final.

52   UNDERSTANDING ENVIRONMENTAL ADMINISTRATION AND LAW

Suggested Reading

Public policy in general

Mazmanian, Daniel, and Paul Sabatier. *Implementation and Public Policy.* Glenview, Ill.: Scott, Foresman, 1983.

Ripley, Randall, and Grace Franklin. *Congress, the Bureaucracy, and Public Policy.* 4th ed. Homewood, Ill.: Dorsey Press, 1991.

——. *Policy Implementation and Bureaucracy.* 2nd ed. Chicago: Dorsey Press, 1986.

Environmental policy

Harris, Richard, and Sidney Milkis. *The Politics of Regulatory Change: A Tale of Two Agencies.* New York: Oxford University Press, 1989. A wonderful discussion of the impact of deregulation on the FTC and EPA.

Rosenbaum, Walter A. *Environmental Politics and Policy.* 2nd ed. Washington, D.C.: Congressional Quarterly, 1991. The standard workhorse for background on environmental policy.

Vig, Norman, and Michael Kraft, eds. *Environmental Policy in the 1980s: Reagan's New Agenda.* Washington, D.C.: Congressional Quarterly, 1984. This book and another by the same authors (below) provide recent analyses of environmental activity in Washington. Most of the articles are specialized but rewarding if one perseveres.

——. *Environmental Policy in the 1990s: Toward a New Agenda.* Washington, D.C.: Congressional Quarterly, 1990. See comment above.

CHAPTER FOUR

LEGAL CONCEPTS IN ENVIRONMENTAL LAW

Every discipline has basic techniques and skills. A miter joint is as necessary for a picture frame as for a house. Basic stitches must be mastered before sewing a hand towel or a suit. So it is with the law. This chapter explains some of the basic stitches of the law.

The first section discusses how to understand legal cases and how to distinguish between the facts of a case and the point of law it establishes. Briefing or summarizing a case is the best way to distinguish between its facts and its law; the section includes a sample brief to illustrate briefing. The other sections deal with legal concepts especially applicable to environmental law: standing, nuisance, property, the public-trust doctrine, and the doctrine of state ownership of wildlife.

UNDERSTANDING CASE LAW

One of the most difficult ideas to grasp in following legal cases is that not all the facts of the case are relevant to the point of law by which the case was decided. It is frustrating to ask for "the rest of the story" and to be unable to discover what happened to the parties in the case.[1] However, from a legal viewpoint, the facts of the case are not the most important information; what matters is the legal precedent that is set. Perhaps the easiest way to remember how cases should be used is to place ourselves in the role of a prosecuting or defending attorney: How would this case support our argument?

To illustrate the importance of the law and the relative unimportance of the facts of the case, consider two cases, *Boyce Motor Lines v. United States* (1952) and *Dalehite v. United States* (1953). Boyce Motor Lines was a trucking firm that transported, among other things, explosives. The regulations of the Interstate

Commerce Commission (ICC) prohibit carrying explosives through tunnels, because a tunnel explosion would endanger more lives than an explosion on an open highway, and because in an underground or—even worse—an underwater tunnel, the damage could be extensive. Unfortunately for Boyce, the ICC also has a rule that requires trucks carrying explosives to move between the pick-up and delivery points as quickly as possible, which usually means traveling by the shortest route. Boyce, a New York City firm, chose to take carbon bisulfide, an explosive, through the Holland Tunnel, reasoning that avoiding the tunnel would keep the truck on the road for many more miles and minutes than was safe. The third time Boyce used the tunnel, the load exploded and about sixty people were injured. Boyce was indicted for violating the tunnel regulations; the district court dismissed the indictment but the appeals court reinstated. Boyce appealed to the Supreme Court, arguing that the two rules were conflicting, that the ICC had not given clear guidance, and that it was impossible to transport explosives into Brooklyn without traveling on some dangerous, congested thoroughfare. The basis of Boyce's argument was that the regulations were impermissibly vague; the Supreme Court disagreed. Although three members of the Court dissented, the majority upheld the ICC and thus Boyce's conviction.

The *Dalehite* case also arose out of an explosion. Explosives and fertilizer may both contain ammonium nitrate; after World War II the Army converted fifteen of its ordnance plants to fertilizer production as part of the American effort to rebuild the agriculture of Europe and Japan. In 1947, in the harbor of Texas City, Texas, two ships loaded with the Army's fertilizer caught fire and blew up. Five hundred and sixty people were killed and over three thousand injured; Texas City practically disappeared. Dalehite and others sought damages from the government, claiming the government had acted negligently in its handling of the potentially explosive materials. In 1953, when the case reached the Supreme Court, existing law exempted the government from liability when the government was performing discretionary actions; the reason for the exemption was that otherwise government officials would be discouraged from making decisions with any element of risk in them at all. Dalehite lost the case. An act of Congress was required to authorize the payment of damages to the victims of the explosion.

At a superficial level, these two cases seem similar. They both deal with explosions and with the transportation of explosives. Yet they cannot be categorized as "explosives" cases. The legal issue in *Boyce* is the alleged vagueness of two ICC regulations concerning the transportation of explosives; however, the issue in *Dalehite* is government liability for accidents—of any kind—that result from the exercise of legitimate discretion. Although a superficial reading of these two cases would find them to be similar, their legal impact is quite different. A careful reading which tried to distinguish the precedent established by each case would distinguish between regulatory vagueness and administrative discretion.

One way to understand a case is to make a *case brief*. This is a written summary, in a standard format, of the important facts and decisions of the case. Briefing a case helps the attorney, or the law student, to grasp the essentials. While managers do not need all the information in a case brief, the habit of briefing is useful. Learning to brief a case may seem only an academic exercise, but the habit of figuring out the reasoning behind an opinion and the point of law is of incalculable value. Without a sense of the progression of legal thought, any explanation of the legal concepts that our regulatory and management processes rely upon will be hard to grasp fully. Legal concepts are fluid, varying with time, with justices, and with substantive areas of the law.

Managers preparing new rules or planning to implement a program need to be able to predict, or at least to understand, judicial reactions to their behavior. By following judicial guidelines, a manager may avoid problems. For example, after the *Calvert Cliffs* decision (discussed in chapter 2), federal agency managers had no doubts about the requirements of the EIS provisions of NEPA. Understanding case law also helps managers interact with the attorneys in their agencies and in the private sector institutions with which they must deal. The entire scope of environmental law would be difficult for one person to master, but the specific case law applying to any given agency's activities is accessible. Being able to distill the importance and impact of judicial decisions for themselves puts managers in control of the law rather than at the mercy of others.

BRIEFING A CASE

The first thing to understand about briefs is that they are short (hence the word *brief*) formal brief starts out with the full name and legal citation of a case, including the year (see box). For administrators, the year a case is decided is very important; an awareness of the technology, social conditions, and political temper at the time the case was decided is critical to understanding how the case may be applied in current situations. The citation, or source, provides the volume number, the name of the series which reports the cases of the deciding court, and the page on which the court opinion begins.

Next comes a summary of the essential facts of the case. These are the behaviors and decisions that led to this particular case coming before the court. For example: Was a species declared an endangered species? Was a cement plant constructed using the best available technology? Will individual members of the Sierra Club be affected when a recreational facility is build in Mineral King Valley? Only those facts necessary to understand the judicial reasoning in the opinion, concurrences, or dissents are included. This section also catalogues how the case came before the court that wrote the opinion. Have all administrative appeals been exhausted? Which court heard the case originally and how did that judge rule? What has been the history of the appeals process for this case?

Next, the issues of the case are stated in the form of a question that can be answered "yes" or "no." For example, in the *Boyce* case, the question is: Are the ICC regulations governing transportation of hazardous materials impermissibly vague? The judicial response, which is the next piece of information in the brief, was "no." The court's response to each issue is followed by the action it ordered, if any.

A summary of the legal reasoning used by the judge writing the opinion follows. In a brief only the reasoning that directly supports the opinion is included. Judicial excursions into interesting tangents are not put into a brief. The name of the judge writing the opinion is important, because judges often develop a chain of reasoning over a series of cases or form temporary alliances with other judges. How the individual judge views an issue may be a key factor in anticipating later judicial reactions. Also, the opinions of some judges are more respected than others', so that the prestige of the judge writing the opinion may give more weight to the decision.

Next are noted concurring and dissenting opinions, if any, and their reasoning. In appeals courts there is usually more than one judge. A judge may agree with the outcome of the case but not agree with the reasoning by which it was reached. A judge may dissent from the outcome. It is in concurring opinions and dissents that we find the clearest expressions of judicial opinions. Concurring opinions are written by judges who agree with the opinion of the court but who disagree with the court's reasoning or who wish to emphasize some aspect of the reasoning. Dissenting opinions reflect judicial disagreement with the outcome of the case; judges write dissents only when their disagreements are intense. In a court opinion, the author is often fusing the decisions and rationales of more than one judge, but the author of a concurring or dissenting opinion is unfettered by such considerations. Since managers need to understand the *reasoning* as a guide to their own future actions, it is important to understand all the legal motivations of the judges who are sufficiently concerned about an issue to write a concurrence or a dissent.

Finally, a brief summarizes the legal principles applied in the case and distinguishes them, if necessary, from those applied in related cases.

It is critical that environmental managers do not carelessly assume that legal decisions and concepts from other policy areas also hold true for environmental policy. A good example of this is the concept of standing. The criteria used to establish standing in environmental matters are not the same as the criteria in, for example, product liability cases.

STANDING

Traditionally, standing is the right to have one's case heard—the right to "stand" before the judge. To have standing, one must have suffered an actual injury to a legally protected right. The case of the *Fontainebleau Hotel Corp. v. Forty-Five Twenty-Five, Inc.* (1959) illustrates some of the common-law considerations for standing.

The Fontainebleau Hotel, built in 1954, was one of the grand hotels of Miami Beach. Its rival, the Eden Roc, was built next door in 1955. The Fontainebleau planned to add a fourteen-story addition that would block the sun from the Eden Roc's beach, cabana, and pool after 2:00 P.M. The Eden Roc asked for and obtained an injunction to stop the construction, and the Fontainebleau appealed. The appeals court supported the Fontainebleau, because under Florida law the Eden Roc had no *legal right* to the sunshine falling on the beach, cabana, and pool. The Eden Roc argued that such a right existed at common law, but the court rejected the argument. There was, the court said, no common law easement given to the Eden Roc; and the hotel had not been built long enough to claim an automatic easement from length of usage.[2] The Eden Roc also invoked the "ancient lights" doctrine, which states that after a building has existed for twenty years, its windows may not be shadowed. However, this has never been an accepted doctrine in American law. The court also found that the Eden Roc had no statutory state constitutional, or federal constitutional right to the sunshine.

Tennessee Valley Authority v. Hill
437 U.S. 153 (1978)

Facts Construction began on Tellico Dam in 1967. In August 1973 a new perch species (the snail darter) was discovered in the river behind the dam site. In December 1973 the Endangered Species Act was passed. In November 1975 the snail darter was listed as endangered. In April 1976 seventeen miles of the Little Tennessee River behind the dam was declared critical habitat for the snail darter. In February 1976, trying to save the snail darter, Hill brought suit in federal district court. He sought an injunction to halt construction. The court denied the injunction, and Hill appealed. The Court of Appeals reversed the district court and ordered the injunction. The TVA appealed to the United States Supreme Court.

Issues
1. Would the TVA be in violation of the Endangered Species Act if it completed and operated the Tellico Dam as planned? Yes.
2. If "yes," is an injunction the appropriate remedy? Yes. The decision of the Court of Appeals is affirmed.

Reasoning: Justice Burger for the Court: The language of the act and the legislative history are clear. Congress intended to "halt and reverse the trend toward species extinction, whatever the cost," and the act "reveals a conscious decision by Congress to give endangered species priority over the 'primary missions' of federal agencies" (p. 184).

Concurrence: None.

Dissent: Justice Powell joined by Justice Blackmun: Congress has funded the Tellico Dam project for twelve years, and it continued this funding even after the Endangered Species Act was passed. There is no indication that the Endangered Species Act was intended to be retroactive. Although Congress will probably exempt the dam from the act, the Court should not force the congressional hand.
Justice Rehnquist also dissented.

Summary: Absent explicit congressional exemptions, the Endangered Species Act is a bar to any federal project that threatens the survival or habitat of a listed species.

It concluded that the hotel had no standing to sue because no legally protected right had been infringed.

In very narrow circumstances, standing may be granted when there is a legally protected right but no actual injury. For example, some environmental statutes grant citizens the right to bring suit without needing to demonstrate an actual physical or economic injury.[3] Most of these acts permit citizen suits only when the agency actions are not discretionary, but there are some exceptions. For example, the Endangered Species Act of 1973 allows a citizen to sue the secretary of the interior "to compel application of prohibitions against the taking of resident endangered species or threatened species," and the permission to bring suit seems to be "without qualification."[4] Section 10 of the Administrative Procedure Act (discussed in chapter 5) provides: "A person suffering legal wrong because of agency action, or adversely affected or aggrieved by agency action within the meaning of a relevant statute, is entitled to judicial review thereof" (5 U.S.C. § 702).

Three cases are key to the interpretation of standing in environmental law. The first of these is *Association of Data Processing Service Organizations v. Camp* (1970), in which the association attempted to reverse an administrative decision allowing banks to provide data processing services to their clients. The question of the association's standing to bring the suit was raised. In this case, the Supreme Court significantly altered the criteria for standing. The Court stated that two questions must be answered: (1) Is the person bringing the suit "aggrieved in fact"? (2) Is the interest to be protected "arguably within the zone of interests to be protected or regulated by the statute or constitutional guarantee in question"?[5] *Data Processing* thus effectively eliminated the test of "legally protected right" in cases of judicial review of administrative action.[6]

The second standing case is the famous Mineral King case, *Sierra Club v. Morton* (1972). The Sierra Club tried to halt the development of a $35-million recreation facility by Walt Disney Enterprises on national forest land in Mineral King Valley. The Sierra Club did not allege any actual injury to its members; it instead asserted a right to be heard because of its organizational interests in protecting the environment. The Supreme Court relied on *Data Processing* and refused to grant the Sierra Club standing; but the Court clearly spelled out how standing might be achieved: all the Sierra Club had to do was assert that some of its members would be unable to enjoy their usual outdoor recreational pursuits if the Disney resort was built. It was in this case that Justice Douglas wrote his famous dissent suggesting that even trees should have standing. He noted that American law already gave legal standing to some inanimate objects, such as ships, and even to some organizations, such as corporations, and he asserted that environmental objectives would be enhanced if litigators could sue on behalf of the trees or valleys or rivers.[7]

In 1973 the Court took its expanded notion of standing to new heights. *United States v. Students Challenging Regulatory Agency Procedures* (SCRAP) was started by five students who formed an organization to challenge an ICC decision to allow across-the-board rate increases for the railroads.[8] The ICC already had in place a higher rate for recycled materials. The students argued that by increasing the rates, the railroads would make recycled materials even less profitable to ship, thus discouraging recycling and increasing the litter in the parks they enjoyed near their home city of Seattle. They also claimed that the lowered demand for recycled materials would cause an increase in logging and mining (to provide raw material for new products), thereby reducing their pleasure in the surrounding countryside. Improbably, the Supreme Court granted standing; however, the challenge to the regulation was unsuccessful.

The decision to grant standing rested on reasoning that must have been a shock to the ICC. The Court said that SCRAP's argument was strengthened by the notion that many people would be affected, and that the rather minimal nature of each person's harm was not a relevant factor. This is opposite to the argument that was accepted by the Court for years as an absolute bar to suits by taxpayers: there are so many taxpayers, and the individual harm done by one new tax to the economic status of any one taxpayer is so small, that taxpayer suits against the government are unacceptable.[9]

After *SCRAP* the Court seemed to pull back from its liberal interpretation of standing in nonenvironmental cases. However, in environmental cases it continued to accept rather tenuous arguments for standing. *Duke Power Co. v. Carolina Environmental Study Group, Inc.* (1978) challenged the 1957 Price-Anderson Act, which limited the liability for damages caused by nuclear power companies to $560 million for any one accident. The Carolina Environmental Study Group claimed that its damages from an accident would probably exceed the Price-Anderson limit, which meant that the statute was depriving them of property (their projected damages) without compensation. The nuclear power plants, they also contended, would never be built without the Price-Anderson protections, and the reactors were harming the environment. The Court granted standing. However, in the decision of the case, the justices determined that the Price-Anderson Act was an acceptable substitute for common law remedies for damages.

There are several reasons why the courts have been more liberal in granting standing in environmental cases than in nonenvironmental ones. First, in the early seventies and following on the heels of NEPA and Earth Day, the courts were eager to give environmentalists a chance to be heard—although being allowed to bring the suit did not guarantee victory for environmentalists. The Sierra Club in the Mineral King case, after the Court had carefully pointed out what the club needed to do to establish standing, immediately and successfully refiled. But the students in *SCRAP* lost their challenge to the ICC regulations. And the Duke Power Company continued to build its reactor. The courts are as sensitive as any other branch of government to public opinion (although they are less vulnerable to expressions of public ill-will), and in these cases they were willing to open the judicial doors for the discussion of issues. Once having been established, the precedent of a relaxed standing requirement in environmental cases continues.

Second, during the early 1970s, the Supreme Court had a number of liberal, activist justices; moreover, Justice Douglas was an ardent environmentalist and often brought his brother justices along with him. Third, in most cases the decisions required statutory interpretation (particularly interpretation of the Administrative Procedure Act as it related to standing), and the judges were not asked to interpret the Constitution in their decisions. Thus one of their traditional barriers to changing the law—a reluctance to change the interpretation of the Constitution—was avoided.

Finally, environmental harms have always had remedies available at common law, and courts are inclined to follow this tradition. Although the circumstances of the environmental harm had changed, the judges still had the common law and its precedents upon which to draw for remedies. One of the common-law concepts that applies to environmental cases is that of nuisance.

NUISANCE

There is a general rule at common law that no one may use his property to impair the right of another person; that is, no one may create a *nuisance*. There are two kinds of nuisance: private and public. A private nuisance is the unreasonable interference with the use or enjoyment of one's land. It does not include physical invasion or trespass, for example, throwing trash over the fence. Playing drums at dawn or polluting a neighbor's well would be private nuisances.[10]

A public nuisance is an activity that adversely affects the health, morals, safety, welfare, comfort, or convenience of the public in general. Large-scale air and water pollution may be considered public nuisances. It is sometimes difficult to distinguish nuisance from trespass. For example, air pollution technically involves particulate matter falling in inappropriate places and is therefore really trespass, but the law tends to treat it as a nuisance. This allows a governmental remedy rather than requiring individuals to sue for damages from trespass.

Whether or not an activity is a nuisance may depend on its location. Courts are typically more lenient in the kinds of undertakings they will permit in rural areas. A hog farm in rural Vermont does not impair the neighbors' use of their property, but transported to Boston, the same hog farm would be banned. Residential areas tend to be the most restrictive. Even when the "nuisance" was in place first, the residential use may have priority, as illustrated in the case of *Spur Industries v. Del Webb Development* (1972).

In 1954 a suburban Phoenix development catering to retirees was established west of Phoenix, Arizona. Two years later a feed lot, later sold to Spur Industries, was started about two miles south of the development. In May 1959 Del Webb began to develop Sun City, building south from the first retirement community. As Sun City grew, so did the feedlot, and by December 1976 the two were only five hundred feet apart. Although Webb had chosen to develop south, and at least in the early years did not consider Spur to be a problem, by 1967 he was having trouble selling residential lots near Spur. Not even Sun City could tolerate thirty thousand head of cattle and a million tons of wet manure per day, baking in the Arizona heat. Webb sued to close Spur, alleging that Spur was both a private and a public nuisance.

Spur contested the action with the defense of "coming to the nuisance": Spur Industries had preceded Del Webb into western Phoenix, and Webb had known all along that the feedlot was there.

The court was sympathetic to the interests of the people living in Sun City and ordered Spur to move, but the court also ordered Webb to pay for the costs of the move. The court reasoned that in the interests of public health and enjoyment of property, Spur must move, but since Webb had put himself and his homebuyers in the predicament, he must pay to extricate them.

Not all such cases end so satisfactorily. Usually when an activity is economically beneficial and yet still a nuisance, the courts find themselves using the "balancing of hardships" or "balancing of the equities" doctrine. In *Boomer v. Atlantic Cement Co.* (1970), a large cement plant was spewing dirt and smoke into the surrounding neighborhood and vibrating the ground. The neighbors claimed this was a nuisance and asked for an injunction to have the nuisance halted. Unfortunately, since the plant was already using the best available technology, the only way to stop the nuisance was to shut the plant. This plant had cost $45 million to build and employed over three hundred local residents. The court weighed the hardship to the community if the plant closed versus the hardship if the nuisance continued. The court decided to allow the plant to continue to operate, but it ordered the plant to pay damages to the neighbors. One judge dissented, saying that to allow the nuisance to continue was the equivalent of giving the power of eminent domain to any private company that chose to pollute.

As is often the case with common-law remedies, the exigencies of the situation may confound our ideas of equitable settlement. The benefits of allowing a nuisance to continue must be balanced against the costs of the nuisance. Who is to blame for the problem? What are the relative hardships for each of the parties? Are there third parties or the public involved?

The next section deals with a concept dear to the heart of Americans; we place it in the pantheon of national values, side by side with life and liberty.

PROPERTY

The concept of property is rooted in English common law.[11] Although the notion of property has expanded since the 1960s to include entitlements such as welfare, this section focuses on real property—land and the economic issues related to land.

The discussion of the origins of land-use control looks at the changes in land tenure systems from feudal days to the Industrial Revolution in the United States. Next, the discussion of eminent domain looks at the ancient right of the sovereign to take private property for public use; in American law this right is constrained by our notions of due process, both procedural and substantive. Then the discussion of zoning looks at government regulation of private property use. Some people have argued that zoning is really a taking or exercise of eminent domain. A discussion of regulation versus taking (which requires compensation) concludes the section on property.

ORIGINS OF LAND-USE CONTROL

The concept of land-use controls or regulations is not a phenomenon of the twentieth century, despite the resistance to zoning and other forms of regulation in rural areas. The regulation of land goes back to ancient times; the earliest code of Roman law, written about 450 B.C., provided for setbacks in housing construction.

Land-use law is not constant; as social and economic conditions change, the law must adapt to protect new arrangements of land use and ownership and to encourage the policies preferred by the authorities. In the eleventh and twelfth centuries, English villages were largely feudal. They had "common" land for the villagers to use for grazing their livestock—though our modern-day notion of *common* as a public right does not accurately describe the medieval commons.[12] In the commons system, either by common-law right as a freehold tenant or through usage and grants, a villager was entitled to pasture limited numbers of specific animals on the land not otherwise used by the feudal lord. The villager also had rights to cut wood, to fish, and to cut peat or turf for fuel. Even from the beginning, the use of the common land was restricted: "Common pasture of stubble and fallow was a feature of open-field husbandry from the start . . . and with it went communal control."[13] The villages determined what kinds of animals and how many might be put on the common, the time of year they could be set loose, how long they might graze, and when they must be removed.

Although the common-land system lasted for centuries, abuses of the system by the wealthier landholders were frequent. In the sixteenth, seventeenth, and eighteenth centuries,

> the poor owning rights may largely be kept out of their rights by the action of large farmers who exceed their rights and thus surcharge the common to the detriment of all, or by the lack of winter feed in the absence of which summer grazing could be of little worth. Again, jobbers would hire cottages in order to obtain, as it were, a right of entry to the common and then proceed to eat up the common; or new cottages would spring up near the common, and though legally without rights, would encroach in practice on those to whom the common really belonged.[14]

The unfortunate tenants were denied any remedy at law for the illegal abuses of the more powerful landowners. The ultimate conclusion was the enclosure of the common land, mostly between 1720 and 1880. Political demands for land reform were frequently no more than a sophisticated land grab, justified in part by the admittedly striking increase in productivity of enclosed common land.

The increased productivity was often touted by land reformers—wealthy or otherwise—as proof of the evils of the commons system. However, the change was the result of many factors and not just of enclosure. Some of the increase would probably have occurred without enclosure, but enclosure hastened the process. The common land was not the best land. The lord's waste was often reclaimed land, cultivated from forest and marsh. Enclosure took the better land and subjected it to new and improved methods of agriculture, which had been all but impossible under the commons system, for the management of the common could not be changed unless all commoners agreed and, just as important, remained agreed. Improved roads and transportation facilities made marketing easier, and of course, the land had fewer people to support.

Economies of scale made it profitable to use improved stock. In 1760 Robert Bakewell, the founder of modern methods of livestock improvement, began selective breeding of farm animals. Previously forbidden by ecclesiastical authorities as incest, inbreeding of animals with desirable qualities soon led to dramatic improvements in stock. Planting the enclosure with nitrogen-fixing crops, such as clover, improved the soil; drainage improved livestock health. Animals were no longer driven to and from pasture land. All of these factors combined to improve the productivity of the formerly common land. Economic pressures from abroad encouraged enclosure, and by the end of the eighteenth century the commons system was effectively gone.

While the system of communal land control was changing in rural areas, the urban landscape was also under examination. Urban crowding reached unthinkable heights, and in London the Great Fire recorded by Samuel Pepys in the seventeenth century produced building codes and land-use restrictions.

The American colonists brought with them an acceptance of land-use controls, but they found that in the New World such regulations were not necessary. Land was plentiful, and only when the census of 1890 declared the American frontier officially closed did Americans really begin to come to grips with the need for land reform and regulation.

Conflicts over land use were at first easy to settle. Usually the common-law remedy of nuisance was sufficient to settle private disputes. Initially, the strength of the concept of property rights, and the Lockean notion that if a person had worked for something and paid for it, it was his to do with as he wished, overrode any suspicion

that the public might be better served if certain activities were prohibited or restricted. However, as the American cities grew, public
controls became necessary. Cities began to pass ordinances restricting certain kinds of activities (such as slaughterhouses, with their at-
tendant odors and refuse; or tanneries; or candlemakers) to
particular parts of town. The source of the power to regulate such
activities is the *police power*: the authority to regulate on behalf of
public health, safety, morals, and general welfare. Objections to the
exercise of the police power generally rested on the notion that the
government was taking an individual's property for public use, but
in the nineteenth century, taking only meant the actual physical
seizure of property. The expansion of the notion of "taking" is discussed later in this chapter.

Most controls on land use come from government regulation,
but some arise at common law. One is the concept of nuisance, discussed in the preceding section. Another is the notion of *waste*,
which can arise when people share interests and rights in a
resource. Waste is committing acts upon the land that are harmful
to the rights of the party not in possession. For example, tenants
who cut down all the trees in their landlord's yard would be guilty
of waste. Waste can be affirmative (such as cutting down the trees)
or permissive (such as allowing a roof to deteriorate so that rain
damages the interior of the house). The remedy for waste can be
money damages, an injunction to stop the conduct that is causing
the harm, or some combination of the two.

There are also some private law or contractual devices to control property, such as covenants and easements. An easement is the
legal right to use or to traverse someone else's land and must be
transferred when the property is transferred. Often utility companies have easements across private property for power lines or tele-
phone wires or water pipes. Covenants are restrictions that "run
with the land." Unlike easements, which in effect allow a physical
trespass on the owner's property, covenants restrict the uses to
which the land may be put. These covenants are voluntary, in the
sense that buyers don't have to buy if they don't like them, but they
are usually binding and also transfer with the property. Examples of
covenants include prohibitions on children in retirement communities, restrictions on the types and heights of fences that may be
erected around a property, and minimum house sizes. Covenants
that are discriminatory, such as banning any racial or religious
groups from buying property in a neighborhood, are not legally
enforceable.

EMINENT DOMAIN

The right of the state to take private property is ancient. All property at one time belonged to the Crown, and in England today this is still technically true. When the sovereign took a subject's property, he was simply reclaiming property that already belonged to him. The sovereign was not required to use due process, nor was he required to pay compensation. In the United States, the Fifth Amendment to the Constitution imposes an obligation on the sovereign to exercise due process of law in taking private property and an obligation to pay compensation for it:

> No person shall . . . be deprived of life, liberty, or property, without due process of law; nor shall private property be taken for public use, without just compensation.

From an analytic perspective, there are several points to be noted in interpreting the Fifth Amendment. First, the amendment protects *persons*, not just citizens; some sections of the Constitution (for example, the Eleventh Amendment) apply only to citizens. Second, the amendment does permit persons to be deprived of life, liberty, or property; the restriction is that this must be done with "due process of law." What is due process? At a minimum, it includes a hearing; just what kind of hearing is required is discussed later in this section. The government does in fact deprive persons of life (capital punishment), liberty (imprisonment), and property (taxes). There is, however, a restriction on taking real property; the amendment states that private property may not be taken for public use "without just compensation." If the federal government wants a person's farm for a military base, for example, it may take the farm but must pay a reasonable price for it. The power to do this is known as the power of eminent domain. It is not essential that the government be taking property for actual use by the government. "Public use" can mean either actual use by the public (highways, national parks) or private use for public advantage (for example, easements for electric power lines). In the nineteenth century the federal government even gave the power of eminent domain to the railroads as an incentive for them to build a transcontinental line.

JUST COMPENSATION   Usually just compensation is determined by fair market value: what a willing buyer would pay a willing seller to buy the land. If only part of the property is taken, and the value of the remainder is changed, compensation is adjusted to include the loss (or increase) of value. A simpler calculus that is sometimes employed is the difference between the value before the taking and the value after. There are other kinds of property rights which must be compensated; people other than the owner may have vested rights in the property. For example, some states still recognize dower rights, which give the wife a certain percentage of the value of all of her husband's real property, regardless of when or how he acquired it. When this property is taken, the dower rights must also be compensated. A lessee may need compensation, as may a person holding an easement across the property, or someone with other rights such as mineral rights. Who is entitled to compensation and how that entitlement is calculated is a complex issue that varies widely between political jurisdictions.

State governments can exercise the power of eminent domain. Must they observe due process and pay compensation? The Fifth Amendment is found in the federal Constitution, and until the end of the nineteenth century it was held to apply only to the actions of the federal government. Although many states had similar clauses in their state constitutions, in 1868 when the Fourteenth Amendment passed, five states still lacked the requirement for just compensation when the state seized private property. The Fourteenth Amendment reads in part:

> No State shall make or enforce any law which shall abridge the privileges or immunities of citizens of the United States; nor shall any State deprive any person of life, liberty, or property, without due process of law; nor deny to any person within its jurisdiction the equal protection of the laws.

The Supreme Court has held that the Fourteenth Amendment protects persons from state government actions as well as from federal government actions. Thus the national Constitution's prohibition on taking private property without just compensation also applies to the states. This has important ramifications for zoning and other forms of land-use regulation.

DUE PROCESS There are two forms of due process: procedural and substantive. Procedural due process is concerned with the forms and procedures followed by government when exercising its legitimate functions; substantive due process is concerned with the legitimacy of those functions. Usually a reference to "due process" refers to *procedural* due process. Substantive due process is rarely invoked.

PROCEDURAL DUE PROCESS Any government action that will affect a person's property requires some form of hearing before the action is taken. Environmental management usually involves administrative hearings rather than court proceedings; there are important differences between the two. In an administrative hearing there is no right to a trial by jury. Evidence is presented in a less formal manner than in court. The decision maker is not totally independent of the agency holding the hearing—administrative law judges are civil servants and vulnerable to transfers, salary changes, and some political pressures. Usually the individual affected in an administrative hearing has the option to appeal the decision, but often he or she must first exhaust nonjudicial remedies before being allowed to take the case to the courts. Some statutes even forbid judicial review of agency decisions.

The Coconino County restaurant license revocation, described in chapter 3, is an example of an administrative hearing.

The case which lays the constitutional foundation for hearings in the administrative decision process is *Londoner v. Denver* (1908). The Colorado legislature had authorized the city of Denver to order street paving and to apportion costs to the adjoining property owners. The city did not allow a hearing for the property owners. The Supreme Court decided that when a tax is determined by a *subordinate body* (that is, an administrative agency acting under delegated legislative authority), the constitutional due process provisions give the taxpayers the right to a hearing. Later cases restricted the taxpayers' right to a hearing;[15] but the important point is that a hearing may be required prior to an action of a subordinate body.

The precise nature of the required hearing differs dramatically, depending upon the issue and the parties involved. Schoolchildren may be entitled to due process before being suspended from school, but their hearing can be a simple conference in the hall with the school principal. A chemical company challenging new EPA regulations will probably receive a full-scale trial-like administrative hearing.

Although an agency may be required to provide a hearing, the adversely affected person is not required to take advantage of the offer. The right to a hearing may be waived, and in fact it usually is. Although the percentages vary among federal agencies, fewer than 5 percent of the parties eligible for a full-scale hearing actually have one.[16]

SUBSTANTIVE DUE PROCESS Substantive due process is particularly of interest in environmental administration because so much of the environmental law deals with regulation. In the early years of the twentieth century, the courts took the view that the legislative power did not include economic regulation. The judges held that individuals had certain fundamental rights that were entitled to judicial protection from legislative interference. Property was considered one of these basic rights (along with life and liberty). In *Lochner v. New York* (1905) the Supreme Court invalidated a New York law regulating the hours of bakery workers, on the grounds that it interfered with the right of contract between employers and employees. From 1905 to the mid-1930s, the theory of substantive due process provided justification for the courts to invalidate many state laws involving economic regulation, especially labor legislation, price regulation, and limitations on entry into business. In 1934, because of such actions, the Court was on a collision path with President Roosevelt. Justice Owen Roberts performed the "switch in time that saved nine," and as a result of his swing vote the Court refused to invalidate a New York law that fixed the selling price of m..lk.[17] By 1941, the about-face was complete:

> [T]he Supreme Court has consistently maintained that, so far as the due process . . . [clause is] concerned, legislative policy in economic matters is solely for the legislature. It has repeatedly taken the position that it will not review the legislative judgment in such matters and has denounced as overruled, or no longer in good standing, the leading due process decisions of the earlier 1905-1934 era in which the Court struck down significant economic legislation by substituting its judgment for that of the legislative bodies.[18]

This posture has given both the federal and the state legislatures a free hand in regulating businesses for environmental reasons. Business has tried unsuccessfully to claim that the legislatures lack the authority to regulate their enterprises, but the environmental interests have prevailed.

ZONING

The first comprehensive zoning plan in the United States was passed by New York City in 1916.[19] Since then the validity of zoning has repeatedly been upheld by the courts as a legitimate use of the police power. Zoning is invalid only if it is unreasonable or arbitrary or capricious—the usual standards against which administrative action is judged—or if it deprives the owner of all or practically all of the use of his or her property. The general rule is that to be valid, zoning must be authorized by enabling statutes; comprehensive zoning is usually governed by statute and therefore is better able to withstand judicial challenge than incremental or piecemeal zoning.

The landmark case for comprehensive zoning is *Euclid v. Ambler Realty Company* (1926). This was the first case in which the Supreme Court directly addressed the constitutionality of zoning. Ambler Realty owned property abutting an industrial area. The property was zoned residential, cutting its value by two-thirds. Ambler sued the city on the grounds that the zoning restriction was an unconstitutional taking without either due process or compensation. The Supreme Court upheld the use of the state's governmental police power.

Why would this case rest on an exercise of *state* power when it was the village of Euclid that had enacted the zoning ordinance? The reason rests on a peculiarity of American land-use law. The counties and cities have no sovereign status. The powers that they have are given to them by the states, and so the exercise of land regulation is indirectly an exercise of a state power.

The basis for many zoning challenges is that the localities exceeded the authority given to them by their state governments. However, because the zoning process is based on state legislative authority, a local zoning ordinance will usually not be overturned unless it is found to be arbitrary or capricious.

REGULATION VERSUS TAKING

A big quandary in land-use law is distinguishing between (1) a permissible use of the police power to regulate land use for the general welfare and (2) government action that takes a person's property and requires compensation. One way to distinguish between regulation and taking is to examine the purposes of government actions. A government action is regulatory if it interferes with the property to prevent *harm* to the public; but if the interference were for the public's *benefit*, then the action is a taking and requires compensation. Thus a zoning decision that inhibited housing development to protect a watershed would be regulatory, but a similar decision to provide parking for a football stadium would be a taking.

The landmark case in this area is *Pennsylvania Coal Co. v. Mahon* (1922). The Pennsylvania Coal Company owned the subsurface mining rights under Mahon's house. The Mahons' contract with the coal company relieved the coal company of any liability should there be any collapse or subsidence as a result of mining operations. The state of Pennsylvania passed a law that forbade mining that caused subsidence of residential property. The company claimed that the statute took away its property rights in the coal and was therefore a taking. The Supreme Court agreed. Justice Louis Brandeis dissented, writing that it was not a taking because the purpose of the statute was to protect the public.

Six years later Justice Brandeis was vindicated in *Miller v. Schoene* (1928). The Court upheld a Virginia law that authorized the state to destroy a grove of ornamental trees to prevent the spread of a destructive disease to a neighboring apple orchard. This was not viewed as a taking of the ornamental trees but rather as a balancing between two forms of property: ornamental trees versus commercially valuable apple trees. The statute was held to be a permissible form of regulation to protect the public from economic harm.

Similar issues arise in governmental actions to protect flood plains, wetlands, and other natural areas. The Supreme Court ruled in *Morris County Land Improvement Co. v. Township of Parsippany-Troy Hills* (1963) that an ordinance restricting the kinds of fill and the uses of filled land was an unconstitutional taking. The ordinance's prohibitions had the effect of converting the land into terrain suitable for public use (such as fishing and recreation), and the company was therefore entitled to compensation.

A similar case is *Dooley v. Town Plan and Zoning Commission of Fairfield* (1964). An ordinance restricted the uses to which a flood plain could be put: parks, playgrounds, marinas, boat houses, landings and docks, and clubhouses. The value of the property owners' land was diminished because of the restrictions. The court ruled that the ordinance was confiscatory, and compensation must be paid to the property owners.

A more recent case, *Just v. Marinette County* (1972), illustrates the change in judicial perspective that occurred in the environmental decade of the seventies. In 1961, the Justs had bought thirty-six acres of land along the shore of a lake in Marinette County. Over the next six years, they made several more purchases of shorefront property, intending to use the property for their own home and to subdivide for other houses. In 1967 Marinette County adopted a shoreland zoning ordinance to protect navigable waters. To save the waters from degradation, the ordinance prohibited the filling of more than a certain amount of wetlands without a conditional use permit. The Justs' property was classified as wetlands, so they were required to get a permit if they planned to fill in any of their shorefront property. The Justs filled in a significant portion of their property without obtaining a permit and were subsequently charged with a violation of the ordinance. The Justs contended that the ordinance was unconstitutional, because it made their shorefront land unusable and was therefore a taking without compensation. The court disagreed, finding that Wisconsin was exercising its public-trust responsibilities and was properly using the state police power to protect the natural environment.

In a 1978 decision, *Pennsylvania Central Transportation Co. v. New York*, the Supreme Court held that "taking" cases must be decided by a three-part test. First, a taking probably exists if there has been a physical invasion of the property, for example, running a power line. Second, a taking may exist if the restriction on the property does not produce widespread public benefit or it is not applied to all property in similar situations. Third, the court must examine the extent to which the property owner is restricted from earning a reasonable rate of return on his or her investment in the property.

Cases in the late eighties brought into sharper focus the concerns of municipal and state planning authorities over the exercise of their land use powers. In *First English Evangelical Lutheran Church of Glendale v. City of Los Angeles* (1987), the Supreme Court gave damages to the landowner for income lost as a result of land use regulations. Also in 1987, the Court ruled in *Nollan v. California Coastal Commission* that the Coastal Commission's requirement of public access to the beach over Nollan's property was a taking.

The law remains unclear. For decades, property has not been granted the same judicial attention as the other protected rights, life and liberty. As the conservative members of the bench become more plentiful and more powerful, property may reassert its position in the hierarchy of protected rights.

THE PUBLIC-TRUST DOCTRINE

One of the arguments accepted in *Just* (above) was that Wisconsin was quite properly exercising its public-trust responsibilities. This notion of the public trust, which in American law dates from *Martin v. Waddell* (1842), is based on the common-law doctrine that the navigable rivers and waterfronts are held by the sovereign for the use of all the people.[20] Much of the debate on public-trust resources is concerned with alienation, that is, the relinquishing of publicly owned resources into private hands.

The landmark case in public trust is *Illinois Central Railroad Co. v. Illinois* (1892). In 1869 the state of Illinois had granted some submerged Chicago shorefront lands in Lake Michigan to the Illinois Central Railroad. Four years later, repenting of its gift, the state repealed the grant. The state then filed suit to "quiet the title" so the chain of state ownership would be clearly recorded, and the railroad objected. The state's taking title to land that was formerly privately owned seemed to raise the constitutional question of a violation of the due process clause. However, the Supreme Court avoided the constitutional question by finding the original grant of land to be invalid because it violated Illinois's public-trust obligations. This case established the central tenet in public-trust litigation:

> When a state holds a resource which is available for the free use of the general public, a court will look with considerable skepticism upon *any* governmental conduct which is calculated *either* to reallocate that resource to more restricted uses *or* to subject public uses to the self-interest of private parties.[21]

Traditionally the public trust has applied only to tidelands and waters used in navigation, water-related commerce, and fisheries; under the original English common law, inland resources were the property of the Crown and were not within the public trust.[22] The public-trust doctrine has, however, been expanded to include national parks, inland lakes, and wildlife. As with many of the common-law doctrines accepted from England but modified to fit New World needs, the public-trust doctrine is unclear and its application varies.

> Public trust law is not a sophisticated or well-coordinated branch of the substantive law. The use of wetlands for navigation, fishery, or commerce may conflict with one of the other public trust uses. . . . The confusion in public trust law derives partly from state legislatures' leaving to the courts the role of defining public trust use and of establishing a hierarchy of preferred uses. The courts, left to fashion the law from a hodgepodge of fact situations, have understandably been unable to formulate a comprehensive body of law.[23]

Traditionally the public-trust doctrine has been put to a variety of uses. It may be used to challenge a government action (such as alienation) or as a defense by a citizen against government action (for example, to resist a condemnation or to assert a public use). Citizens may use the doctrine against other citizens. Government may exercise the trust either to recover damages from private parties or from other units of government, or to protect its legislative prerogatives to define and to exercise the trust.[24]

Under current law, the public-trust doctrine is invoked only when a violation is alleged. The doctrine may not be used to compel agency activity without some triggering event. For example, in the Mono Lake case, *National Audubon Society v. Department of Water and Power of the City of Los Angeles* (1983), the trust doctrine was invoked to halt the city of Los Angeles drawing municipal water from Mono Lake; and in the Redwood National Park litigation, *Sierra Club v. Department of the Interior* (1974, 1975, and 1976), logging on private lands adjacent to a national park triggered the lawsuit.

The public trust includes "an affirmative protective duty of government—a fiduciary obligation—in dealing with certain properties held publicly."[25] Some authorities go even further; one has said that resource managers have to carry out the public trust "as the Bank of America trust officer would for a trust you set up for your children—strict adherence to trust principles."[26] Public trust resources

> are protected by the trust against unfair dealing and dissipation, which is classical trust language suggesting the necessity for procedural correctness and substantive care. . . . The public trust doctrine demands fair procedures, decisions that are justified, and results that are consistent with protection and perpetuation of the resources.[27]

At least one state court has found that the public trust in natural resources is an "active" trust. In 1927, the Wisconsin state Supreme Court ruled:

> The trust reposed in the state is not a passive trust; it is governmental, active, and administrative. . . . [T]he trust, being both active and administrative, requires the lawmaking body to act in all cases where action is necessary, not only to preserve the trust, but to promote it. . . . A failure so to act, in our opinion, would have amounted to gross negligence and a misconception of its proper duties and obligations in the premises.[28]

THE STATE OWNERSHIP DOCTRINE

Closely connected to the idea of public trust is the notion of the state ownership of wildlife. Although partially discredited today, the doctrine has had a great impact on international, federal, and state wildlife law.[29]

In *Martin v. Waddell* (1842), Chief Justice Roger Taney found that the rights to the navigable waters, submerged lands, fish, and wildlife could not have been conveyed by King Charles to the Duke of York as alienable rights because such rights were a public trust. The public character of the rights was passed on to the various sovereign states, which thereafter also owned the wildlife. Technically this decision applied only to the original thirteen states. However, in 1845 a question arose about the status of wildlife in new states. In *Pollard's Lessee v. Hagan,* the Court applied the ruling to newly admitted states as well, citing the legislative convention that new states are admitted on an equal footing with previously existing states.

The state ownership doctrine was challenged again in 1855 in *Smith v. Maryland.* The case involved a shipowner who had been taking oysters with a scoop or drag in defiance of Maryland law. Smith's vessel was licensed by the federal government, and he contended that the state law was an unconstitutional interference with the federal power to regulate interstate commerce. The Supreme Court held that because Maryland owned the soil on which the oysters were located, Maryland was allowed to regulate the oyster fisheries. Maryland's claim of state ownership in this case overrode the commerce clause of the Constitution. The Court carefully protected its own prerogatives on future related questions:

> Whether this liberty [to take oysters] belongs exclusively to the citizens of the State of Maryland, or may lawfully be enjoyed in common by all citizens of the United States; whether this public use may be restricted by the States to its own citizens, or a part of them, or by force of the Constitution must remain common to all citizens of the United States; whether the national government, by a treaty or act of congress, can grant to foreigners the right to participate therein; or what, in general, are the limits of the trust upon which the State holds this soil, or its power to define and control that trust, are matters wholly without the scope of this case, and upon which we give no opinion.[30]

Of course, the Court was not allowed to leave so many loose ends forever. *McCready v. Virginia* (1876) gave Virginia ownership of not only the tidewaters but also the fish and oysters in those waters.

At issue was a Virginia statute that prohibited non-Virginia residents from planting oysters in the Virginia tidal waters. The Court held that the state was only regulating the common property of the people it represented. This was a substantial expansion of the earlier decisions in *Martin* and *Smith*. However, in 1891 the Court decided that the commonwealth of Massachusetts could regulate fishing in Buzzards Bay, not because it owned the fish but because, absent any conflicting federal regulation, the state probably had the right to regulate within its territorial waters.[31] This represented a change from the strong endorsement of state ownership laid out in *McCready*. The Court was growing cautious, and it seemed to distinguish *McCready* on the basis that *McCready* dealt with shellfish (stationary and imbedded in soil) rather than finfish, which move through waters that are under federal as well as state jurisdiction.

In 1896 *Geer v. Connecticut* indicated a return to the notion that the states owned their wildlife and were independent of federal interference in the management of the wildlife. Geer was prohibited under Connecticut law from exporting lawfully killed game birds; the Court offered three separate arguments to support the state law. First, since the state owned the game, "commerce" within the meaning of the Constitution was—perhaps—not initiated when the game was killed. Second, even if commerce were initiated, it was at the most *intra*state commerce, because—due to the Connecticut statute—the game could not be exported. Finally, even if interstate commerce were occurring, so that the statute was an interference with interstate commerce, nevertheless the right of the state to exercise the police power and to preserve a food supply for its citizens overrode the commerce clause. Although *Geer* recognized that some states' rights in wildlife were transferred by the Constitution to the federal government, the case was still used to uphold the state ownership doctrine.

At the turn of the century, Teddy Roosevelt's conservation movement was in full cry. The Sierra Club was eight years old; the federal government had passed the Forest Management Act (1897); and the River and Harbor Act (1899) had established the legal basis for controlling pollution on navigable waterways. The passage of the Lacey Act in 1900 fitted right in. The Lacey Act prohibits the interstate transportation of any game killed in violation of state law; in addition, it permits a state to prohibit the importation of game lawfully killed in another state. This expanded the holding in *Geer*, which allowed states to prohibit the export of lawfully killed game; the Lacey Act allows them to prohibit the import of lawfully killed game.

In 1912 the Court confirmed the expansion of the state power to regulate the taking of wildlife; Justice Edward White, author of the *Geer* opinion, held in *The Abbey Dodge* that the state ownership doctrine preempted federal wildlife law. This extreme position did not hold for long; in 1926 *Foster-Fountain Packing Co. v. Haydel* softened *Geer* by holding that once wildlife enters the stream of commerce, the state loses absolute control over that wildlife.

FEDERAL REGULATION OF WILDLIFE

Geer was the high-water mark for state regulation of wildlife. Since then, various Supreme Court decisions have established three constitutional bases for federal regulation of wildlife: the federal treaty-making power, the federal property power, and the federal commerce power.

In 1913 Congress passed the Migratory Bird Act, which declared all migratory game and insectivorous birds to be under federal protection and regulation. Promptly challenged in federal district courts, the act was found unconstitutional. While the United States' appeal was pending, the government concluded a treaty with Great Britain to protect migratory birds; in 1918 Congress repealed the Migratory Bird Act and passed a new act, the Migratory Bird Treaty Act, to implement the treaty. The Court never ruled on the constitutionality of the Migratory Bird Act.

The Migratory Bird Treaty Act was challenged when the state of Missouri filed to prohibit a federal game warden from enforcing the act. In *Missouri v. Holland* (1920), the Court stunned the states by agreeing with the federal government that, under the treaty power of the Constitution and the supremacy clause (which asserts federal supremacy in all conflicts between federal and state laws), the treaty and its implementing legislation took precedence over the state interest. Federal wildlife regulation seemed assured.

Although the federal power to regulate wildlife through the treaty provisions of the Constitution had been established, the federal power to hunt or to manage wildlife on federal lands was not so clearly established. The federal government as landowner within state boundaries was held by the states to be simply another property owner and therefore subject to state wildlife regulations. However, the Supreme Court held in *Kleppe v. New Mexico* (1976) that the federal government had the power to regulate and to protect the wildlife living on federal land within a state.

Until 1977, there was no Supreme Court decision that speci-
fied the reach of the Constitution's commerce clause in federal
wildlife regulation. In that year, *Douglas v. Seacoast Products, Inc.*
determined that a Virginia residency requirement for menhaden
fishing was preempted by the federal licenses held by the fishing
vessels. In *Douglas* the Court clearly rejected the state ownership
doctrine:

> A State does not stand in the same position as the owner of a private
> game preserve and it is pure fantasy to talk of "owning" wild fish,
> birds, or animals. Neither the States nor the Federal Government,
> any more than a hopeful fisherman or hunter, has title to these crea-
> tures until they are reduced to possession by skillful capture.[32]

The present status of the state ownership doctrine was summa-
rized in the *Tangier Sound* case (discussed in chapter 1), which
granted fishing rights in Virginian waters to Maryland fishermen:

> In sum, the dilution of the ownership theory has been such that in
> the Court's analysis of a statutory scheme, "ownership" of a natural
> resource is but one factor that the Court must consider in determin-
> ing whether a State has exercised its police power in conformity with
> federal law and the Constitution.[33]

Suggested Reading

Bean, Michael J. *The Evolution of National Wildlife Law*. New York: Praeger,
   1983. This is the only book that I know of on this topic; fortunately for
   us all, it is a clear, complete, and well-written treatise.

Cooper, Phillip. *Public Law and Public Administration*. 2nd ed. Englewood
   Cliffs, N.J.: Prentice-Hall, 1988. This is *not* a casebook, which makes it a
   rarity among books on administrative law.

Hoban, Thomas More, and Richard Oliver Brooks. *Green Justice: The Environment and the Courts*. Boulder, Colo.: Westview Press, 1987. This book
   is a mixture of casebook and explanatory text. The authors have a
   scarcely concealed antiregulatory bias, but the general discussions are
   excellent.

CHAPTER FIVE

CONTROLLING POLLUTION AND HAZARDOUS AND TOXIC SUBSTANCES

Regulating the production, use, and disposal of harmful substances is a responsibility shared by the national government and the states. This chapter presents the administrative framework within which such regulation occurs. The chapter begins with a discussion of the Administrative Procedure Act (APA). Although the APA does not deal directly with environmental matters, it is the basic legislation that governs all federal agencies. Most states have similar legislation, so to understand the framework that informs environmental regulations, it is necessary first to grasp the basic points of the APA.

The second section discusses the legal liability of administrative officials. The next section presents the basic legislation aimed at controlling air and water pollution. Most regulatory processes are punitive and focus on outputs (emissions); this section also examines some alternative approaches to pollution control. The fourth section focuses on hazardous and toxic wastes and outlines the regulation of pesticides, the provisions of the Clean Air Act and Clean Water Act that deal with hazardous and toxic substances, the Toxic Substances Control Act, and Superfund.

The chapter concludes with a discussion of pollution control in Great Britain, which operates under the same original legal premises as the United States but implements control policy quite differently.

THE ADMINISTRATIVE PROCEDURE ACT

The Administrative Procedure Act of 1946 was the culmination of years of anxious debate among government officials, legal scholars, and the business community. The administrative state had been growing rapidly since the late nineteenth century; the New Deal led to a proliferation of both independent agencies and the overall bureaucracy. The lawyers were especially concerned as power shifted from the courts to the executive agencies. They were being closed out of the decision process by Roosevelt's bright young men in the agencies.

In 1934, the second year of the New Deal, the American Bar Association (ABA) formed an administrative law committee that issued annual reports stressing the reduced power of the judicial branch. Joining these critical voices were the conservatives who used complaints about fairness, due process, and conformity to the common law to cloak their opposition to Roosevelt's economic and social policies. Some of the critics, however, were genuinely concerned about what they perceived as threats from the administrative process to traditionally protected rights. Their basic question was how the political system could maintain justice and the constitutionally mandated separation of powers if one person or agency acted as legislature (making rules), prosecutor (investigating infractions), judge (conducting hearings), and enforcing agent. As it became increasingly clear that the agencies were involved in *making* policy as well as interpreting legislative policies, concerns about the substantive law increased as well.

The ABA's Special Committee on Administrative Law had managed in 1935 to engineer the passage of the Federal Register Act. The *Federal Register* for the first time provided a daily record of the administrative activities of the executive branch; for example, it contained the texts of executive orders and proposed and final rules. Encouraged by this success, the committee lobbied for the Walter-Logan Bill, which was passed by Congress in December 1940. Proponents of the bill defended it as providing safeguards for individual liberties, unsullied by technical expertise: "Judicial review deals not so much with technical facts as with fairness of hearing— a matter not for technical experts but for impartial courts."[1] It was felt that a rigid procedural code would remove political pressures from the agencies by providing standards upon which to base decisions and by promoting rule making rather than case-by-case adjudication.

However, although the bill passed Congress, President Roosevelt vetoed it. Opponents of the bill charged that it was nothing more than a blatant attempt to wrest control of the administration from the president. In his veto message, Roosevelt singled out for opprobrium two particular groups: lawyers and large business interests: "The bill that is now before me is one of the repeated efforts by a combination of lawyers who desire to have all processes of government conducted through lawsuits and of interests which desire to escape regulation."[2]

Roosevelt had another, more mundane reason for his veto. The final report of the Attorney General's Committee on Administrative Procedure was almost complete. The work of this committee was unique; instead of merely taking testimony and generating a report, it conducted primary investigation and produced legislation. For the first time, the administrative process was studied on the

> basis of knowledge rather than of hypothesis or preconceived ideas. . . . [The committee] studied the administrative establishment from the inside, thoroughly and dispassionately. Its acute discussion of the characteristics of the administrative process, its conclusions as to defects existing in the process, and its proposals to remedy them all sprang from and were buttressed by facts laboriously ascertained and carefully weighed.[3]

The attorney general's report affirmed the necessity for and value of the administrative process. It found that agencies were an inevitable development and were essential for the effective management of a modern, industrial government. This was at least the view of the majority of the committee; the minority extended the recommendations of the majority in an attempt to impose a uniform code of administrative behavior on the agencies. The majority felt that the substantive issues dealt with by the various agencies were so complex and idiosyncratic that no uniform code could govern them all; the minority disagreed—and it is their bill which actually provided the basis for the APA.

Although extensive hearings were held in the summer of 1941 on the proposed administrative legislation, America's entry into World War II delayed further consideration of any administrative procedure legislation. Close to the end of the war, the ABA began again to agitate for legislation, and in 1946 the Administrative Procedure Act was passed.

The major impact of the act was that it codified existing practice and law; in other words, it found a common ground among the agencies. The APA has six major portions, all of which have relevance to environmental administration and law: definitions of terms used in the act; the rules for fair information practices; guidelines for rule making; procedures for adjudication; creation of administrative law judges; and provisions for judicial review of agency actions.

DEFINITIONS OF TERMS

The first section of the APA defines the terms used in the legislation. While this definition of terms is important in any legislation, it is especially important in the APA because it provides a point of reference for the agencies. Any agency which had previously used different phrases to describe agency activities could turn to this section and discover the common terminology.

FAIR INFORMATION PRACTICES

One sign of the success of the APA is how little it has been amended since 1946. Virtually all of the amendments occur in the second section of the act; they are primarily additions made in the sixties and seventies in response to criticisms of governmental abuses of power. Section 552 is the Freedom of Information Act of 1966; section 552(a) is the Privacy Act of 1974; and section 552(b) is the Government in the Sunshine Act of 1976.

RULE MAKING

The third section of the APA is perhaps the most important. It provides the guidelines for the federal rule-making procedures.[4]

> A "rule" means the whole or a part of an agency statement of general or particular applicability and future effect designed to implement, interpret, or prescribe law or policy or describing the organization, procedure, or practice requirements of an agency and includes the approval or prescription for the future of rates, wages, corporate or financial structures or reorganization thereof, prices, facilities, appliances, services or allowances therefor or of valuations, costs, or accounting, or practices bearing on any of the foregoing. 5 U.S.C. § 551(4)

It is important to distinguish between rule making and adjudication. Rule making is the administrative equivalent of legislation; it is sometimes called "secondary legislation." It establishes future standards of general applicability; a rule covers a class of people or actions, not a particular person or action. Adjudication is the administrative parallel to the judicial process. It takes place after some activity has occurred. Agencies can make policy either through rule making or through adjudication; the courts prefer the agencies to stick to rule making. Agencies can also make policy by informal actions, such as the summary action taken by the EPA in 1979 when it banned 2,4,5-T (dioxin) on an emergency basis, without a hearing, just before the spring crop-spraying season.[5]

The courts are more likely to review rules on procedural due process grounds than substantive due process. Regulations and rules must stay within the statutory authority given to the agency by the legislature; however, this authority is often vague, leaving a great deal to the agency's discretion. The rules must have a reasonable basis; that is, they may not be arbitrary, capricious, or involve an abuse of discretion, and they must be promulgated in accordance with the APA and with the restrictions laid down in their own enabling or organic act.

TYPES OF RULES There are three types of rules: substantive (or legislative), procedural, and interpretive.

Substantive rules implement or prescribe law or policy—for example, safety requirements for nuclear power plants. They are legally binding and can be enforced in court as though they were primary legislation. The amount of authority that an agency has to promulgate rules varies with the enabling legislation. Some agencies have very broad authority; for example, NEPA states:

> The Administrator is authorized to allow appropriate use of special Environmental Protection Agency research and test facilities by outside groups of individuals and to receive reimbursement or fees for costs incurred thereby when he finds this to be *in the public interest*. 42 U.S.C. § 4379 (emphasis added)

Other agencies find their authority quite restricted; for example, the Endangered Species Act of 1973 requires that:

> [T]he Secretary shall make a finding as to whether the petition presents substantial scientific or commercial information indicating that the petitioned action may be warranted. If such a petition is found to present such information, the Secretary *shall* promptly commence a review of the status of the species concerned. The

Secretary *shall promptly* publish each finding made under this sub-paragraph in the Federal Register. 16 U.S.C. § 1533(b)(3)(A) (emphasis added)

The courts have the final word on whether a substantive rule is legitimate.

Procedural rules describe "the organization, procedure, or practice requirements of an agency." For example, they may define who is allowed to intervene in an agency adjudication and under what circumstances; the provisions in some environmental legislation that permit citizen suits are examples of procedural rules. The APA does not apply to procedural rule making; indeed, an agency is allowed to go beyond the APA and its own organic act in restricting the procedures under which it operates. However, an agency is required to honor its own rules once they have been issued. For example, during the Watergate investigation U.S. Attorney General Elliot Richardson appointed Archibald Cox as special prosecutor and at the same time issued a procedural rule giving the special prosecutor the authority to contest claims of executive privilege. When Cox tried to get President Nixon's tapes and rejected Nixon's claims of executive privilege, Nixon ordered him fired. The first two attorneys general that he ordered to fire Cox refused; the third was Robert Bork, who complied with Nixon's order. A federal court invalidated the firing and held that the procedural rule was binding.

Interpretive rules are "statements issued by agencies that present the agency's understanding of the meaning of the language in its regulations or the statutes it administers."[6] They are exempt from APA requirements but must be published in the *Federal Register*. They do not to add to or subtract from existing law; they simply give the public a more detailed idea of how the agency intends to act. In this sense they are the administrative equivalent of advisory opinions. It is not clear how binding an interpretative rule is on the agency. On occasion the courts have judged that an ostensibly interpretive rule was actually substantive and have held the agency to it. The safest approach is for the agency to assume that a court will find the rule binding, but for the affected party to assume it will not. Why would an administrative agency bother with such an ambiguous process? Because it allows the agency to make small adjustments to policy without going through the cumbersome rule-making procedures.

RULE-MAKING PROCEDURES   There are three basic procedures for making rules: informal, formal, and hybrid.

Informal rule making is informal only in contrast to the formal rule-making procedure. It is also called notice and comment rule making. It is governed by section 553 of the APA, which exempts from the act all military and foreign-affairs functions (since these are committed to the executive by the Constitution); agency management and personnel; and "public property, loans, grants, benefits, or contracts" (which are covered by a separate statute, the Federal Property and Administrative Services Act).

The informal rule-making procedure requires the agency to publish in the *Federal Register* a notice regarding the proposed rule. An exception is allowed if everyone subject to the proposed rule is individually notified, but this exception is rarely used. There are several necessary components of the notice. It must give the time, place, and nature of the rule-making proceedings and must refer to the legal authority under which the rule is to be made. The notice must either provide the term or substance of the proposed rule, or give a description of the subjects and issues involved. Finally, the notice must include an opportunity for written, and sometimes oral, comment by interested parties.

Once the agency has fixed upon the rule, it must publish the text of the rule, and a general statement of its basis and purpose, in the *Federal Register* at least thirty days before the effective date of the rule, to allow affected parties to come into compliance. After the rule has been published, interested persons have the right to ask for an issuance, amendment, or repeal of the rule.

This is a relatively simple, informal procedure. There is no formal hearing to present evidence and testimony about the rule. The time period is short; a rule might complete the process in less than sixty days if it is a simple and noncontroversial rule. There is no record of comments, testimonies, or meetings required; the agency merely announces its intention, receives comments, and issues the rule.

Formal rulemaking is more complex. Its distinguishing characteristic is the administrative hearing. Several statutes require full hearings as part of the rule-making process. Such a hearing need not be held unless the statute explicitly requires it. There is nothing to prohibit an agency from having one voluntarily. Administrative hearings are conducted under the regulations spelled out in sections 556 and 557 of the APA. An administrative law judge presides over the hearing, and the final opinion is conveyed to the administrator charged with making the final rule. The judge's opinion must be considered, although it is not binding. The final rule must be based on "reliable, probative, and substantial evidence" (§ 556[d]).

There are many arguments to favor the formal process over the informal. The formal record that is generated by the hearing process provides a pedigree for the development of the new regulation. There is full opportunity for public participation and, because the rules of evidence apply (although not the same rules of evidence as would apply in a criminal trial), all information can be verified. The burden of proof rests with the agency, and the formal hearing provides a record for the interested parties to be sure that the weight of the evidence is sufficient to support the rule.

There are also many counterarguments. Formal rule making is a costly procedure in terms of both money and time. The flexibility of the administrators is reduced—an evil that the administrative process is designed to avoid. And the process itself, resembling a court trial, is increasingly judicialized. For example, the original APA created independent "hearing examiners" who had specialized knowledge in their own regulatory fields. These hearing examiners have metamorphosed into "administrative law judges," who are attorneys with at least seven years' experience presenting cases before federal courts or agencies.

Hybrid rule making   The impetus for hybrid rule making came from the judiciary. Federal courts prefer the administrative agencies to use their rule-making powers to make policy rather than to use case-by-case adjudicatory powers, because judicial review is simplified when a rule is the basis of the administrative decision. However, the informal process does not require the establishment of a reviewable record. The lack of a formal record complicates the judge's task when reviewing agency action. As the administrative agencies continued to utilize their rule-making powers, and as the need for regulation increased, in part because of increased environmental regulation, the courts found their job increasingly complex. Deference to administrative expertise was a nice concept, but a court had difficulty judging the "substantial" basis of a rule that was technically complex and lacked a formal record. Partly in self-defense, the agencies began to generate records of the informal rule-making processes, and the courts, followed by the Congress, applauded.

The keystone of the hybrid process is the record before the administrator. When a record of the rule-making process has been kept, the court can review the process. The record not only allows judicial review, it also allows peer preview, legislative oversight, and public criticism. Surprisingly, it also increases administrative flexibility because it simplifies changing rules to meet changing circumstances.

Congress has followed the judicial lead, and most rule-making legislation in the seventies and eighties includes hybrid rule-making requirements. For example, the Toxic Substance Control Act of 1976 states:

> Any rule under subparagraph (A), and any substantive amendment or repeal of such a rule, shall be promulgated pursuant to the procedures specified in section 553 of [the APA], except that (i) the Administrator shall give interested persons an opportunity for the oral presentation of data, views, or arguments, in addition to an opportunity to make written submissions, (ii) a transcript shall be kept of any oral presentation, and (iii) the Administrator shall make and publish with the rule the finding described in subparagraph (A). 15 U.S.C. § 2604(b)(2)(C)

Hybrid rule-making follows informal rule-making procedures, with several additions: the basis and purpose of the rule are formally set forth, with supporting documentation; a record is made, showing that evidence of adequate notice was given, or made available, to all interested parties; sufficient time is allowed for comments and alternative interpretations; a record is made, showing evidence that the agency did consider and respond to comments; and the reasoning followed by the administrator is recorded.

EXECUTIVE ORDERS Substantial presidential efforts have been made to take control of the regulatory process. Since the early seventies, presidents have constrained the powers of the agencies through executive orders. In 1974 President Ford authorized the Office of Management and Budget (OMB) to assess the inflationary impact of proposed rules; in 1978 President Carter issued an order requiring, among other things, that agencies ensure an opportunity for public participation in rule making—including public hearings, sixty-day comment periods, and wider dissemination of notice of hearings. One of President Reagan's first actions in office was to issue Executive Order 12291 (and later Executive Order 12498), requiring agencies to conduct a cost-benefit analysis of all proposed rules and to choose the least costly alternative. This requirement conflicted with some enabling statutes for environmental legislation and has been challenged in court by environmental groups.

Not only did these initial changes substantially modify the intent and practice of the APA, they also nullified large portions of substantive law. These changes are also of questionable legality. While the President has authority to oversee execution of the laws by the executive branch, his constitutional authority is "to take care that the laws be faithfully executed," not to devise procedures that make executive agency enforcement of the laws difficult if not impossible.[7]

ADMINISTRATIVE ADJUDICATION

The fourth section of the Administrative Procedure Act deals with adjudication.[8] The specific kind of adjudicatory procedure required in agency processes varies from relatively informal, oral hearings to very structured procedures that resemble formal civil trials. Some statutes require hearings; it is only these statutes that automatically trigger the full hearing described in the APA. In some circumstances the courts have mandated adjudicatory hearings, based on constitutional requirements. Finally, the agencies themselves may have, independent of their enabling legislation or court decisions, rules that require them to hold hearings. The necessity for hearings originates in the due process clause of the Constitution (discussed in chapter 4). When an administrative agency's action affects a citizen's property rights, the citizen is entitled to a hearing. In chapter 4, property was narrowly defined as real property, but developments since the sixties have created a new form of property right.

The key case in the "due process explosion"—the transformation of entitlements to property rights— is *Goldberg v. Kelly* (1970). This case, involving a New York City welfare recipient, established that welfare is a property right that may not be taken away without due process. Just when a government benefit becomes a right was spelled out in *Board of Regents v. Roth* (1972). In that case the Court said that, in order for a due process hearing to be required, the interested person must have more than a unilateral expectation of the benefit; he or she must have a legitimate claim of entitlement. Moreover, this entitlement must originate in some independent source such as a law or already existing rules and regulations.

The expansion of entitlements into property rights is rarely at issue in environmental law. However, it is possible to argue that in some states citizens have a property right, protected by due process, in a healthy environment. Some states have established statutory rights to clean, safe environments; others have written such rights into their state constitutions. If these changes create entitlements for citizens, then administrative agencies may be required to exercise due process safeguards when managing or regulating the environment. Usually constitutional safeguards are designed to protect citizens against government actions, but interpretations of the due process clause may create positive obligations to act.

> The courts have struggled with the issue of imposing liability for state inaction because they have failed to identify any workable Constitutional standard. But in fact the Supreme Court developed such a standard when it set forth the due process requirements for the withdrawal of statutory entitlements. Even assuming that a state has no obligation to provide protection in the first place, it may violate the due process clause when it assumes such an obligation and then fails to fulfill it.[9]

A special problem arises because of the general nature of environmental protection. Some government benefits, such as police protection, do not create property interests because there is no special class of citizen entitled to the benefits. However, one might argue that environmental protection is not analogous to police protection, which states must provide, but rather that the provision of environmental protection is voluntary and therefore creates rights. A supporting argument is found in a 1971 California case, *Marks v. Whitney*, in which one party sought to build a marina which would have limited the access of his neighbor to the ocean. The neighbor's standing was challenged when he objected. The California Supreme Court held on appeal that the neighbor had standing because, if the plaintiff were allowed to build his marina, he would be "taking away from [his neighbor] rights to which he is entitled as a member of the general public."[10]

Another problem in administrative adjudication arises when the responsibilities of the agency overlap with private and professional standards and liabilities. For example, management effectiveness in the state water quality system discussed below—a complex mix of professional standards, citizen public relations, and state regulations—relies in large part on the potential for administration adjudication.

In addition to other environmental rules, the Arizona Department of Environmental Quality (DEQ) was empowered by the legislature through Arizona Revised Statutes 49-253 to develop and to enforce rules governing water systems. The rules provide that plans must be submitted and the construction of water systems must be inspected by a professional engineer.

The owner of a water system must protect the water system and keep it in proper operating condition. Also, the owner must sample for various pollutants. Operation not in accordance with departmental rules may subject the water system owner to an administrative order, which may be enforced by a court injunction.

Responsibility for the water system rests partially with the engineer as well. If the engineer who designs and inspects the construction of a water system is negligent, the state Board of Technical Registration, which licenses professional engineers, may take disciplinary action, such as the suspension or revocation of the engineer's license, and may assess administrative penalties not to exceed $2,000.

In addition, should someone be injured due to the improper design, construction, or operation of the water system, the engineer or the owner could become liable for the tort of negligence. Sometimes, it may be shown by an injured party's attorney that the engineer or system owner violated a rule of the department. In that case, the law of torts holds that such violation of a governmental rule is evidence of negligence which can be presented to a jury.

The expansion of a water system in Navajo County, Arizona, was designed by a consulting engineer whose professional license was granted not by examination but through action of a grandfather clause. The plans were found to be unworkable by the contractor and the DEQ field engineer. It was necessary for the system owner to threaten the consulting engineer with a complaint to the Board of Technical Registration before plans were redesigned. Following the consulting engineer's death, his estate filed a lawsuit for payment in excess of what the system owner anticipated. The owner then alleged that the consulting engineer's original design was improper and the design contract's scope was exceeded. It was important that DEQ's field engineer could demonstrate that the original plans would not work and the rules of the department were violated. The owner's attorney could then use this information in an attempt to show the consulting engineer was negligent in designing the system expansion. The suit was settled out of court.

JUDICIAL REVIEW

The sixth section of the APA deals with judicial review of agency actions.[11] Judicial review is the "power of a court to determine the legality and constitutionality" of an action of a government official, agency, or legislative body."[12] Some agency actions are not subject to review. The Supreme Court does not have jurisdiction over all agency actions because the Congress has the power to exempt some activities; article III of the Constitution states: "In all the other Cases before mentioned, the Supreme Court shall have appellate Jurisdiction, both as to Law and Fact, with such Exceptions, and under such Regulations as the Congress shall make."

Section 701 of the APA, which defines the applicability of judicial review of agency actions, exempts actions where the "statutes preclude judicial review" or which have been "committed to agency discretion by law." However, Section 706 (2)(A) of the act forbids arbitrary and capricious action and abuses of discretion. The reviewing courts must determine when an action is committed to agency discretion and when these actions are reviewable under section 706. The overall effect of these two seemingly contradictory sections is to encourage agencies to maintain records of their actions and interactions.

SCOPE OF REVIEW The scope of judicial review for administrative actions is defined in section 706:

> To the extent necessary to decision and when presented, the reviewing court shall decide all relevant questions of law, interpret constitutional and statutory provisions, and determine the meaning or applicability of the terms of an agency action.

The court may "compel agency action unlawfully withheld or unreasonably delayed" as well as "hold unlawful and set aside agency action, findings, and conclusions" that are arbitrary, capricious, abuses of discretion, or violations of constitutional rights, or that exceed statutory authority, violate due process, or are unsupported by substantial evidence.

For adjudicatory decisions, the primary judicial question is whether the agency position is supported by substantial evidence. Since most adjudicatory hearings are adversarial and therefore produce conflicting evidence, a court often has a difficult time determining which evidence is applicable. In formal rule making also, the scope of review rests on substantial evidence, while review of informal rule making is limited to the "arbitrary and capricious" standard. In hybrid rule making the scope of review is determined by the authorizing statute. For example, the Toxic Substances Control Act of 1976 gives as part of the standard of review:

Section 706 of [the APA] shall apply to review of a rule under this section, except that—
  (i) in the case of review of a rule under [several sections of the act], the standard for review prescribed by paragraph (2)(E) of such section 706 shall not apply and the court shall hold unlawful and set aside such rule *if the court finds that the rule is not supported by substantial evidence in the rulemaking record.* (emphasis added)

LIABILITY OF ADMINISTRATIVE OFFICIALS

One of the more complex issues in environmental administration is the liability of individual employees to lawsuits. Under the ancient common-law doctrine of sovereign immunity, the government and its employees were absolutely immune from prosecution for actions related to their governmental functions. The doctrine has its origins in the ancient divine right of kings: God ordains the king, God can do no wrong, the king can do no wrong. However, even divine kings recognized that their subordinates could make mistakes (or that, for political reasons, the king might want to dissociate himself from some subordinate's action), and so the custom evolved that the king could give permission for the government to be sued. However, in the twentieth century the immunity of government officials from liability suits has changed. Immunity ranges from absolute immunity (for such activities as legislating) to none, that is, no more immunity than is borne by a private citizen. In the middle range is qualified immunity, the notion that an employee acting in "good faith" is immune from being sued.

The first chink in the armor of the sovereign immunity doctrine came in 1971 with *Bivens v. Six Unknown, Named Agents of the Federal Bureau of Narcotics*, which established the notion of qualified immunity. The six agents had arrested Bivens after a warrantless search. In its opinion, the Supreme Court created the "Bivens tort": if officials violate an individual's constitutional rights, the individual may seek redress by suing the officials. The officials may offer the defense that they believed in good faith that their actions were lawful, provided such a belief was reasonable at the time.

However, the state officials, even if their actions are lawful under their own state laws, may nevertheless be liable under federal law. Under section 1983 of the Civil Rights Act of 1871, individuals may sue state officials if their *federal* constitutional rights are violated by those officials operating under the authority of state law:

> Every person, who under color of any statute, ordinance, regulation, custom or usage, of any State or Territory, subjects or causes to be subjected, any citizen of the United States or other person within the jurisdiction thereof to the deprivation of any rights, privileges or immunities secured by the Constitution and laws, shall be liable to the party injured in an action at law, suit in equity or other proper proceeding for redress.[13]

This provision of the 1871 Civil Rights Act was largely ignored until the late sixties, when civil rights activists used it to redress racial injustices in recalcitrant southern states.

To utilize section 1983 in environmental suits, a plaintiff must establish that the state has created a property interest, which would then be protected by the Fifth and Fourteenth amendments to the Constitution. For example, a state may create a property interest (analogous to the entitlements to welfare recognized by the Supreme Court in *Goldberg v. Kelly*) by establishing a statutory or state constitutional right to a clean, safe environment.

CONTROLLING POLLUTION

This section presents the current situation in air and water pollution regulation and examines an alternative regulatory approach to air and water pollution control: pollution rights purchase schemes.

AIR POLLUTION

An air pollutant develops "when the concentration of a normal component of air or of a new chemical added to or formed in the air builds up to the point of causing harm to humans, other animals, vegetation, or materials such as metals and stone."[14] The major sources of air pollution are transportation (49 percent), industrial processes (13 percent), fuel combusion in stationary sources (28 percent), solid waste disposal (3 percent), and miscellaneous (7 percent).[15] Some pollutants are harmful as soon as they enter the atmosphere; these *primary air pollutants* contribute the majority of air pollution in the United States. *Secondary air pollutants* are formed from the chemical reaction of several air components; for example, sulfur dioxide combines with oxygen to form sulfur trioxide, which then combines with water vapor to produce acid rain.

/The dangers of air pollution and its dramatic consequences have been known for centuries. In 1273 the king of England tried to reduce air pollution by banning the burning of coal. London was known as "the Smoke" for good reason, and Sherlock Holmes's romantic "pea soup" fogs were deadly. In 1911 over a thousand Londoners died from coal smoke; in 1952 the infamous Killer Smog killed four thousand Londoners. After this, Parliament passed air pollution control laws. The United States waited through disasters in 1948 (twenty deaths) and 1963 (three hundred dead in New York City) before passing the Clean Air Act Amendment in 1970./ These amendments gave teeth to federal efforts to improve air quality; earlier efforts, such as the Clean Air Act of 1955, had simply provided technical and financial assistance to the states.

The Clean Air Act and its 1977 amendments gave power to the federal government to impose air quality standards. The EPA was required to establish national ambient air quality standards (NAAQSs) for seven major pollutants: suspended particulate matter (SPM), sulfur oxides, carbon monoxide, nitrogen oxides, ozone, volatile organic compounds, and lead. The cost of meeting the standards was not supposed to be a criterion in setting the standards. The EPA had to set two types of NAAQSs: the *primary ambient air quality standards* were to protect human health and to provide a margin of safety for the most vulnerable populations, such as infants and the elderly; the *secondary ambient air quality standards* were to protect visibility and crops, buildings, and water supplies.

To implement the Clean Air Act, the EPA divided the nation into 247 air quality control regions, each of which was supposed to meet the primary standards by 1982. Areas that did not achieve primary standards by that date (or by some later date if an extension were granted) were labeled *nonattainment regions*, with restrictions on new plant construction and old plant expansions until the emission standards were met.

Of course, some areas of the country were already cleaner than the NAAQSs required, and the EPA sought to protect these through a policy of *prevention of significant deterioration* (PSD). Three classes of existing air quality were established. Class I areas, which had the highest existing air quality, were protected from virtually any deterioration. Class II and Class III areas were allowed progressively more pollution, with the NAAQSs being the absolute limit of permissible pollution. Each state was responsible for developing state implementation plans (SIPs) to meet federal standards by the late eighties.

Under the Reagan administration, industry and the executive branch cooperated to ease federal auto emission standards, to extend EPA deadlines, and in general to relax the expansion and enforcement of existing air pollution regulations. The conservatives asserted that the economic cost of clean air was too high,[16] and that the accepted levels of pollution were too low. They also charged the regulating agencies with inflexibility. There is some justification for their arguments. Federal policies change even as industry strives to comply; this makes industry tend to avoid compliance as long as possible. Also, prior to the 1990 reauthorization, regulatory strategies focused on emissions rather than on production processes, and there were few economic incentives (or economic slack) for industries to look at internal production and management strategies to stop pollution at its source.

Environmentalists, too, were critical of the EPA; and the chaos in the EPA during the first Reagan administration seemed to justify their complaints. Enforcement of existing regulations was problematic, and new regulations were halted or delayed under executive orders requiring cost-benefit analysis and other evaluations not always in agreement with legislative intentions. The environmentalists and the administration were often at odds; "[b]y the end of 1986, environmentalists and key congressional allies had prevented the gutting of the 1970 and 1977 Clean Air acts but had been unable to persuade Congress to pass any new legislation strengthening air pollution control."[17] All this changed in 1990.

On November 15, 1990, President Bush signed a new Clean Air Act Amendment. Bush had initiated the new bill on June 12, 1989, when his administration presented a proposal for new legislation, "departing from a decade of Reagan administration hostility toward new industry regulation . . . [and strengthening] the hand of congressional proponents of clean air legislation, whose proposals had repeatedly been killed or stalled to death at the behest of industry."[18]

The 1990 Clean Air Act Amendment added three major new areas to federal regulatory control: reduction of acid deposition, reduction of chlorofluorocarbons (CFCs), and increased control of air toxics.[19] A national permitting program was also established, and enforcement was strengthened.

To meet the act's acid deposition requirements in Title IV, industries must achieve a permanent ten million ton reduction from 1980 levels in sulfur dioxide emissions during a two-phase implementation process to be fully effective on January 1, 2000. Title VI addresses the problem of stratospheric ozone and global climate protection. The act uses the economic incentives and requirements established by EPA under the 1977 amendments to phase out CFCs and halons according to the schedules established in the Montreal Protocol (discussed in chapter 7). This involves complete elimination of CFCs and carbon tetrachloride by 2000 and methyl chloroform by 2002. On January 1, 1994, a total ban on aerosols, with exemptions for flammability and safety, goes into effect.

The air toxics title was prompted by the information generated from Title III of SARA, the "community right to know" title. The discovery that over 2.7 billion pounds of toxic air pollutants were released annually was a powerful trigger for increasing the regulation of air toxics. In a radical departure from previous programs, the new act is technology-based rather than emissions-focused, and 189 substances are now regulated (as opposed to the 8 controlled under the old legislation). All pollutant sources must apply maximum achievable control technologies (MACTs) to their processes. As in the old act, different standards and timetables are established for new and existing sources.

The permitting system and improved enforcement are the last two substantial changes. The operating permits program is "in many ways the most important procedural reform contained in the new law."[20] Polluting sources must obtain an operating permit, states must administer the permitting program, and the EPA reviews all programs and may veto any permit. In addition, the EPA is required to develop and implement a federal permit plan if a state fails to comply with the provisions of the act. The fee structure for permits must offset program costs; initial suggestions are for fees of $25 per ton of emission for a five-year permit.

The enforcement provisions are important and new in clean-air legislation.[21] Four provisions are especially noteworthy: the field citation program, the imposition of criminal liability for dangerous releases, the requirement of compliance certification, and the citizen suit provisions. Under the field citation program, inspectors may visit plants to inspect the plants and the plant records. They are empowered to issue citations at once, which may carry fines of up to $5000. The act establishes civil and criminal liability for releases that endanger the public: "knowingly endangering" the public through a deliberate, illegal release may result in a prison term of up to fifteen years and a fine of up to $250,000 for an individual and $500,000 for a corporation. The regulated industries are required to certify their compliance with the permit conditions on a regular basis and to provide monitoring and other forms of evidence to prove compliance. Citizen suits may be used to enforce the permits; the citizen suit provisions are stronger under the new law. Citizens may now sue corporations for past violations if the violation is continuing, and penalties may be imposed to require mitigation of harmful effects.

The new law is a sweeping reform. It affects a much wider range of businesses and requires the EPA to move rapidly to meet the regulation deadlines. Given the administration's support of the bill, its implementation will be a priority for the EPA throughout the nineties.

WATER POLLUTION

Issues of water pollution control are more immediate than issues of air pollution control because polluted water more seriously threatens public health, and because water is easier to control than air. Water pollution is "any physical or chemical change in surface water or groundwater that can adversely affect living organisms."[22] The levels of pollution that are acceptable in any water supply depend in part on the use to which the water is put. A waterway used primarily for large ships can tolerate a higher level of pollution than one that provides drinking water for a small community. Water for industrial needs does not have to meet swimming-water criteria. Environmentalists like to point out that water *could* be used for industrial needs if it met swimming-water criteria; the cleaner, the better. Economists talk instead about "beneficent degradation," the desirable level of pollution in a body of water.

Pollution is usually classified as either *point source* pollution, that is, pollution with a readily isolated egress point such as a sewer treatment plant or oil tankers, or *non-point-source* pollution, which is more difficult to control because it is spread over a large area. The pollution caused by agricultural pesticides in rainwater runoff, for example, is difficult to measure or to identify. The best management practices try to reduce the behavior that causes agricultural non-point-source pollution; urban non-point-source pollution is less amenable to control.

Water supplies are classified as surface water and groundwater. Sources of surface water—such as lakes, rivers, and oceans—are to some extent self-cleansing, although some pollutants are so deadly even in small concentrations that neither dilution nor dispersal are helpful. These surface water systems are easily overloaded, but they are at least accessible. Groundwater is much more vulnerable to pollution and harder to restore. Most drinking water in the United States is from groundwater.

Although only a small percentage of the nation's groundwater is polluted, the proximity of these contaminated aquifers to population centers means that five million to ten million Americans have polluted water sources. This problem may be more severe than reported since many chemicals found in groundwater are not detected in routine federal inspections, and private wells are not regularly tested.[23]

There are eight major types of water pollutants: disease-causing agents, such as bacteria; oxygen-demanding wastes, such as manure, which need the dissolved oxygen in water to degrade; water-soluble inorganic chemicals; inorganic plant nutrients; organic chemicals, sediment, or suspended matter; radioactive substances; and thermal pollution, which elevates water temperatures.[24]

In 1974 the federal Safe Drinking Water Act imposed federal safety standards on the states. Previously there were no uniform water quality standards for drinking water. The act requires the EPA to set standards for drinking water for pollutants with potentially adverse effects on human health. Although a "margin of safety" is also mandated, the EPA must also take technical feasibility and cost into account. In 1985 the EPA reported that 87 percent of the municipal water systems were in compliance with its standards.[25] However, environmentalists advocated that standards be added for another seven hundred potential pollutants. In 1986, amendments to the Safe Drinking Water Act required the EPA to set standards for eighty-three new contaminants by 1989 and for an additional twenty-five by 1991.

The centerpieces of U.S. water pollution control strategies are the Federal Water Pollution Control Act of 1972 and the Clean Water Act of 1977; amendments were passed in 1981 and 1987, the latter over a presidential veto. American waters were to be "fishable and swimmable" by 1983, and discharge of pollutants into navigable waters was to be halted by 1985. This legislation "is the purest example of 'technology forcing' in the federal regulatory code . . . [and] serves as an enduring monument to the American politician's belief in the possibilities of social engineering and to the political muscle of the environmental movement in the early 1970s."[26]

Needless to say, these goals were not achieved; however, progress was made in cleaning up the nation's waters. Between 1972 and

1986, almost $45 billion was provided to municipalities by the federal government, supplemented by $15 billion of state and local government funds, to upgrade or to construct municipal wastewater treatment facilities.

The record is not unblemished. By 1986, two-thirds of American municipalities had completed construction of their effluent control systems; but of these, 12 percent were still not in compliance. The failure of the remaining one-third to complete construction on schedule is "attributed to fraud, overbuilding, bureaucratic and construction delays, and a 37% cut in federal funding for water pollution control between 1981 and 1986 by the Reagan administration."[27]

Industrial dischargers were not much better. Although 94 percent were reporting compliance with their EPA waste-discharge permits, a 1984 study by the General Accounting Office (GAO) found that most were actually violating the conditions of the permits.[28]

Finally, control of non-point sources of water pollution was marginal. Although the water pollution control laws require local and regional planning by the states to reduce non-point-source pollution, neither goals nor standards have been established, and funding to establish them has not been forthcoming. The national level is no better; there are "no comprehensive legislation, goals, or funding designed to protect . . . groundwater supplies from contamination."[29]

Whether these programs are viewed as partial successes or partial failures, the reasons for the outcomes are found in the political climate of implementation. First, by assigning the major implementation strategies to the states, the process was opened to the vagaries of state economics and politics. While the intention behind state implementation is to respect the differences between the states, the effect is to blunt the effectiveness of the legislation. Second, the EPA had wide discretion in setting the regulatory framework for the water-control acts. Third, the action-forcing provisions left the EPA vulnerable to claims of technological impossibility; the immediate stew of litigation that arose from enforcement efforts hampered successful implementation. Finally, since water pollution control is protective regulatory policy, the policy actors include the White House and the senior members of the Congress; their high visibility and the conflicts between them reduced the effectiveness of the implementation efforts.

ECONOMIC APPROACHES TO POLLUTION CONTROL

Three approaches to controlling pollution are available to managers: suits based on common law theories such as nuisance, discussed in chapter 4; suits to enforce the Clean Air Act and the Clean Water Act; and economic incentives. Unlike most regulatory plans—which constrain the private sector, forcing it to utilize and to develop technologies—economic incentives can promote environmental protection by using the market.

Two economic factors that distort the operation of a free market are externalities and free riders. Simply put, externalities are spillover effects which have an impact on individuals or groups which have not contributed to the project. For example, a factory may dump pollutants into the air, harming the health of local residents. This behavior marks economic sense for the factory, since the disposal of pollutants is free, but the residents gain no benefits and are, instead, harmed. Thus the costs of the polluting activities are not borne by those who reap the benefits, and polluters have no economic incentives to reduce pollution. Free riders are individuals who participate in the benefits of an activity without contributing to the activity's cost; for example, non-residents who use a tax-supported public park are free riders. Air pollution provides a good example of the relationship between pollution, externalities, and free riders:

> There may be many agents who produce the pollution. It can come from automobiles, factories, electrical power plants, and so on. Also, large numbers of individuals "consume" the pollution by breathing air filled with particulates, sulfur dioxide, and oxides of nitrogen. Producers of the externality can also be consumers of air pollution. Anyone who drives a car and lives in an area of low air quality is both a producer and consumer. The reason this public externality arises is simple: Air is an open access resource. Because no property rights to air exist, those who generate air pollution are free to use the air as a waste dump without paying any fees. Once air pollution is generated, large numbers of individuals (animals, vegetation, and property) are affected. Each person affected might be willing to pay something to reduce the pollution, but if he or she did so, others who did not pay would also benefit.[30]

One of the remedies proposed to adjust the imbalances between producers of pollution and consumers of pollution is the use of marketable permits to pollute. First proposed by Dales in 1968,[31] pollution permits would provide transferable property rights for the disposal of waste. The government would choose the level of pollution it is willing to tolerate by issuing pollution rights equal to that amount. The number of rights would be reviewed at certain intervals, perhaps five or ten years. A market for transferable rights would then develop.

> In turn, the buying and selling of the Rights in an open market and the consequent establishment of an explicit price for the right to discharge a ton of wastes into a water (or air) system results in a theoretically efficient allocation of "anti-pollution effort" as between different dischargers. In other words, the market automatically ensures that the required reduction in waste discharge will be achieved at the smallest possible total cost to society. Moreover, the rise in the price of the Pollution Rights over time will automatically solve the problem of economic growth; as the price rises, it will be economic for existing dischargers to reduce their wastes, and thereby make room for newcomers. And, finally, it seems obvious that the Pollution Rights market will require very little administrative expense by comparison with alternative schemes.[32]

This proposal, according to Dales, would be less effective with multiple-source pollution (such as automobiles) and non-point-source pollution (such as agricultural runoff). However, as a substantial proportion of both air and water pollution is generated by single-source industrial polluters, Dales's scheme has great appeal to those with market inclinations. Air pollution is especially amenable to Dales's market solutions because the existing regulatory mechanisms would be easy to adapt to his approach.[33]

The policy of prevention of significant deterioration, or non-degradation policy, established under the Clean Air Act allowed the EPA to set incremental standards for increased pollution emissions in class II and class III areas. Industries were allocated pollution increments on a first come, first served basis.

In 1979 two reform mechanisms were added to the clean air legislation. The first was the *bubble policy*, which allows trading in pollution emissions. At first such trading was restricted to intra-plant emissions, but the EPA later permitted plants within the same geographic area to increase emissions in one plant in return for correspondingly reduced emissions at another. The second reform was the *emissions offset policy*, which allows a new firm to enter an area and to pollute if an established firm will agree to reduce its emissions to match. The EPA allows localities to "bank" reductions that occur when a company goes out of business, and then the locality can transfer these credits when a new company locates in the community. How the credits are transferred is up to the states: "the State is free to govern ownership, use, sale, and commercial transactions in banked emission offsets as it sees fit."[34] These are not yet marketable rights, but they are a first step.

This sort of rights scheme has several advantages. Many businesses would be more environmentally responsible if their internal affairs and their relations with the EPA were modified. Some obstacles to waste reduction are internal to the business, but others are imposed externally by the government's emphasis on emissions control rather than source reduction. In addition to reducing administrative costs, pollution rights schemes encourage businesses to find alternative ways to reduce emissions and other wastes. They might allow businesses to focus on waste production; to revamp internal accounting systems so as to charge pollution to operations, thus encouraging improved production technologies; and to improve their internal information management systems.

Harmful though they are, air pollutants and water pollutants are benign compared to hazardous and toxic wastes. Separate regulatory programs to deal with these substances have been established; these are discussed in the next section.

HAZARDOUS AND TOXIC SUBSTANCES

The problems associated with the production, use, and disposal of hazardous wastes and chemicals are a result of the high standard of living in industrialized societies. The large-scale production of synthetic chemicals did not begin until after World War II. Before that, pesticides were the predominant hazardous chemical, and these were under the control of the U.S. Department of Agriculture and the Food and Drug Administration (FDA). Today approximately sixty thousand chemicals are commonly used in the United States, resulting in the production of 290 million metric tons of hazardous waste per year.[35] In 1980 alone, one thousand new chemicals were reviewed for manufacture by the EPA, but only a few of these chemicals had been tested for adverse effects.

Public awareness of the chemical problem was aroused in 1962 by Rachel Carson's book *Silent Spring*, but the more popular issues of air and water pollution dominated environmental action throughout the sixties. Congress was not alerted to the dangers of accumulating chemicals until 1971, when the Council on Environmental Quality (CEQ) reported on the dangers of toxic chemicals.

Prior to 1976, chemicals and hazardous wastes were controlled and regulated on an individual basis. There was no coordinated attempt to deal with the problem. Chemicals or wastes found in water supplies were regulated under the Federal Water Pollution Control Act of 1972. Chemicals or wastes emitted into the air were controlled by the Air Quality Act of 1967. Agricultural chemicals and wastes were controlled by the strong 1972 amendments to the Federal Insecticide, Fungicide, and Rodenticide Act of 1947 (FIFRA). If the substance was a residue on food, then it was the responsibility of the FDA.

In 1976, five years after the CEQ report on chemical dangers, Congress enacted two pieces of legislation designed specifically to deal with the problems associated with chemicals and hazardous wastes. The Toxic Substances Control Act (TSCA) was designed to identify and to evaluate the environmental and health effects of existing chemicals and of any new substance entering the United States market. The Resource Conservation and Recovery Act (RCRA) was designed to control solid-waste management practices that could endanger public health or the environment. Both of these laws were implemented slowly, due to underestimation of the chemical and waste problem and the low priority given the issue by the executive branch. Few rules and regulations had been promulgated by the late seventies and early eighties. There was also a failure to resolve the problem of leaking and abandoned dumps, which presented a threat to human health or the environment. This problem was aggravated because usually no potentially responsible parties (PRPs) could be found to bear the clean-up costs.

The most important acts governing toxic and hazardous substances are the Federal Insecticide, Fungicide, and Rodenticide Act of 1947 (FIFRA); the Clean Air Act of 1970 and the Clean Water Act of 1977; the Resource Conservation and Recovery Act of 1976 (RCRA); the Toxic Substances Control Act of 1976 (TSCA); and the Comprehensive Environmental Response, Compensation, and Liability Act of 1980 (CERCLA or Superfund) and its 1986 amendments (Superfund Amendment and Reauthorization Act or SARA). Each of these statutes is discussed below.

THE FEDERAL INSECTICIDE, FUNGICIDE AND RODENTICIDE ACT

Although the publicity surrounding pesticide control might lead us to suspect that controlling toxic substances is a relatively new government activity, the federal government has been regulating pesticides since the first labeling act, the Insecticide Act of 1910, was passed. This act was repealed in 1947, when the comprehensive Federal Insecticide, Fungicide, and Rodenticide Act (FIFRA) was passed. Like the 1910 act, FIFRA focused on labeling. It was originally managed by the Department of Agriculture, but in 1970 the EPA assumed responsibility for administering the act. As a result of a series of cases, an extensive body of case law regulating pesticides has developed.

> In each case, the court has held that the burden of proof is on the manufacturer once substantial evidence of a health hazard has been shown. Essentially, once EPA has found sufficient evidence of risk to justify initiation of cancellation proceedings, the burden is on the proponent of continued registration to demonstrate that the risk is minimal or that the benefits of use outweigh the risks.[36]

THE CLEAN AIR ACT AND THE CLEAN WATER ACT

Section 112 of the Clean Air Act provides standards for the emission of hazardous air pollutants; such a pollutant is defined as

> an air pollutant to which no ambient air quality standard is applicable and which in the judgment of the Administrator causes, or contributes to, air pollution which may reasonably be anticipated to result in an increase in mortality or an increase in serious irreversible, or incapacitating reversible, illness.

Once a standard is promulgated by the EPA, all new sources must adhere to the standard. Rather than enforce emission standards, the EPA may "issue regulations controlling design, equipment, work practices, or operations."[37]

The Clean Water Act's concerns with toxic substances are more complicated than those of the Clean Air Act. The original

1972 legislation proved very difficult to implement, and the EPA agreed to new methods of control. Codified in the 1977 amendments, the best available technology (BAT) is the standard used to determine effluent limitations. BAT considerations include "the age of equipment and facilities, the process employed, engineering aspects of control techniques, process changes, [cost], and non-water quality environmental impact (including energy requirements). There is no requirement of a balancing between the costs and benefits of effluent reduction."[38] The EPA may impose stronger standards if necessary to provide a margin of safety.

THE RESOURCE CONSERVATION AND RECOVERY ACT

The RCRA is focused primarily on solid waste, and it is notable for its tracking system from "cradle to grave," that is, from production to final disposal. This system has standards for generators, transporters, and disposal sites. Generators must keep detailed records and must meet reporting, labeling, and packaging requirements. Transporters, who are also required to meet labeling and records standards, must track materials through a permitted manifest system. The system sets standards for the location, construction, and operation of disposal sites, and for record keeping.

Enforcement is implemented through the permitting system set forth in section 3005. The EPA may inspect, and it can bring both civil and criminal actions for violations. States may assume responsibility for hazardous-waste control, but they must meet federal standards in their controlling systems.

Reauthorization of RCRA was discussed during the 101st Congress (1990); however, despite efforts by Thomas Luken, the chairman of the House Energy and Commerce Subcommittee, the efforts to reauthorize were unsuccessful. Although environmentalists argued that tightening the hazardous waste provisions of RCRA was essential, the House and Senate concerned themselves primarily with solid-waste issues. Analysts predicted that RCRA would be the major environmental effort of the 102nd Congress.[39]

THE TOXIC SUBSTANCES CONTROL ACT

The intent of TSCA was

to complete the chain of federal environmental-protection statutes enacted piecemeal between 1970 . . . and 1976. In contrast to laws designed to improve and protect the quality of water, air, and natural resources, TSCA was designed as a gap-filling law and empowered EPA to evaluate the safety of raw materials. It gave the agency broad authority to control chemical risks that could not be dealt with under other environmental statutes.[40]

TSCA emphasizes three policies: data collection, primarily by the industries involved; government authority to prevent risks—especially imminent ones—to public health or the environment; and consideration of economic impacts.

SUPERFUND AND SARA

In 1978 Love Canal, a housing development near the city of Niagara Falls, New York, was declared to be in a state of emergency because long-buried chemicals were seeping into the basements of the public school and several houses. A high incidence of health problems triggered an investigation that unveiled the presence of 21,900 tons of chemical wastes buried in fifty-five gallon drums.[41] The publicity surrounding Love Canal led to the discovery of thousands of similar dump sites.

In direct response to the public outcry over Love Canal, the Comprehensive Environmental Response, Compensation, and Liability Act of 1980 (CERCLA or Superfund) was enacted. Superfund was developed to ensure financial responsibility for the long-term maintenance of waste disposal facilities and to provide for the clean-up of old and abandoned hazardous waste disposal sites that were leaking or that otherwise endangered the public health. This law was designed to close the gap between TSCA and RCRA concerning the closed dumps. Superfund also had provisions to respond to emergency spills of hazardous wastes. A National Priorities List of all uncontrolled hazardous waste sites was established. Two types of government action were possible under Superfund. First, a removal action, which was primarily an emergency response, had a time limit of six months and a cost limit of $1 million. Second, a remedial action could be undertaken to clean up sites that were not considered an immediate threat to human health but were listed on the National Priorities List. Remedial actions were to follow the recommendations of the remedial investigations and feasibility studies (RI/FSs) and were to be performed in accordance with the

National Contingency Plan (NCP). The NCP under Superfund is an expanded version of the original NCP created in the Federal Water Pollution Control Act of 1972. It includes the hazardous-substance response plan, which established procedures and standards for responding to releases of hazardous substances, pollutants, and contaminants. It specifies the procedures, techniques, materials, equipment, and methods to be employed in identifying, removing, or remedying releases of hazardous substances to minimize the damages of the releases.

Superfund allocated $1.6 billion over five years for clean-up, primarily financed by a feedstock tax on certain chemicals and on petroleum. The main accomplishment of Superfund was to develop an understanding of the magnitude of the problem. An Office of Technology Assessment report on Superfund estimated that as much as $100 billion may need to be spent over fifty years to clean up an estimated ten thousand sites.

After four years of Superfund, Congress began to grasp the serious nature of the problem and the EPA's lack of desire under the Reagan administration to get tough with violators.[42] Superfund expired in 1985, and in 1986 Congress passed the Superfund Amendment and Reauthorization Act (SARA). SARA expanded the funding of Superfund to $9 billion. This funding not only included an increase in the feedstock tax but also added an environmental tax on corporate income over $2 million. This represented a major deviation from the principle that "the polluter pays." SARA set performance deadlines and achievement standards for the EPA. It required the completion of 650 RI/FSs and 375 remedial investigations in the five years following enactment. The removal action was expanded to one year in duration and $2 million in cost. Section 206 gave citizens standing to file suit for any violation of CERCLA or SARA, subject to some restrictions. For example, citizen suits are not allowed within sixty days of the notification of the potentially responsible parties of the site violation. Citizen suits are also prohibited if the president is diligently prosecuting the case under CERCLA or RCRA. SARA also allocated $500 million to the leaking underground storage tank (UST) problem. The rights of citizens were expanded in Title III, which required that community planning and right-to-know programs be implemented.

In late 1990, Superfund was added to the congressional budget-reconciliation bill during conference negotiations. The taxes on oil and chemical companies to fund the clean-up operations were extended until December 31, 1995. The purpose for the extension was to avert a repeat of the 1985 slowdown in clean-ups; left without taxing authority by the expiration of Superfund, the EPA was forced to conserve the $130 million remaining in the fund by reducing its clean-up efforts. Congress now has until the end of 1995 to reauthorize Superfund, which expires in December 1991.[43]

POLLUTION CONTROL IN GREAT BRITAIN

Great Britain, which is also a common law country, has enacted pollution control legislation similar to that of the United States, but it has taken a different route for implementation and enforcement. Unlike the environmental revolution in the United States in the sixties and seventies, the environmental movement in England was comparatively moderate.[44] However, the British results are as good as if not better than the American, and a look at the British approach is useful to highlight the peculiarly American aspects of U.S. regulatory policies.

Concern for air quality can be identified as early as 1819, when the member of Parliament for Durham City, Michael Taylor, campaigned for clean air legislation;[45] however, legislation had to wait until 1863, when the Alkali Inspectorate—the first national air pollution agency—was established. The legislation provided for inspection of factory premises by experts responsible to a central government authority, a model that is still followed in Britain. However, this legislation was of no avail against domestic smoke. The Killer Smog of 1952, which contributed to the deaths of approximately four thousand Londoners, was the final trigger event that led to Britain's Clean Air Act of 1956. However, because the smog was not perceived as a national problem, this act did not have widespread public support, and its passage was largely the result of activity by special interest groups such as the Smoke Abatement Society.[46]

Water pollution control was implemented more slowly; water pollution was not a national concern until it became a commercial hazard, fouling the waterways so badly that no acceptable water could be found for industrial processes.[47] Economic distress in industry led to political activity; however, remedies for pollution were largely found in common law rather than in legislative enactment, until enactment of the Salmon and Freshwater Fisheries Act, 1923, the Public Health Act, 1936, and the Rivers (Prevention of Pollution) Act, 1951. (The Waterworks Clauses Acts, 1847 and 1863, dealt largely with the provision of water, not its quality.)

It was not until the 1967 *Torrey Canyon* disaster that the British environmental movement caught fire at the national level, and new environmental groups such as Friends of the Earth and the Conservation Society were formed. In 1969 the Conservative and Labor parties included environmental planks in their political platforms. In 1970 the government of Edward Heath established a new Department of the Environment that "assumed a series of wide-ranging administrative and statutory powers . . . including land-use planning, surface transportation, housing construction, the preservation of amenity, the protection of the coasts and countryside, the preservation of historic towns and monuments and the control of air, water, and noise pollution."[48] This "superministry" made Britain the first nation to establish a cabinet-level department for the environment; a similar department was not even seriously proposed in the United States until 1989. Following on the heels of the new ministry came the Control of Pollution Act of 1974, which established broad centralized authority in toxic-waste disposal. Its full implementation was delayed until 1979, and only since the late eighties has the act been fully operational. Despite this apparent saliency of environmental concerns, the British environmental movement continues to be moderate.

The development of pollution control in Great Britain has been incremental. Absolute removal of potential pollutants has never been regarded as a sensible policy. The characteristics of Great Britain's natural environment (fast rivers, proximity to the sea, prevailing winds, and so on) has encouraged the use of the physical environment as a dispersal route for potential pollutants. Government measures to control environmental damage have been taken in response to public outcry about dramatic and dangerous pollution problems. These measures may be statutes directly addressing pollution, such as the Alkali Act of 1863, passed to control the release of hydrochloric acid from alkali plants; or they may be more general statutes such as the Town and Country Planning Acts, which give some pollution-control authority, at least implicitly, to the local planning agencies.

One of the governing principles of pollution control has been that executive responsibility rests largely with local authorities and water authorities. Local authorities regulate the collection and disposal of domestic and industrial waste, the permitted air pollution from domestic and some industrial premises, and the abatement of noise. Until privatized by the Thatcher government in 1989, regional water authorities controlled sewerage in England and Wales and water pollution in England.

Three key concepts underlie pollution control in Great Britain. British policy recognizes that the issue in pollution control is how much pollution to allow, and this question is answered in both political and scientific terms. The subsequent issue of how to achieve a given level of pollution is also a political question. "Best practicable means" is the political answer to implementation: pollution control must be conducted with "regard to local conditions, to the current state of scientific, technical and medical knowledge of the potential harm or nuisance involved and to the financial implications."[49] In theory this allows sufficient discretion on the part of the regulatory agencies to negotiate with offenders in a reasonable manner rather than forcing compliance with rigid standards.

A related concept, "best practicable environmental option," was endorsed by the Conservative government in 1982. Under this approach, regulatory authorities are encouraged to select the option for disposal of pollution that provides the least harm, given present scientific, technical, practical, economic, and geographic factors. The third concept is "polluter pays," an idea that is also accepted in European Economic Community environmental policy. British authorities pride themselves on the fact that the cost of controlling pollution is borne almost entirely by the polluter. The one exception to this policy is grants to residents in smoke control zones to help them pay for conversion to smokeless appliances. The practical effect of the "polluter pays" policy is to foreclose some improvements on economic grounds (under the notion of "best practicable means") and to remove financial incentives for industry to take the initiative in pollution control.

In absolute numbers, the improvement in Great Britain's environment has been impressive. Between 1958 and 1978, urban ground concentrations of sulfur dioxide fell by 50 percent. From 1958 to 1981, industrial smoke decreased by 94 percent, while in the same period domestic coal smoke was reduced by 80 percent. Water quality has improved; in 1958, 86 percent of Great Britain's rivers had both fish and water that was potable after treatment. In 1975, 91 percent of the rivers met those standards. Between 1958 and 1980, the kilometers of "grossly polluted" and "poor quality" nontidal waterways decreased by 39 percent, and the length of polluted tidal waterways was reduced by 42 percent.[50] David Vogel attributes this success to three factors: "a highly respected civil service, a business community that was prepared to cooperate with government officials, and a public that was not particularly mistrustful of large corporations,"[51] all factors that are lacking in the United States. The relatively high social status of public officials allows them to deal with industrial managers on an equal footing, and the presumptions of good intentions on one hand, and economic flexibility on the other, enable the two groups to work cooperatively rather than as antagonists. What appears as laxity of enforcement to non-British eyes may be extremely effective enforcement in the British context. Certainly, the results of the British system have been positive.

Suggested Reading

Battle, Jackson. *Environmental Law.* Vol. 2, *Water Pollution and Hazardous Wastes;* vol. 3, *Air Pollution.* Cincinnati: Anderson Publishing Co., 1988.

Dales, J. H. *Pollution, property & prices: An Essay in Policy-making and Economics.* Toronto: University of Toronto Press, 1968. A classic and very readable essay that sets out the concept of pollution rights. He is persuasive even if you're not an economist.

Rosenbaum, Walter A. *Environmental Politics and Policy.* 2d ed. Washington, D.C.: Congressional Quarterly, 1991. Primarily an undergraduate text, this furnishes an excellent overview of several areas of environmental policy: air pollution, water supply and pollution, toxic and hazardous wastes, energy, and public lands. The discussions on the relationships between science and politics alone make the book worthwhile.

CHAPTER SIX

MANAGING WILDLIFE AND PUBLIC LANDS

The management of wildlife and that of public lands are related issues that generate complex webs of statues, regulations, and even international treaties. It would be impossible to discuss every enactment that affects public lands and wildlife. The purpose of this chapter is not to present the individual provisions of every act but rather to acquaint readers with the political context of various policy areas and the general intent behind the major acts and their subsequent implementation and revision.

The chapter is divided into three sections. The section on wildlife management discusses the regulation of the taking of wildlife and the commerce in wildlife; the acquisition and management of wildlife habitat; the protection of marine mammals; and the conservation of endangered species.[1] The section on public lands discusses six periods of federal land history: acquisition, disposal, reservation, custodial management, intensive management, and consultation and confrontation. The chapter concludes with a telling example of how a manager might circumvent the protections Congress put in place for the wilderness system.

WILDLIFE MANAGEMENT

Federal wildlife law is distinguished by its dispersal among many federal agencies. The federal agencies with major responsibility for wildlife are the Fish and Wildlife Service (FWS) of the Department of the Interior, and the National Marine Fisheries Service in the National Oceanic and Atmospheric Administration (NOAA) of the Commerce Department. The National Park Service, the Forest Service, and the Bureau of Land Management (BLM) also have strong roles in this policy area. Because of the interagency activity, the following discussion of wildlife management and law is divided into topic areas, beginning with the taking of wildlife.

REGULATING THE TAKING OF WILDLIFE

The most important acts dealing with the taking of wildlife are the Migratory Bird Treaty Act, the Bald Eagle Protection Act, and the Wild Free-Roaming Horses and Burros Act.

MIGRATORY BIRD TREATY ACT In 1916 the United States made a treaty with Great Britain, on behalf of Canada, to protect migratory birds. The Migratory Bird Treaty Act of 1918 was passed to implement the treaty. The act provided federal protection through the secretary of agriculture for all migratory game birds and insectivorous birds. It also restricted the shipping of birds across state lines if the shipment broke the laws of the states in which the birds were taken. The act withstood a court challenge by the states, and with that issue settled, the national government proceeded to sign similar treaties with Mexico (1936), Japan (1972), and the Soviet Union (1976).

It was soon clear that simply protecting birds from hunters was not sufficient to guarantee a supply of the birds. Habitat protection was also necessary, and in 1929 the Migratory Bird Conservation Act created a national system of bird refuges. Few refuges were actually purchased until the Migratory Bird Hunting Stamp Act of 1934 provided funds for habitat protection. Amendments to this act (also known as the Duck Stamp Act) have varied the percentages of revenue allocated for refuge purchase and for management. Some amendments, and additional statutes such as the National Wildlife Refuge System Administration Act of 1966, have given the secretary of agriculture the power to permit hunting on the refuges. At the same time as the Duck Stamp Act was passed, Congress enacted the Fish and Wildlife Coordination Act to authorize the Bureau of Biological Survey (the precursor to the FWS) to coordinate wildlife refuges on federal water impoundments. These refuges were under the control of the secretary of the interior.

The opposite side of the bird protection issue is the damage that migrating birds may do to unharvested crops. The 1916 treaty allowed the killing of birds that endanger agricultural interests, and the Coordination Act was amended in 1946 to permit the secretary of the interior to work with other agencies to minimize bird damage. The legislative solution was to provide alternative sources of

feed for these birds. In 1948 the Lea Act authorized renting or purchasing land for feeding areas; and two other acts, the Waterfowl
Depredations Control Act of 1956 and the Surplus Grain for Wildlife Act of 1961, provided the authority for federal feeding of
migrating birds and resident game birds.

The agency with primary responsibility for regulating hunting
and commerce in migratory bird species is the Fish and Wildlife
Service (FWS). Through the duck stamp revenues and congressional appropriations, the FWS is able to purchase land and easements
to protect habitat for migrating species. The FWS is consulted by the
Department of Agriculture and all other federal water-resource agencies to ensure that water projects affecting wetlands will not uduly
harm the migratory species or their habitat. The FWS may authorize the killing of birds (as opposed to routine hunting) if agricultural
crops or human health are threatened by the birds' activities.[2]

THE BALD EAGLE PROTECTION ACT In 1940 an act was
passed to protect the national symbol of the United States. In addition to protecting the lives and nests of the birds, the Bald Eagle
Protection Act prohibits the sale, possession, or transport of bald
eagles or of any part of an eagle (such as feathers). After 1959 Alas-
kan bald eagles were protected by the act; in 1962 golden eagles
were also covered, although state governors may authorize the
shooting of golden eagles to protect livestock. The golden eagles
were added because immature bald eagles are difficult to distinguish from golden eagles. The act was also amended in 1972 to
prohibit taking the protected birds by poison. Penalties for violation
of the act are severe: criminal penalties up to $10,000 and two years
in jail, and civil penalties of up to $5000 per violation. The civil
penalties were also increased in 1972 by the automatic revocation of
federal grazing privileges held by ranchers convicted of a violation.
At the same time a "citizen bounty" of half of any fine (up to $2500)
was authorized for anyone giving information that leads to a
conviction.

After the 1916 Migratory Bird Treaty between Great Britain
and the United States was amended in 1972, the Migratory Bird
Conservation Act of 1929 was amended to protect bald eagles and
other raptors. The Endangered Species Act of 1973 (discussed later
in this section) also affords some protection for the bald eagle.

WILD FREE-ROAMING HORSES AND BURROS ACT Just as
the Bald Eagle Protection Act was passed to protect a national
symbol, the Wild and Free-Roaming Horses and Burros Act of 1971

had a great deal of popular sentiment behind it. The brutal slaughter of wild horses was publicized by the efforts of a few westerners, and the romantic attachment of Americans to horses in general and to symbols of the Old West in particular persuaded Congress to protect the animals on federal lands. Subsequent complications over animals wandering onto private property and the problems for legitimate owners of unbranded animals straying onto federally managed land have been resolved through the courts.

Under the act, the BLM is permitted to remove "excess" animals, which cause management problems since horses and burros reproduce rapidly. At the end of 1985 the BLM was holding nine thousand animals in its feedlot corrals,[3] and the removal of excess animals from the range was necessarily slowed. Adoption rates for the horses in BLM custody dropped, and pressure is mounting for the government to sell the animals for commercial purposes, usually for pet food. The 1986 budget for wild horse and burro management was $16 million.[4]

This is an example of a policy area that is especially difficult for Congress. Most Americans are oblivious to the conditions in slaughterhouses, but even a sanitized photo of frightened horses in slaughter conditions will mobilize public opinion. In the early eighties, when the Reagan administration tried to remove wild ponies from the eastern coastal islands to make room for off-road vehicles, the public outcry forced it to reconsider. An issue that is so emotional that school children write letters in protest will also involve their parents. Congress must consider the political context of horse and burro issues more than the simply technical or economic context.

REGULATING COMMERCE IN WILDLIFE

The issue of commerce in wildlife was discussed in some detail in chapter 4. The key legislation is the Lacey Act, originally passed in 1900. It had two purposes: "to strengthen and supplement state wildlife conservation laws . . . [and] to promote the interests of agriculture and horticulture by prohibiting the importation of certain types of wildlife determined to be injurious to those interests."[5] Although there is nothing in the language of the Lacey Act to exclude fish, the act was generally considered only in relation to game birds and fur-bearing mammals. In 1926 Congress passed the Black Bass Act to extend Lacey Act–like protections to black bass, an important game fish. Subsequent amendments have extended the Lacey Act to include "wild animals, birds, and parts or eggs thereof, captured or killed contrary to federal law or the laws of any foreign country."[6]

These acts had important implications for protecting wildlife in foreign countries. In 1930 the Tariff Act supplemented the Lacey Act by requiring that, if the laws of the exporting country protected an animal, the United States consul at the place of export must certify any such animal or any products derived from it before they could be brought into the United States. Products or animals lacking the certification may be seized. Responsibility for the Lacey Act originally rested with the secretary of agriculture, and responsibility for the Tariff Act with the secretary of commerce. In 1970, following a thirty-year consolidation under the secretary of the interior, the Lacey Act moved to the Commerce Department.

Substantial changes were made in these acts in 1981. The Lacey Act Amendments repealed the Black Bass Act and drastically revised the original Lacey Act. The enforcement provisions were enhanced and the general scope of the act expanded. Now the act extends to all wild animals, including those bred and raised in captivity, and some plant species. Criminal penalties were also increased; the maximum fine is now $20,000, and jail terms range from one to five years. Under the 1981 amendments, these penalties no longer require that the violator "knowingly and willfully" violated the act; thus the government does not have to prove that the violator intended to break the law.

ACQUISITION AND MANAGEMENT OF WILDLIFE HABITAT

The federal government owns approximately one-fourth of the nation's land, but this ownership is heavily concentrated in the western states and Alaska. For wildlife to thrive, habitat must be available and protected. Wildlife habitat comes from three types of lands: lands expressly acquired for habitat, multiple-use lands, and special-purpose federal lands such as the National Park System and military bases.

NATIONAL WILDLIFE REFUGE SYSTEM
The Migratory Bird Treaty Act originally did not provide for land for bird refuges; in 1929 new legislation rectified the oversight. Lands acquired under the Migratory Bird Conservation Act of 1929 were originally intended to be "inviolate sanctuaries" for the birds, but amend-

ments have allowed the secretary of the interior to permit public hunting if compatible with other purposes. The Duck Stamp Act (the Migratory Bird Hunting Stamp Act of 1934) provided funds for refuge acquisition. Despite acquisition authority in other related acts, the Migratory Bird Conservation Act remains the primary source of authority for wildlife refuge acquisition.

Acquisition and management of the various wildlife areas was scattered about the country and between the numerous land-management agencies. The FWS administered several different categories, and the BLM occasionally shared responsibility with the FWS. In 1966 the National Wildlife Refuge System Administration Act consolidated the various units under the FWS, but it did not provide much guidance for administration. The act's major impacts were to restrict the transfer, exchange, or disposal of land; to clarify the authority of the secretary of the interior to accept monetary donations for land acquisition; and to authorize the secretary to permit hunting if hunting were compatible with other uses. The "authorization of 'compatible' uses thus made clear that the national wildlife refuges were not necessarily to be managed as 'single use' lands, but more properly as 'dominant use' lands."[7] The system currently encompasses ninety million acres of lands and waters and is administered by the Fish and Wildlife Service.

Wetlands are another important wildlife habitat. Public perceptions about wetlands have changed dramatically since the 1860s, when the Swamp Land Act gave federal wetlands to the states for development. Today, wetlands are usually purchased under the Migratory Bird Conservation Act with Duck Stamp Act funding. The 1961 Wetlands Act allows advance appropriations to the Migratory Bird Conservation Fund for upland habitat surrounding wetlands and for some wetlands purchase as well. Other funds are available from the Land and Water Conservation Fund, supplied primarily by receipts for offshore oil and gas leases. A third source of wetlands protection is the Water Bank Act of 1970, which allows the secretary of agriculture to reimburse land owners who protect their wetlands and adjacent uplands. These programs do not adequately address the problem of wetland loss to development.

Private organizations such as Ducks Unlimited are vital in the protection of wetlands as wildlife habitat. Ducks Unlimited manages private lands throughout the Canadian-American migratory pathways. The Nature Conservancy acquires wetlands to protect them from development, and the National Audubon Society also manages bird refuges. The impact of groups such as these is not limited to their land acquisitions. Their intensive and skillful lobbying and political involvement also provide protection to the wetland habitats.

MULTIPLE-USE LANDS The Forest Service manages 191 million acres, including half the big game and cold-water fish habitat, and habitat for sixty-four threatened or endangered species.[8] Wildlife conservation is a relatively recent addition to the Forest Service's responsibilities; the Multiple-Use Sustained-Yield Act of 1960, the Forest and Rangeland Renewable Resources Planning Act of 1974, and the National Forest Management Act of 1976 include wildlife habitat for both game and nongame species as part of the Forest Service mission.

Funding, always a problem, received some relief from the 1974 act which amended the Knutson-Vandenberg Act of 1930. The original Knutson-Vandenberg Act required private purchasers of Forest Service timber to help pay for reforestation of the logged area. The amendment allowed the funds also to be used for protecting and improving fish and wildlife habitat. Although helpful, the funds have been restricted in use. Secondary impacts of logging activities are not mitigated, an issue that is particularly important in fish habitat management because of the heavy siltation that often results from timbering and road building. An additional criticism of the program is that funds are only generated by profitable timber sales; many sales are, on paper, financial losses to the federal government.[9]

The Bureau of Land Management is the second agency required to protect wildlife under the multiple-use concept, which requires federal land management agencies to manage for recreation and wildlife habitat as well as for the specific consumptive use (for example, timber harvesting). Like the Forest Service, its mandate comes from the Federal Land Policy and Management Act of 1976. It manages about 60 percent of all lands under federal jurisdiction but is largely unknown in the eastern United States. Its lands are leftovers from the land disposals of the nineteenth century (discussed in the second section of this chapter). Most of the productive or economically valuable land was transferred into private hands, so the BLM holdings usually have low productivity and are not found in contiguous blocks of land. This makes BLM land decisions often controversial, as they affect the adjacent privately held land as well as the blocks of federal land. Technically, the BLM manages habitat rather than species (although it does have responsibility for the wild horses and burros), with most management of resident species being under state responsibility.

The BLM's policy implementation is also hampered by the condition of the land it manages. Grazing permits for BLM lands are issued to western ranchers at well below market value. The ranchers then have little incentive to improve or to maintain the public lands. As a result, typically the public grazing lands are not as well kept as the private lands, and political domination by the powerful livestock industry lobby has affected the BLM policy process. The organizational history of the agency, which was formed in 1946 from the old Grazing Service and the General Land Office, has earned it the nickname of "Bureau of Livestock and Mining."

SPECIAL-PURPOSE FEDERAL LANDS   The National Park Service also has a stake in wildlife. The first national park, Yellowstone, was established in 1872. Even then hunting was an issue, and in 1883 the U.S. Army was used to protect the scenery and wildlife in Yellowstone. For the next thirty-three years, the army tried with varying success to protect the newly established parks from the hunting activities of citizens. In 1916 Congress enacted the National Park Service Organic Act, which listed wildlife protection as one of the purposes of the national parks.

Until the fifties, wildlife management in the parks lacked an ecological perspective. "Good" animals were protected, but "bad" ones like wolves and coyotes were killed. In the fifties an advisory board was appointed after the conservation community complained about the Park Service management practices. In 1963 this group released the Leopold Report, which emphasized an ecological perspective for wildlife management.

The Wilderness Act of 1964 applied to all of the federal land-management agencies. Wilderness protection is critical for habitat protection for wildlife, and this act was passed partly to overcome the reluctance of the Forest Service to designate wilderness areas in national forests. Under the act, almost forty million acres of National Park land alone have been designated as wilderness, and the Park Service has recommended designation of another twenty-five million acres. The Land and Water Conservation Act of 1964 provided much-needed money to purchase additional park land.

Military lands are incorporated into wildlife concerns through the Sikes Act Extension, enacted in 1974. The act is primarily aimed at the development of cooperative comprehensive plans with the departments of the interior and agriculture and with state fish and game departments. It provides an optional mechanism for cooperative wildlife management on military reservations. The secretary of defense may be brought in with the secretary of the interior and the state agencies to "carry out a program of planning, development, maintenance, and coordination of wildlife, fish and game conservation in military reservations."[10] In 1989 the Department of Defense agreed to work with The Nature Conservancy on land-management issues on military installations.

The final category of special lands are the vast holdings of the federal government on the outer continental shelf (OCS). The total area of the OCS is approximately 819 million acres, or 36 percent of the dry land area of the United States.[11] The Outer Continental Shelf Lands Act of 1953 asserted national control of the OCS up to two hundred miles from the shore, excluding the three-mile territorial limit for the states established in the Submerged Lands Act of 1953.[12] Management is shared between the BLM and the United States Geological Survey (USGS), with the USGS having primary responsibility for tract-specific geologic, engineering, and economic evaluations.

The enabling legislation was amended in 1978 due to congressional dissatisfaction with Interior Department's administration of the 1953 Submerged Lands Act. The amendments required more flexible bidding procedures for oil and gas leases, expanded economic planning provisions, increased the role of state and local governments in planning for lease sales, exploration, and development, and established a policy to favor small refiners. The amendments also created an Offshore Oil Pollution Compensation Fund, supported by a barrel tax at the point of production, to mitigate the costs of oil spills.

The OCS Lands Act claims federal authority over the mineral resources of the shelf, not over the fishing and navigation rights in the waters above. However, the "living resources" of the shelf may be protected.[13] The 1978 amendments required the secretary of the interior to conduct a study "to establish information needed for the assessment and management of environmental impacts on the human, marine, and coastal environments" and to "predict impacts on the marine biota which may result from chronic low level pollution of large spills."[14] Although the OCS Lands Act does not give the authority to conserve wildlife, two related acts, the Fishery Conservation and Management Act of 1976 and the Marine Protection, Research, and Sanctuaries Act of 1972, do provide such authority.

PROTECTION OF MARINE MAMMALS

Clearly the federal government cannot mandate an international system of marine mammal protection; but the government can, and did, institute such a program for the territorial waters of the United States. The reasons for such legislation, enacted in 1972, are many. The primary reason was the need to provide protection and regulation of a commercial resource which was in danger of depletion. Another reason, stressed by ecologists and other scientists, was the ecological importance of marine mammals and the necessity to protect that ecological niche. Finally, an intensive lobbying effort arose from citizens concerned about the harvesting of mammals with apparently extraordinary intelligence and complex social arrangements.[15]

In 1972 Congress enacted the Marine Mammal Protection Act (MMPA), which "articulated policy goals of broad generality and implemented them with specific directions that were neither purely protectionist nor purely exploitive, but were almost always complex."[16] With some extremely specific exceptions, the keystone of the act was an absolute moratorium on the taking of marine mammals by United States citizens or by foreigners within the Fishery Conservation Zone of the United States. The state control over marine mammals was preempted.

Implementation of the act was split between the secretary of commerce and the secretary of the interior. The commerce secretary bears responsibility for all cetaceans (whales and porpoises) and for all pinnipedians (seals) except walruses. The interior secretary has authority over all other marine mammals (manatees, dugongs, polar bears, sea otters, and walruses).

An independent advisory body, the Marine Mammal Commission, was established in the act. It became the focus of controversy during the first Reagan administration. The members of the commission had previously been highly respected marine scientists appointed by the president on the recommendation of the CEQ, the Smithsonian Institution, the National Science Foundation, and the National Academy of Sciences, but Reagan chose to appoint members chosen by the CEQ alone. In 1982 Congress passed a rider to the Commercial Fisheries Research and Development Act that made Marine Mammal Commission appointments subject to Senate confirmation.[17]

MMPA is unique in its provisions for waivers by either secretary. A waiver must be extremely specific, applying only to a particular species or population stock and then only to a limited amount. If the secretary is convinced that the proposed waiver will not harm the resource and that the taking is "in accord with sound principles of resource protection and conservation as provided in the purposes and policies" of the act, the secretary may issue regulations to control a waiver and then issue the waiver itself.[18]

The rule-making process the secretary must follow is the formal process described in chapter 5. A full adversarial hearing must be conducted by an administrative law judge, allowing the presentation of evidence and cross-examination of witnesses. A full record of the hearing must be kept. The hearing must cover the proposed waiver as well as the regulations related to it, and the secretary must publish all scientific statements and all relevant studies and recommendations made by the Marine Mammal Commission. These are "procedural requirements more stringent than those applicable to the promulgation of regulations under any other wildlife statute."[19]

The MMPA is not the only legislation that protects marine mammals. The Endangered Species Act of 1973 provides protections for endangered and threatened marine mammals; the Marine Protection, Research, and Sanctuaries Act of 1972 provides habitat protection; and various international treaties (discussed in chapter 7) affect marine mammals. Threatened or endangered marine mammals include "the northern sea otter, the southern sea otter, the dugong, all species of manatees and monk seals, the Gulf of California harbor porpoise, and blue, bowhead, finback, gray, humpback, right, Sei, and sperm whales."[20]

Private interest groups have been highly visible in the protection of marine mammals. The harp seal hunts in Canada were halted by Greenpeace activists protesting in often bloody confrontations with seal hunters, by protectionists spray painting the young seals to ruin their pelts during the harvest period, by a national boycott of Canadian fish products, and by the distribution of one of the most poignant animal posters ever made: a mother seal nuzzling the skinned carcass of her pup. "Setting on" porpoises by tuna fishermen was halted in 1990 (or at least the tuna companies claimed that the practice had been stopped) due to a consumer boycott of tuna products; 1990 saw "Dolphin Safe" labels in the supermarket. The plight of the whales has been publicized by Greenpeace, whose members cast themselves adrift between whaling ships and their prey. These interest groups are skilled at manipulating the policy process, providing trigger events, and using the media to increase public concern over marine mammal issues.

CONSERVATION OF ENDANGERED SPECIES

Three federal statutes and one international treaty have been enacted to attempt to halt the destruction of wildlife. The first statute was the Endangered Species Preservation Act of 1966. The strongest portion of this act provided for habitat protection. Beyond this, it was primarily a statement of good intentions. The most notable limitation was that it did not provide any restrictions on the taking of wildlife, leaving such regulations to the states.

In 1969 Congress enacted the Endangered Species Conservation Act. The major innovation of this act was "its authorization to the Secretary [of the interior] to promulgate a list of wildlife 'threatened with worldwide extinction' and to prohibit their importation into the United States, except for certain limited purposes."[21] Unfortunately, the 1969 act fell short of providing the kind of legislation that would protect endangered species in time. The secretary of the interior listed only species in imminent danger of extinction and provided no protection for species approaching the danger point.

By 1973 it was clear to the Congress that the federal endangered species program was not sufficient. Apart from the MMPA, there were no restrictions on taking endangered species, and the constraints on federal activities that might harm species were narrow and embellished with many loopholes. The magnitude of the problem of vanishing species was becoming all too apparent. Scientists estimate conservatively that 15 percent of all species in the Latin American rain forests will be gone by 2000; in the large national parks in the United States between one-quarter and one-third of the large animal species are already gone.[22] According to William Mansfield, the deputy director of the United Nations Environmental Programme, the extinction rate in 1990 was over 150 species per day, and "biological diversity faces the worst stage of mass extinction in 65 million years."[23] In 1973 Congress passed the Endangered Species Act, which established the "threatened" and "endangered" categories of wildlife and authorized criminal sanctions for violations of the regulations implementing the act. The act also provided protection for critical habitats, a departure from previous federal regulatory efforts. The listing process was formalized, providing interest groups with increased access to the protection process. In 1982, responding to Reagan's requirement that FWS consider the economic consequences of listing endangered and threatened species, Congress amended the act to clarify congressional intentions that "listing decisions were to be based solely on biological considerations and that economic impacts were to be considered only in the designation of critical habitat."[24]

The 1969 Endangered Species Conservation Act had called for an international meeting on endangered species, and in 1973 the meeting produced the Convention on International Trade in Endangered Species of Wild Fauna and Flora (CITES), which was focused on international trade in the species and not on their management. The convention established three classes of endangered species and listed them in appendices. Appendix I species are in the highest danger of extinction and may not be traded for primarily commercial purposes. Appendix II species may be traded commercially, subject to certain convention restrictions. Appendix III species are those designated by signatory countries as requiring other countries' cooperation with the internal, national management of the species.

Special concerns about endangered species are raised by third-world nations which face direct competition for life-sustaining resources between their human populations and their wildlife. Poorer nations faced with economic constraints limit funding for wildlife conservation and management, and some see the preservation concerns of developed nations as cloaked imperialism. International treaties to protect threatened wildlife often are supplemented by loans or grants to encourage and to enable the developing nations to preserve their own natural heritage.

THE PUBLIC LANDS

The federal lands comprise over 700,000 acres (excluding inland waters), or about one-fourth of the United States.[25] This statistic is misleading, however, as most of the federal land is in the western states and Alaska. The federal government owns over half of the land in some western states. Thus federal land policies have a great impact on the states, and especially the western states.

Federal ownership of land arises from two sources. The first is Article I of the Constitution:

[Congress shall have Power] . . . to exercise [exclusive authority] over all Places purchased by the Consent of the Legislature of the State in which the Same shall be, for the Erection of Forts, Magazines, Arsenals, dock-Yards, and other needful Buildings. Art. I, § 8, cl. 17

The power of the federal government over land that it acquired under Article I varies, depending upon reservations placed on the land at the time the land was ceded to the national government or on subsequent changes by Congress.

The second source of authority over lands is Article IV:

> The Congress shall have Power to dispose of and make all needful Rules and Regulations respecting the Territory or other Property belonging to the United States; and nothing in this Constitution shall be so construed as to Prejudice any Claims of the United States, or of any particular State. Art. IV, § 3, cl. 2

The federal power over these lands is virtually absolute. At one time the states were thought to have police power over federal land within their jurisdictions just as they do over land belonging to any other owners, but the law is currently interpreted to mean that the federal government has sovereign power over these lands.

In this century the demands on the federal lands have increased dramatically. Increased leisure time, greater mobility, and the popularity of camping and hiking have increased public interest in all forms of outdoor activities, especially in wilderness experiences and wildlife observation. The demand for grazing permits has increased in the West, and shifts in population to the Sunbelt have created an enormous pressure on the water supply and water quality. The competition among user groups is fierce. The outer continental shelf has become increasingly important for mineral production. Demands on the national forests for timber have increased to about ten billion board-feet annually, and the demand continues to rise.[26] Revenues from federal lands are also increasing, primarily as a result of the offshore oil and gas leases, although timber sales are also a significant factor. Since 1950 the income generated by the federal lands has surpassed their total expenditures.[27]

The statutes governing the federal lands are as checkered as the federal land holdings. There is no uniform or controlling statute; as a result the agencies have a fair amount of discretion, but they are also subject to the vagaries of congressional whims. Although the public perception is that these lands are both managed and used by the federal government, in actuality most of the benefits from the federal lands go to private concerns through mining, grazing, recreation, and timbering. Mining and oil claims on federal land are developed by private individuals and corporations. Grazing permits are given to ranchers to expand their herds; the federal government does not run livestock on the federal grazing lands. Timber is purchased and cut by private timber companies, not the United States Forest Service. It is from "this interface between public ownership and private use of the same lands that the conflicts with federal policy arise and persist."[28]

The winning hand in these conflicts between public ownership and private use has changed many times since the colonial days. Marion Clawson, director of the BLM from 1948 to 1953, divides the history of federal lands into six relatively distinct areas: acquisition, disposal, reservation, custodial management, intensive management, and consultation and confrontation.

ACQUISITION

The early phase of acquisition was from the beginning of the republic through the 1860s—encompassing the Louisiana Purchase; the acquisition of Florida, the Southwest, and the Pacific Northwest; the Gadsden Purchase; and finally the acquisition of Alaska. While of course these acquisitions had the effect of increasing the lands held by the federal government, their primary purpose was imperialistic; the United States simply chose to purchase rather than to acquire by conquest.

Other forms of land acquisition by the federal government continued through the twentieth century. Under the Weeks Act of 1911 the national forests have been increased by purchases of private lands, and since 1961 the federal government has been purchasing land for national parks. There has been less opposition to these purchases than one might expect, because the private sector usually continues to have access to the benefits of the resources.

DISPOSAL

Following the acquisition of large chunks of land, the federal government was eager to begin development on those lands. This necessitated subsidizing railroad companies to build railways, and encouraging homesteaders and ranchers to settle on the land. The government also removed Native Americans from the most profitable land, despite legal and moral arguments against such activities. Some land was given to war veterans, and some was auctioned. Some was simply given away to homesteaders who would promise to live on the land and improve it; eventually, more than a quarter of the public domain was distributed under the Homestead Act of 1862 and later extensions of the original Homestead Act, such as the Stock-Raising Homestead Act of 1916, the Timber Culture Act of 1873, the Desert Land Sales Act of 1877, and the Timber and Stone Act of 1878. The period of American history from the early nineteenth century until the New Deal, in which land disposal took place, was tumultuous, and the "process of land disposal was a lusty affair—a headlong, even precipitous process, full of frauds and deceits, but one which transformed a great deal of land into valuable private property—and one which built a nation."[29]

RESERVATION

The Progressive Movement, and an increasing demand by the public for conservation measures at the turn of the century, led to an interest in permanent reservation of part of the federal lands. The first large, systematic reservation was that of the national forests created in 1891 by the Forest Reserve Act.[30] By 1897 nearly forty million acres had been withdrawn for inclusion in the forest reserves. The authority of the president to make these reservations was finally established by the Supreme Court when it ruled in *United States v. Midwest Oil Company* (1915) that "Congress, by failing to challenge a host of 19th century executive withdrawals, had in effect acquiesced to earlier presidents' claims that they held broad implied powers to withdraw public lands from disposal."[31] This presidential power was limited by the Federal Land Policy and Management Act of 1976 (FLPMA), which requires congressional review of proposed withdrawals and imposes other restrictions on the implied executive powers of withdrawal. Other reservations were established by the 1934 Taylor Act, which placed grazing on federal lands under the control of the Department of the Interior; the department's Division of Grazing joined in 1946 with the General Land Office to become the Bureau of Land Management.

CUSTODIAL MANAGEMENT

Custodial management has been a characteristic of federal land management from the very beginning of the reservation period. During this period, federal land management focused on maintaining resources and allowing access for development, but active management was not a priority. It continues to reflect the earliest conservationist ideals of Gifford Pinchot, the first head of the Forestry Service, and his contemporaries. Pinchot wrote in 1910: "The first great fact about conservation is that it stands for development. . . and for the prevention of waste. . . . The natural resources must be developed and preserved for the benefit of the many, and not merely for the profit of a few."[32]

Dissatisfied with the management in the Department of the Interior, Pinchot took his Division of Forestry to the Department of Agriculture, where it has continued to protect timber resources for private industry. The Forest Service emphasized its relationships with lumber concerns, but it also encouraged recreational opportunities on forest lands.

When the National Park Service was established in 1916, it found itself in competition with the Forest Service, which was convinced that it was the logical guardian of the nation's parks. The Park Service responded by stressing its preservationist attitude (in contrast to the Forest Service's conservationist-utilitarian perspective) and by expanding the parks with Forest Service land as much as possible. During the New Deal, the Park Service benefited from the support of Roosevelt's close friend and advisor, Harold Ickes, who served as secretary of the interior. Ickes convinced Roosevelt to give a large portion of the Civilian Conservation Corps to Park Service management. Finally, in 1936 the Park Service won recognition of its recreational role with the passage of the Park, Parkway and Recreation Area Study Act of 1936. This act gave primary responsibility to the Park Service for federal recreation activities on all federal lands not controlled by the Department of Agriculture. It also identified the Park Service as the agency responsible for delivering federal aid for recreation projects to state governments.[33]

INTENSIVE MANAGEMENT

From about 1950 to 1960, the Park Service, Forest Service, and other land management agencies actively encouraged development and use of federal lands. In 1951 Conrad Wirth was appointed the new director of the Park Service. He implemented Mission 66, a plan to upgrade the park facilities and to encourage increased use of the parks. More than two thousand miles of road were built or upgraded during this period.[34] New and ambitious visitor centers were established in many parks, and Mission 66 was a success.

The Forest Service was also experiencing good times. Forest sale revenues increased, and in most years the service showed a profit. During the fifties, the Forest Service surplus was over $20 million.[35] Oil and gas leasing, mining, recreation, and grazing also increased during this period, and in general the national forests experienced an economic boom. This increased the pressure on the land and the managers, and led inexorably to clashes with interest groups in the sixties.

CONSULTATION AND CONFRONTATION

To some extent, all of the previous phases of public land management continued from 1960 on. However, for reasons outlined in chapter 2, the public was no longer willing to allow federal agencies to manage resources without direct public input. Concerns with environmental quality were bound up in land management issues. Energy mining issues and air quality are interrelated, and the preservation of the ocean ecosystems was imperiled by drilling on the outer continental shelf. Water supplies and watershed management became connected with the question of safe disposal of hazardous and toxic wastes. All of these issues increased awareness of the impact of federal land management policies for both environmentalists and commodity producers.

In 1960 Congress passed the Multiple-Use Sustained Yield Act, which provided a legislative foundation for the institutional policies already in place in the Forest Service. Multiple use is an ambiguous concept, which is not clarified in the legislative definitions; this is both a problem and an asset to the agencies required to manage under its instructions. It is a problem when uses conflict, as when critical habitat is also prime recreational or mining or timbering terrain. It is an asset in that the ambiguity gives managers discretion and hence flexibility.

The 1964 Wilderness Act, like the Multiple-Use Sustained Yield Act, was the result of controversy and compromise. It gave protection to wilderness areas within the national forests, protecting these areas from Forest Service redesignation. Lands managed by the BLM were also considered for wilderness designation. Some extractive uses, such as coal mining, were allowed through the eighties; charges that the Department of the Interior under James Watt was deliberately building roads to exclude undeveloped land from wilderness consideration led to dramatic confrontations between environmental groups and Reagan's administration.[36]

Several acts, such as the Forest and Rangeland Renewable Resources Planning Act of 1974 (RPA) and its successor, the National Forest Management Act of 1976, mandated long-range planning by the management agencies. The RPA requires that all renewable resources be assessed every ten years and that a national forest plan be submitted every five years. The Federal Land Policy and Management Act of 1976 (FLPMA) is also a planning act that increased the discretionary powers of the BLM. It contains a multiple-use provision, includes BLM lands in wilderness consideration, and increases the requirements for public participation that were so characteristic of the legislation of the seventies.

The trend in federal land legislation was to turn away from agency initiatives and toward congressional initiatives, largely in response to the demands of special interest groups. Even the venerable Park Service was not immune from congressional assertions of power. Congress began to increase its power over the agency during the Nixon years, when the formerly cordial relations between the Park Service and the Congress deteriorated. As other forms of environmental benefits (such as new dams) for constituents decreased, members of Congress increasingly found the national parks to be a vehicle for distributing goodies back home. One critic said:

> The Park Service has become a servant of Congress in the worst sense. It has become Congress' flunky in carrying out its pork barrel chores while it is supposed to be the guardian of the national interest. Unfortunately the Service doesn't have the power to uphold that interest.[37]

During the eighties, public attention shifted to concerns about environmental quality; but the public lands, with their well-established "iron triangles," held their own in the policy process in Washington. Between 1970 and 1980, the number of acres included in the national parks increased by 169 percent. Over one hundred rivers were designated as wild and scenic, and another 10,000 miles were proposed for consideration. The National Wilderness Preservation System added significant amounts of land, primarily in Alaska. Wetlands were not such a success story; over 300,000 acres per year fell to the developers.[38]

During the Reagan years, many administration policies were designed to help developers utilize the resources of federal lands. The story which follows illustrates how managers may utilize the legal and political system to achieve policy goals that were not part of the original congressional intent.[39]

USING THE LAW TO ACHIEVE
POLICY GOALS

Public-land managers are given a great deal of latitude in their management policies, partly because of the conflicting rules and multiple agencies involved. The discussion which follows shows how skillfully managers may manipulate the administrative law and procedures.

In the late 1940s the federal government acquired the Bitter Lake National Wildlife Refuge in New Mexico. Originally a mix of private and state land, the refuge was part of the Salt Creek Wilderness along the Pecos River in eastern New Mexico. The state retained its mineral rights, and in 1972 it issued an oil-gas lease to Yates Petroleum Corporation on the condition that Yates commence drilling operations before midnight on November 1, 1982, or lose the lease. In September 1982 New Mexico gave Yates a permit to drill. Yates asked the U.S. Fish and Wildlife Service for a right-of-way and surface occupancy permit, and at the same time applied to the BLM for a right-of-way permit.

Monday-morning quarterbacking by the environmentalists and an anonymous Interior Department career employee suggests that one of the two following scenarios then developed. The first possibility is that Reagan's administration "saw this case as an opportunity to set a precedent establishing the rights of an existing lessee to drill in the wilderness . . . [and] did it for the principle of the thing."[40] The second possibility is that

> the politicos in the department [of the Interior] were asleep on this one. . . . Once Yates acted, the Reagan appointees were forced to do something, especially after it got on television and Congress got stirred up. Their hearts weren't in it, though. These, after all, weren't welfare chiselers they were dealing with. So they fumbled around with the case until the heat was off; then they quietly handed Yates the permits they wanted and gave them a little slap on the wrist.[41]

In either scenario, we can imagine an Interior employee whose goal was to let Yates drill. Assuming this to be true: what are the legal obstacles the employee faced and how were they overcome?

Interior did not have authority to issue the permits that Yates requested. Congress had barred expenditures to process permits or leases for energy development in designated wilderness areas. Although the Wilderness Act of 1964 *allowed* oil and gas leasing in wilderness areas, such leasing was not required; until 1981 no secretary had issued such oil or gas leases. In October, Interior sent the following letter in response to Yates's request for permits.

> The purpose of this letter is to inform you of the status of your application . . . for access and drillsite permits. . . . The Solicitor's Office has determined that there is no legal objection to the approval of the above requests. However, recent appropriations legislation has prohibited the obligation of funds for "any aspects of the processing or issuance of permits or leases pertaining to exploration for or development of coal, oil, and gas" in certain areas, including Salt Creek Wilderness, § 126, P.L. 97-276. In short, due to the restriction in the appropriation legislation, we cannot process or issue the applications at this time.[42]

What interpretation could the Interior Department expect Yates to put on such a letter? Without straining the meaning, this letter says that drilling is permissible but Interior just cannot spend the money to process the application. It is a strong signal to the oil company that Interior will not proceed against it if it drills.

Several other options were open to Interior. It could have purchased Yates's lease, or it could have tried to trade for an equivalent oil-gas lease on public lands that were not designated as wilderness. However, Secretary of the Interior James Watt had been very clear that he intended to open wilderness areas for gas and oil exploration, which had been the triggering action for the congressional prohibition on processing permits and leases.

On October 31 Yates acted to protect its lease and began to prepare the site for drilling. The next day Yates drilled a forty-foot hole, and on November 2 it constructed roads and a drill pad.

From its own perspective, Yates had been as conscientious as anyone could expect. Its state lease was about to expire, so it had to move quickly to salvage the investment. It consulted with the BLM and with the FWS on the best route for its road to the site, and "indeed Yates altered its planned route to avoid a potential archaeological area."[43] By the time a federal appeals court upheld a temporary restraining order obtained by federal officials against Yates, the well was 2800 feet deep. The temporary restraining order was followed by a permanent injunction.

In December the limitations on processing permits expired, and Congress was not in session. Although their own procedural rules restrict the BLM and the FWS from issuing permits to companies with trespass injunctions outstanding, the two agencies gave Yates the necessary permits late in the month. In February, after drilling another 1400 feet, Yates capped the well. For payment of nominal rental and processing fees, the BLM agreed to void its trespass complaint against Yates.[44]

While we might not applaud the result, if the Interior Department was trying to allow Yates to drill, it succeeded rather well. Had Yates not been caught drilling by a quail-hunting environmentalist on November 1, the company's activities might not have been discovered until the well was drilled and capped. The October letter from the Department of the Interior would have provided the legitimacy Yates needed until challenged by an outside group. Once the furor started, the agencies followed the letter of the law and restricted the drilling, but as soon as the legal and political variables permitted, they legitimized Yates's operation. The penalties were mitigated, and the agencies could be fairly confident that no interest group was going to take them to task legally for ignoring their own procedural rules. There was no remedial action to be taken and no damages to be claimed. By clever use of the policy process and the law, the administrators achieved the goal that, presumably, they were aiming at.

Suggested Reading

Bean, Michael J. *The Evolution of National Wildlife Law*. Revised and expanded ed. New York: Praeger, 1983. A *tour de force* that is essential for understanding issues of wildlife and how they relate to other environmental issues.

Clawson, Marion. *The Federal Lands Revisited*. Baltimore: Johns Hopkins University Press for Resources for the Future, 1983. Focused on the Forest Service and BLM lands, this book provides an historical as well as a contemporary (1983) look at federal lands.

Foresta, Ronald A. *America's National Parks and Their Keepers*. Baltimore: Johns Hopkins University Press for Resources for the Future, 1984. A good companion for Clawson's book on the Forest Service and the BLM.

National Audubon Society. *Audubon Wildlife Report*. Annual since 1985. New York: National Audubon Society. If you can only get one of these, get the 1985 report, since it gives the most thorough background for each area. Subsequent reports provide updates on the major wildlife issues. An especially nice feature is each report's "featured agency," for which detailed information is given.

CHAPTER SEVEN

INTERNATIONAL ENVIRONMENTAL POLICY

This chapter is intended to provide a brief introduction to international issues as they affect American environmental administration and law. As complex as national environmental administration and law are, international environmental policy is even more so. It is made more complex by the proliferation of interest groups and concerns; the lack of enforcement mechanisms imperils even the agreements that are reached. To illustrate the complexity of the topic, the first section contrasts the success of international efforts to regulate northern fur seal stocks with the spectacular lack of success in controlling whaling.

The chapter continues with a discussion of the major international organizations, predominantly in the United Nations, that are concerned with international issues. The acceptance of the biosphere concept and the establishment of the United Nations Environment Programme are discussed.

Transboundary air issues—including acid deposition and the depletion of stratospheric ozone—are presented in the third section, which also looks at the role of the European Community in environmental affairs. The final section deals with international efforts to utilize the last undeveloped continent on the planet, the Antarctic.

REGULATING SEAL AND WHALE TAKING

The first sealing treaty was signed in 1911; the first step toward regulating whaling was made in 1920. Almost a century later, the two programs—both dealing with northern sea-going mammals and requiring the cooperation of primarily the same nations—have widely divergent results. Why?

In 1911, the United States, Russia, Japan, and Great Britain signed the Treaty for the Preservation and Protection of Fur Seals. This treaty regulated the hunting of northern fur seals, particularly in their rookeries on the Pribilof Islands in the Bering Sea. The annual seal harvests had been noticeably declining at the end of the nineteenth century, partially because of unrestricted hunting at the breeding grounds but also because of pelagic hunting (hunting the animals in the open sea, while they are migrating). Pelagic hunting was especially wasteful, with five to nine seals killed for every seal recovered.[1] After decades of negotiation, the four seal-hunting nations reached agreement, banning outright all pelagic hunting and imposing regulation on the rookeries. Only skins that were certified by a signatory nation as having been taken under government supervision could be imported into the four countries, and the harvest from the breeding grounds was shared among the four. This latter point was extremely important for Great Britain, whose seal hunting had been exclusively pelagic. Although Japan withdrew from the treaty in 1941, the terms of the treaty were later continued by a series of conventions.

The treaty accomplished all it set out to do, although its thrust was to encourage the taking of seals rather than their preservation. The seal stocks recovered by the forties, but they have declined steadily since. The decline is attributed to several factors other than hunting, primarily deaths of young seals from unfortunate encounters with fishing gear and discarded plastics. The general increase in pollution levels has also taken its toll. In 1970 the United States Food and Drug Administration withdrew iron supplement pills made from seal livers from the American market because of the dangerously high levels of mercury detected in seal livers collected for a DDT study. There has been no commercial hunting of seals in the United States since 1985, mostly because of a decreased demand for seal furs and by-products, although subsistence hunting continues.

While the results of international agreements on fur seals may not please conservationists, the policies themselves were implemented successfully. The signatories to the treaties and conventions followed the spirit as well as the letter of the agreements, and reduction in seal stocks cannot be attributed to a failure of public policies directed at seals. International agreements on whales do not reflect such happy results.

Like the seal stocks, whale stocks were also declining at the end of the nineteenth century. Alarmed by the decline, whaling nations established an International Bureau for Whaling Statistics in Norway in 1920. Participation was completely voluntary, and member nations were simply asked to provide data on whales caught. In 1931 the League of Nations passed the Convention for Regulation of Whaling, and by 1935 twenty-four nations were adhering to the convention. Unfortunately, neither Japan nor the Soviet Union was among the adherents. The convention was ineffective, not only because two of the most important whaling nations were not signatories, but also because there were no enforcement measures in the convention. Whaling continued to be profitable, and improvements in technology made the capture and processing of whales even easier and more efficient. From the whales' viewpoint, World War II was a nice break.

In 1946 an international whaling conference was held in Washington at the instigation of the United States. The International Whaling Commission (IWC) was established at this conference, and a code regulating the hunting of whales was adopted. The progress was largely illusory, however; the annual quotas were set so high "that during its first 20 years of existence [the IWC] presided over serious depletion of nearly all the world's whale populations."[2] This can be attributed in part to factors that were really beyond the control of the IWC.

> The record of the International Whaling Commission during the three decades following its establishment was largely a history of its inability to overcome the studied and stubborn defense of the short-range interests of the whaling industry. The commission's ineffectualness was compounded by its frequent disregard of the findings and recommendations of its scientific advisors. Although the preamble of the 1946 treaty refers to "the interest of the nations of the world in safeguarding for future generations the great natural resources represented by whale stocks," the document is filled with qualifications that have been interpreted to legitimize the destructive and wasteful methods of operation.[3]

The whale became a symbol of the international environmental movement at the Stockholm Conference (discussed below) in 1972. Public pressure continued to mount to protect the whale, and finally, in 1982, the IWC declared a moratorium on whaling, to take effect for pelagic whaling during the 1985–1986 seasons and for coastal whaling in 1986. Unfortunately, the "qualifications" mentioned in the quotation above continue to be present in the moratorium, and the killing of whales for "scientific" purposes continues to be permissible. For example, in 1986 Iceland took 120 whales for scientific research, selling the meat (predictably not needed for "research") to Japan. In that first year of the moratorium, at least six thousand whales were killed.[4] In 1990 the Japanese whaling fleet set out to harvest over six hundred minke whales for research, violating at least the spirit of their agreement to halt whaling activities. The Soviets, who have also made similar undertakings, are restricting their fleet activities.

In 1971 Congress enacted the Pelly Amendment to the Fisherman's Protective Act of 1967. This amendment requires the secretary of commerce to notify the president when a foreign country is fishing in a manner that reduces the effectiveness of an international fishery agreement to which the United States is a party. The president then has the option to direct the secretary to halt the importation of fish products from that country. This amendment has not been used against nations violating the IWC agreement. The president's order to prohibit imports is discretionary; the offending nations are of great economic and strategic importance to the United States, and the whales have not been considered sufficiently important to warrant upsetting trade agreements.

However, other legislation had been more useful. In 1979 Congress enacted the Packwood-Magnuson Amendment to the Fishery Conservation and Management Act of 1976. This amendment requires the secretary of commerce to reduce by at least 50 percent the allowed catch of a foreign nation in United States territorial waters if that nation undermines the effectiveness of the IWC. During the Reagan administration, Japan refused to abide by the IWC moratorium, and the American Cetacean Society went to court to force the secretary of commerce to follow the Packwood-Magnuson Amendment.[5] The society won its case in the lower courts, but the Supreme Court reversed the decision, declining to force the secretary to determine that a particular action undermined the IWC's effectiveness, and claiming that such determinations were within the secretary's discretion. However, Japan notified the United States soon afterwards that it would eliminate its whaling operations by March 1988.

The Soviet Union was not as easy to convince. In 1985 the secretary of commerce reduced the Soviet Union's fishing quota under the Packwood-Magnuson Amendment. The Soviet Union told the IWC meeting that it would halt whaling in 1987. For the next two years it did not fish in United States waters. The basis for the USSR's change of heart was probably economic:

> For many years, the principal economic benefit from the Soviet whaling operation has been derived from the sale of meat to Japan. Observers believe that the Soviets decided to cease whaling because

the United States probably would certify Japan if it purchased meat from a country violating the moratorium provision.[6]

The Soviets assumed the Japanese would stop purchasing whale meat rather than face certification; in any case, whaling was no longer as profitable as it had been.

Even if the moratorium succeeds in halting the killing of whales for any purpose, the recovery of whale stocks will be slow. The blue whale, for example, is sexually mature at twenty-five, and even then only reproduces every two to five years. Some whale stocks may be below the critical level where replenishment is possible, and of course, deteriorating environmental conditions will continue to weaken whale populations regardless of human hunting activities.

While neither the fur seal nor the whale regulation program has been especially successful in terms of species protection, the policy process largely achieved its objectives in the fur seal policy area and yet failed when dealing with whales. Some of this may be attributed to differences between the species. Fur seals are a single species found mostly in one geographical area largely under the control of the United States, whereas several species of whales were the subject of IWC regulations, and their territories ranged the high seas and the territorial waters of many nations. Because of their variety, little is known about the life cycles and biological characteristics of whales, whereas seals have been studied extensively and a great deal is known about them.

In addition, the fur seal treaty and subsequent conventions were designed so that all of the nations involved benefited from compliance and no one nation bore a disproportionate cost. However, the whaling conventions could not bear equitably on the concerned nations. Whale meat, rarely used for human consumption in the United States, is a diet staple in Japan. National security interests entered in as well: Norway monitors Soviet fleet movements for the western allies, and Iceland threatened to lease its strategically sensitive inland fisheries to the Soviets if the United States persisted in enforcing the IWC moratorium. Finally, and perhaps most important, the whaling industries of Japan, Iceland, Norway, and the Soviet Union are large and influential; just as regulatory agencies are "captured" in the United States, the "weakness of the IWC as a protective agency was that its voting members represented in most instances the industry that it was intended to police."[7]

These two cases demonstrate how international environmental issues confront all the problems of national issues, but are magnified. Although few issues are truly global (atmospheric problems being notable exceptions), many issues have physical impacts that cross national boundaries. Even if a problem is geographically limited, it may have international or global ramifications, for example, the changes in weather caused by hundreds of oil wells burning out of control in the Middle East. Some issues are beyond the practical range of any national government jurisdiction, for example, mining on the deep sea bed and issues of outer space. Other issues are extremely localized but so similar in many jurisdictions that international cooperation is to the advantage of all concerned, for example, outbreaks of contagious disease. Finally, some issues are so interactive that international efforts are the only possible solution. For example, the destruction of tropical rain forests is believed to affect global climate; this belief has led to international financing for third-world governments to encourage rain forest protection.

The same characteristics (described in chapter 3) that bring national issues to the attention of one government can bring international issues to the attention of many governments. Issues that are specific and concrete and that have an immediate impact arouse public concern and attention more readily than general and highly technical issues such as the bio-geo-chemical cycles. The decreasing ozone layer was not a public international issue until its connection to rising rates of skin cancer was suggested. Much of the control of all international policy (not just environmental) is with the developed nations, and their constituencies will not become involved with third-world concerns until they perceive some direct impact on themselves. The most obvious exception seems to be wildlife preservation; however, some cynical observers note that the western world only becomes excited about saving beautiful, spectacular, or heartrendingly cute species.

INTERNATIONAL ORGANIZATIONS

Just as domestic policies must have initiators and policy entrepreneurs to get an issue onto the systemic agenda and then the institutional agenda, the international environmental movement had to bring its concerns to the attention of a mass public. First, environmental issues had to become *national* issues. Sovereign nations have many issues of international importance to deal with, and until there is consensus within the country that environmentalism is important, a nation will not expend limited international resources to address environmental problems. Second, the nations needed some expectation that international efforts toward solving environmental problems could achieve their policy goals. Lynton Caldwell finds this assurance in the "biosphere concept," which sees the earth as one ecosystem or biosphere, with environmental actions having consequences across the globe, and humans as the dominant altering agents.[8] Once the scientific community acknowledged the interdependence of Earth's subordinate ecosystems and the impact of human activity, constructive action was possible.

The United Nations began to respond to these concerns in the mid-sixties. Environmentalism had become a salient issue not only in the United States but also across the globe, especially in the industrialized democracies such as Canada, France, Japan, Sweden, West Germany, and the United Kingdom. Other countries had their Rachel Carsons to expose the dangers of pollution: Jean Dorst in France wrote *Before Nature Dies* (1965), and in Sweden Rolf Edberg wrote *On the Shred of a Cloud* (1966).[9] The *Torrey Canyon* disaster in 1967 brought home to western Europe the dangers that could result from ignoring the environment.

Progress from the national agendas to the international agenda was rapid as it became increasingly clear that unilateral national actions were not enough. For example, Africa cannot protect its endangered species without help from the countries that provide a market for luxury furs. The industrial states cannot prevent acid rain from blowing over their borders, and—as Chernobyl taught the world—no one is safe from radiation once it gets into the atmosphere. Prognosticators foretold worldwide disaster on the horizon.

To some extent, the Western nations were in better shape than in the early years of the twentieth century. The automobile, not yet identified as an environmental ogre, had replaced horses as the major means of transportation. The pollution problems caused by horses had been severe; not only were the droppings a health hazard but the corpses of overworked animals also littered city streets the way junk cars do today. Water-borne diseases were fewer, thanks in part to urban sanitation and water systems. The use of bituminous coal was reduced or totally banned, reducing the deadly smogs in many industrial centers.

The new dangers identified in the sixties, such as DDT and radiation, were less easily controlled. They were invisible and had long-term latent effects. They came from many sources, and they became more invasive as they permeated water and air supplies. Once the national publics were convinced of the dangers of the new pollutants, international cooperation became feasible.

In 1966 the General Conference of the United Nations Educational, Scientific, and Cultural Organization (UNESCO) adopted a resolution that the biosphere was a social concern as well as a geophysical one. A Biosphere Conference was scheduled to take place in Paris in 1968. At this conference the members declared that environmental concerns, especially issues regarding air, soil, and water pollution in industrialized countries, were becoming critical and that short-term solutions were no longer satisfactory. They also asserted the importance of the social sciences as partners with science and technology to fashion remedies.

In 1969 the secretary-general of the United Nations gave the delegates a report on the state of the environment. He set Stockholm as the site for an international conference on the environment, to be held in 1972. For two years the preparatory committee and subcommittees met, and in 1971 they set the final agenda for the conference. The preliminary meetings had produced some consensus on the issues, and when the delegates assembled in Stockholm, they had an agenda designed to promote achievements rather than simple discussion.

Biosphere protection and social and economic development were the two foci of the Stockholm Conference, and the achievements of the conference in these two areas were substantial. First, the United Nations Environment Programme (UNEP) was established in the secretariat to provide an integrated mechanism to coordinate worldwide environmental concerns. Second, the delegates achieved general consensus on four major documents: the Declaration on the Human Environment, the Declaration of Principles, the 109 Recommendations for Action, and—perhaps most critical of all— the Resolution of Institutional and Financial Arrangements. Of course, all the participants did not accede to all the proposals. France vowed to continue to test nuclear weapons, and Japan to continue whaling; and the United States refused to commit funds for environmental protection in developing countries. By most accounts, however, Stockholm was a success.

It avoided foundering on antagonisms born of Third World resentment over First World "injustice." The price of this avoidance was incorporation of environmental protection into the Third World's development priorities. Yet this First World concession introduced a new environmental element into the conventional interpretation of development. The development concept was thus enlarged, and delegates were exposed to evidence that many social and economic problems had environmental connections . . . .

In retrospect more than a decade later, the primary accomplishment of the Stockholm conference was the identification and legitimization of the biosphere as an object of national and international policy. Its resolutions provided standards for environment-related acts of government, which even regimes indifferent to environmental values felt obliged to acknowledge as evidence for a status of progressive "modernity."[10]

That same year, the United Nations General Assembly adopted the report of the Stockholm Conference. The site of UNEP was moved from Geneva to Nairobi as a concession to the developing nations. By 1974 UNEP was attempting to implement the Stockholm resolutions. UNEP has become the accepted international forum for examining environmental problems, and the existence of a third-world majority in its membership has continued to allay the suspicions of the developing nations. The primary accomplishments have been the promotion of treaties; for example, UNEP helped forge the Convention on International Trade in Endangered Species (CITES) in 1973.

It would be impractical to attempt a comprehensive survey of international treaties and understandings governing environmental concerns, such as CITES, the IWC, and the Fur Seal Treaty, discussed earlier. However, several transboundary and global issues are interesting because they have such an impact on internal, national environmental administration. Of special interest are the transboundary air issues such as acid deposition and the depletion of stratospheric ozone.

TRANSBOUNDARY AIR ISSUES

Transboundary air issues have achieved international prominence as changing weather patterns, the hole in the ozone over Antarctica, and acid deposition threaten public health, world agriculture, and even the very existence of some coastal communities. International treaties, conventions, and "soft law" options, such as the 1988 Declaration on the 30 percent Reduction of Nitrogen Oxide Emissions, have proliferated.[11] International concern with these issues has generated proposals for a Law of the Air treaty. This would be similar in effect and format to the Law of the Sea treaty, which as of 1990 was still not ratified by a sufficient number of nations to bring it into force. In 1989 twenty-four countries sent representatives to a conference in The Hague to discuss an air treaty. The Netherlands, France, and Norway cosponsored the conference, which "adopted a declaration calling for new international authority, either by strengthening existing institutions or by creating new institutions."[12]

The following discussion focuses on the issues of acid deposition and ozone depletion. Although other international problems are also important, these two issues have fairly well defined institutional agreements to begin coping with the problems. In addition, both are of special importance to environmental managers in the United States.

ACID DEPOSITION

Air pollution became an international issue when the air-borne effects from the burning of fossil fuels and from radiation became apparent in countries that had not caused them. Early in the seventies, the first warning signs appeared when lakes in Sweden began to die: "hundreds of previously normal lakes had become too acidic to support healthy biological processes; customary plant and animal life, including most native fishes, were dying or absent."[13] Scientists determined that the acid precipitation affecting these lakes had originated in other parts of Europe. In the next twenty years, evidence showed similar and increasing problems with acid deposition throughout the European continent and North America.

In 1980 the United States and Canada signed a memorandum of intent indicating that each would reduce the sulfur and nitrogen emissions from coal-fired furnaces, which are the major source of acid deposition. However, the Reagan administration immediately backed away from the agreement and advocated more study to confirm the connection between coal-fired furnaces and acid deposition. This was a difficult position for the White House to maintain, given three reports from the American scientific community that confirmed the connection. *The New York Times* trumpeted, "If we take the conservative point of view that we must wait until scientific knowledge is definitive, the accumulated deposition and damaged environment may reach the point of irreversibility."[14] First was the report from the Interagency Task Force on Acid Precipitation, asserting that industrial stacks were the major source of acid rain in the northeast. This was followed by a report from the White House Office for Science. The third report was from the National Academy of Sciences, claiming that acid rain could be reduced if the sulfur oxide emissions from coal-fired plants in the eastern United States were reduced.

Since then the international evidence has mounted. Forests in the eastern United States are endangered, and in Germany over half of the trees are damaged from acid precipitation. Eastern Europe is also plagued with damaged areas, the extent of which is becoming apparent as the political regimes change.

One of the stumbling blocks to international cooperation on stemming acid rain is that countries have had great difficulty in reaching internal agreement on their own remedies. Despite growing scientific evidence to support the peril of acid deposition, public interest in the United States remains low. In the United States, conflicts between industry and environmentalists, between coal-producing regions, and between coal-burning and acid deposition–receiving regions complicate any legislative attempts to deal with the problem.

Some international improvements have been made; Norway, Finland, Sweden, Denmark, Germany, Switzerland, Austria, and Canada have agreed to a 30 percent reduction in sulfur discharges by 1993. In 1988 the European Community agreed on a cutback program for sulfur emissions. Great Britain, which was the largest producer of sulfur oxides in Western Europe, agreed to install scrubbers on its sulfur-producing power plants. The European Community has also agreed that by 1992 small-engine vehicles will be required to meet emission-control standards similar to those of the United States. By 1994 all large cars throughout the European community will be required to be fitted with catalytic converters.

OZONE DEPLETION

Another transboundary air issue with global implications is the ozone level in the upper atmosphere; related to this is the issue of global warming. The issue of stratospheric ozone has been addressed by seeking to reduce the production of chlorofluorocarbons (CFCs). In 1976 UNEP labeled ozone deterioration as one of five priority items on the international environmental agenda. In 1985 compromise was reached through the Vienna Convention for the Protection of the Ozone Layer: "the Convention failed to agree on any global control measures [but] it passed a resolution calling for an economic workshop and continued negotiations to culminate in a diplomatic conference."[15] Scientific data continued to accumulate that indicated a dramatic decrease in stratospheric ozone, and soon reports of a large hole in the ozone layer over Antarctica caught the public imagination as issues of acid deposition could not. In September 1987 twenty-four nations (including the major CFC-producing countries) plus the European Community Commission signed the Montreal Protocol on Substances that Deplete the Ozone Layer. This is especially notable because "for the first time the international community reached agreement on control of a valuable economic commodity to prevent future environmental damage."[16] By the beginning of 1990, fifty-one countries had ratified the agreement.[17]

The Montreal Protocol has had an impact on United States environmental policy through the regulations issued by the EPA under its statutory authority from the Clean Air Act. In the eighties the EPA was not especially enthusiastic about CFC regulation:

> EPA successfully delayed domestic action until international measures were achieved and, undoubtedly, will attempt to continue putting off further domestic regulation to pursue a more stringent international agreement. Only revising the Protocol, congressional action, or a court order will move EPA to action.[18]

The European Community (EC) has become involved in the ozone issue. The EC began to consider its overall environmental policy in the early seventies, and since then it has issued well over a hundred directives on environmental matters. The "action plan" for the EC stated that "major aspects of environmental policy in individual countries must no longer be planned or implemented in isolation . . . and that national policies should be harmonized within the community."[19] However, many of these directives only codified existing national regulatory policies, and enforcement has been lax. Even successful EC suits in the European Court have not led to changes in national behavior.

The EC has brought its environmental focus to bear on issues that truly require international cooperation. Large construction projects with effects that cross national boundaries are now assessed for their international impact. Nations notify each other when transporting toxic materials across national boundaries. The EC was also a major player in limiting ocean pollution in the North Sea. The EC has subsequently been very active on the ozone issue.

> In March 1989, in what the *New York Times* described as "an unexpectedly strong move," the twelve member states of the EC agreed to cut the production of chlorofluorocarbons by 85 percent as soon as possible, and to eliminate them entirely by the end of the century.

(EC members are currently responsible for slightly more than one-third of worldwide chlorofluorocarbon production.) This step went considerably beyond an agreement reached in Montreal in 1987 by thirty-one nations, including the Common Market countries and the United States, that had called for a 50 percent reduction in the production of these chemicals by the end of the century. This new consensus was made possible in large measure by a major shift in the position of the British government.[20]

Britain continues to support international cooperation on the ozone issue. In June 1990 Prime Minister Thatc¹.er offered to contribute $9 million toward the projected $15 million needed for a three-year program to help developing countries reduce their CFC consumption. Speaking to the delegates assembled at the London conference called to review progress on the Montreal Protocol, the Prime Minister said:

> It is the duty of industrialized countries to help [developing countries] obtain and adopt the substitute technologies that will enable them to avoid our mistakes. . . . An important part of that will be to help them financially, so they can meet the extra costs involved.[21]

The Montreal Protocol represents a major shift in the relationship between scientific certainty and public policy decision making. The political and economic pressures to resist establishing policies to reduce CFCs and related compounds were intense. Richard Benedick, chief United States negotiator for the ozone protection treaties, attributes the success of the negotiations to several factors, among which are the close relationships between atmospheric scientists and the government officials, the education and use of public opinion to sway politicians, leadership from the United Nations Environmental Programme and from financially influential countries such as the United States, and consideration of the needs of developing countries.[22] The protocol "may signal a fundamental shift in attitude among critical segments of society when confronted with uncertain but potentially grave threats that require coordinated international action."[23]

CONTROLLING DEVELOPMENT IN ANTARCTICA

Antarctica is truly the last frontier on the planet. Exploration has been limited by technology, and only recently have the polar regions been invaded by quasi-permanent settlements of scientists. The northern polar regions are more accessible than the southern ones, and the comparatively close proximity of Canada and the Soviet Union has made the Arctic more familiar. The Antarctic is a continent surrounded by an extensive ice pack, unlike the Arctic, which is composed entirely of frozen ocean. Until recently, the inaccessibility of the Antarctic has made any territorial claims upon its land "largely symbolic."[24]

> There have been few practical demands on the continent: Although the Antarctic continent is believed to contain significant mineral deposits, and although the waters of the Antarctic have abundant marine life, the principal importance of Antarctica to modern society has been through the opportunities it affords for scientific observation and research.[25]

In 1959, Antarctica was designated an international scientific reserve under the Antarctic Treaty by the twelve nations doing scientific research on the continent (Argentina, Australia, Belgium, Chile, France, Japan, New Zealand, Norway, South Africa, the Soviet Union, Great Britain, and the United States). The seven nations that also asserted territorial claims to the land suspended those claims for thirty years.[26] The treaty was intended primarily to prohibit the use of Antarctica for military purposes or for nuclear testing or the storage of nuclear waste. Recent discoveries that suggest substantial oil and gas supplies on the Antarctic OCS have strained relations between the signatories, and an oil spill in 1989 alerted environmentalists to the dangers that development is bringing to the continent, not the least of which is simple waste disposal by the scientific settlements.

In 1964 the signatories (known as the consultative parties) adopted the Agreed Measures for Antarctic Fauna and Flora to ensure protection of the native species. The same year as the Agreed Measures were adopted, Norway began sealing in the Antarctic. Because there were no binding agreements concerning sealing, an additional convention was negotiated: the 1972 Convention for the Conservation of Antarctic Seals. This convention bans pelagic sealing, and it sets optimum sustainable yield as an upper limit for harvesting. Although the convention does not meet the standards mandated by the Marine Mammal Protection Act, "to prevent the initiation of commercial sealing without any international regulation, the [United States] Senate gave its consent to the ratification of the Convention."[27]

The Convention on the Conservation of Antarctic Marine Living Resources (Southern Ocean Convention) was signed in 1980 and became effective in 1982. It was motivated in part by concern for krill, a small crustacean that lives in the Southern Ocean and is fished extensively by the Japanese and Soviet fishing fleets (and in the eighties by the Poles and West Germans). Probably the most bitter dispute over the Antarctic, prior to the oil spill, involved this abundant and inexpensive source of protein. The political problems arise because krill is the staple diet of the endangered great blue or baleen whales, which are close to extinction, and also of seals, penguins, and some fish. Political pressures became so intense that the Food and Agriculture Organization of the United Nations withheld scientific findings to avoid offending the krill-fishing nations. The convention is intended to protect the marine ecosystem by requiring that the nations harvesting krill consider the impact on other species when setting catch limits.

The Convention on the Conservation of Antarctic Marine Living Resources covers all living marine resources. To implement the convention, a Commission for the Conservation of Antarctic Marine Living Resources was established. The commission has the authority to acquire data, acting on advice from a scientific committee also established by the convention, and to adopt conservation measures, including restrictions on the harvest of living marine resources in the Southern Ocean. The commission is also empowered to establish marine reserves to protect especially vulnerable species and habitat.

Pressure for mineral exploitation on the Antarctic continent continues to increase, although a 1988 draft convention dealing with minerals was rejected by two members of the consultative committee. Because of these and other pressures, "the prospect of Antarctica remaining a natural reserve for science and nature appears to be fading."[28]

Suggested Reading

Caldwell, Lynton Keith. *International Environmental Policy*. Durham, N.C.: Duke University Press, 1984. Extremely thorough discussion of the development and structure of the role of the United Nations in environmental matters.

Ziegler, Charles. *Environmental Policy in the USSR*. Amherst: University of Massachusetts Press, 1987. A dry but thorough little book that provides insight into environmental policy in the Soviet Union prior to the upheavals of the late eighties.

AFTERWORD

This book was written to explain the history of environmental law, the process by which our laws are made and amended, the role of the agencies in implementing the laws, and the role of the courts in interpreting them. Environmental managers in all agencies and in all levels of government face similar issues. Whether those managers are administering a Forest Service timber sale or supervising the clean-up of a Superfund site, their jobs are imbedded in a legal and political context that they must understand if they are to perform well. The purpose of this book has been to help managers to understand that context.

Environmental law, like any subfield of administrative law, is flexible and depends in large part on the substantive policy being addressed. It includes case law but is not restricted to case law. Environmental law includes a vital discretionary component that operates at every level of the administrative process, including agency and court behavior. Because of its intimate relationship with the legislature, the executive, the courts, and the public, environmental law is intensely political in both its origins and its implementation. Any useful analysis or study of environmental law must include these political relationships.

One important factor which has been emphasized throughout this book is the fluid and historical nature of environmental administration and law. Good managers must know the institutional history of their agency, their law, and their program. For example, the economic pressures to develop the western United States following the Civil War led to the large land-dispersal programs, federal subsidies to railroad companies, subsidized grazing permits, and a federal mining law that encouraged mineral exploration and extraction on the federal lands. The legacy of the programs has affected the attitudes of western citizens toward land use for the past century. Regardless of the contemporary intent of Congress in amending old statutes or enacting new legislation, managers must understand the deep-seated cultural attitudes that they will encounter when they try to implement the will of Congress. The managers' role is as much to educate as to regulate if they wish to regulate successfully.

To narrow the example even further, consider the efforts by public land range managers to convince western cattle ranchers to improve range management techniques.[1] Cattle ranchers are by nature individualist and entrepreneurial; they do not take kindly to external controls or to management initiatives that restrict their opportunities for profit. Their cultural biases lead them to prefer to minimize leadership, to exploit their environment, and to follow the economic rationality of squeezing as many cattle as possible onto their allotments. The government land managers, in contrast, are more likely to tend toward hierarchical approaches to resource problems: to defer to their enabling statutes, to implement regulations, and then to enforce the regulations through some combination of economic, civil, or even criminal sanctions. This divergence of cultural biases has often led to political impasses or, on occasion, to violent resistance.

How might responsible and educated managers respond? First, through public education; they might utilize what Michael Thompson calls *surprise*, which occurs when the accumulated weight of contrary evidence breaks through the cultural filter, contradicting existing ideas.[2] In this case, the deterioration of the public range almost past recovery forced some ranchers to realize that nature was not endlessly abundant and resilient. They changed their strategies from exploitation to control, developing new techniques and technology to structure the grazing environment. A second option is for the managers to try to impose some additional form of external controls or regulation on the ranchers. As might have been predicted, there was a concerted effort of resistance from the ranchers, who organized strong lobbying groups. The ranchers were very successful in their lobbying efforts, but once the immediate threat of external controls was removed, their dislike of rules led to disintegration of the lobby. The third option is for environmental interest groups, which are usually at odds with public-land management agencies, to form a temporary political coalition with the regulating agencies. The administrators, disliking the disorder of depleted ranges and the ranchers' opposition to their control mechanisms, did indeed accept an alliance with the environmentalists. For a short time, the specter of a nonsubsidizing grazing fee to force ranchers to value the land at its true market value was a strong possibility, although the rancher lobby finally prevailed. As one would expect, the surprise-based change, small as it is, has endured; but once the environmentalist-manager alliance deteriorated, the unsurprised ranchers reverted to their old ways.

Similarly the 1990 Clean Air Amendment Act, which was badly needed to update the thirteen-year-old amendments, was not enacted until the policy process provided several trigger events—the Antarctic hole in the ozone, the threat of global warming, and the startling accumulation of information generated by title III of SARA on toxic air emissions. The policy process also provided a president willing to affect adversely both large and small businesses, and the retirement of Senator Robert Byrd, who assiduously protected eastern coal-mining operations.

To stay current, managers must be sensitive to political changes in all levels of the policy process: executive, congressional, judicial, public, and personal. Environmental law will respond to changes in presidential leadership and to shifts in power within the legislatures. The impact of the Reagan years on the federal judiciary will be a potent factor for decades, as the newly appointed judges gain experience and prestige. A majority of the Supreme Court justices now lean toward the conservative camp; how that will affect environmental law is still in the realm of speculation.

Managers must also consider their own political agendas when designing environmental law and policy. Ethical managers are constantly aware of their obligation in a democratic society to respond to the demands of the elected officials and to the direct inputs of the citizens whose lives the managers affect. Managers must balance long-term costs and benefits against short-term, and must be willing to negotiate and to compromise, at the same time protecting their employees, their superiors, and their own position. It is a challenging task, and managers must bring to bear all the tools they can muster if they are to do their job well.

Managers are usually trained in their substantive fields of hydrology, silvaculture, fisheries, or civil engineering, but by the time they are managers, their training needs are in public administration. How should a budget be presented for maximum effect? What is a fair hearing? How may the courts respond to a new regulation? Why did something happen, and how can it be changed? These questions are not addressed by technocratic training in environmental specialties, but by education in the techniques of public administration. Public administration is a generalist approach to management—and environmental managers are generalists. They have the specific training for their fields, but they need the rigorous, disciplined approach of organization theory and policy analysis as well.

As a new century approaches, environmental management is more complex than ever. In the late nineteenth century, when the conservation movement was first getting under way, the only significant issues were those of natural beauty, land protection, and wildlife management. As industrialization continued, problems of pollution, waste management, and public health appeared; but the old issues of land, wildlife, and beauty did not go away. The movement toward transboundary issues which are resolved in the global community does not mean the previous problems are resolved or set aside. As a professional endeavor, environmental management has become more difficult because new issues are simply piled upon the old.

In the coming century, environmental managers will confront some of the most pressing and vital problems that have ever faced society. Failure will bring tragedy and catastrophe. Success may do nothing more than buy time. Success is most likely to come in increments while failures, like Chernobyl, will loom large in history.

To be successful, environmental managers must take the long view, looking back at the processes and events that have shaped the earth's environment to its present condition, and predicting how these processes will shape and be shaped by events still unknown. Managers must not be discouraged by the tortoise-like pace of improvement. All around them are signs of encouragement: greater openness in the Soviet bloc nations; corporate activism that rewards responsible private management; international awareness of the global dimensions of environmental problems. Information, and the technology to use it, is available on a scale unimaginable even thirty years ago. If the problems have grown to immense proportions, so has the capacity to forge solutions. This is both a challenge and an opportunity: Environmental managers are placed so that, if they are clever and conscientious, they can change the world—or their part of it—for the better. Few of us are so fortunate.

NOTES

Chapter 1

1. The common-law system is indeed *English* rather than *British*. Scotland, which joined England in 1707, has a civil-law system.
2. *Martin v. Waddell*, 41 U.S. (16 Pet.) 367 (1842), at 416.
3. *American Textile Manufacturers Institute v. Donovan*, 452 U.S. 490 (1981), at 547–48.
4. Tom Arrandale, *The Battle for Natural Resources* (Washington, D.C.: Congressional Quarterly, 1983), p. 47.
5. Susan J. Buck and Edward Hathaway, "Designating State Natural Resource Trustees under SARA," in *Regulatory Federalism, Natural Resources and Environmental Management,* ed. Michael Hamilton (Washington, D.C.: ASPA, 1990), pp. 83–94.
6. The following discussion is drawn from William Keefe, Henry Abraham, William Flanigan, Charles O. Jones, Morris Ogul, and John Spanier, *American Democracy: Institutions, Politics, and Policies* (Homewood, Ill.: Dorsey Press, 1983), chap. 2.
7. *New State Ice Co. v. Liebmann*, 285 U.S. 262 (1932), at 311, Justice Brandeis dissenting.

Chapter 2

1. Ted Williams, "'Silent Spring' Revisited," *Modern Maturity* (October–November 1987), p. 48.
2. 42 U.S.C. § 4321.
3. 42 U.S.C. § 4321.
4. A. A. Harnisch, et al. *Chief Joseph Dam Columbia River, Washington Community Impact Reports.* IWR Reports 78-3 and 78-R2. (Fort Belvoir, VA: U.S. Army Engineer Institute for Water Resources, 1978), p. 413.
5. 42 U.S.C. § 4341.
6. *Calvert Cliffs Coordinating Committee, Inc. v. United States Atomic Energy Commission* (1971), 449 F.2d 1109, at 1114.
7. Kenneth J. Meier, *Regulation: Politics, Bureaucracy, and Economics* (New York: St. Martin's Press, 1985), p. 140.
8. Ibid.

Chapter 3

1. The material that follows is drawn primarily from Randall Ripley and Grace Franklin, *Congress, the Bureaucracy, and Public Policy*, 4th ed. (Homewood, Ill.: Dorsey Press, 1991) especially chap. 1.

2. Another perspective on the temporary coalition of the BLM and environmentalists is found in Susan J. Buck, "Cultural Theory and Management of Common Property Resources," *Human Ecology* 17 (1989): pp. 101–16.

3. Penelope ReVelle and Charles ReVelle, *The Environment: Issues and Choices for Society* (Boston: Jones and Bartlett Publishers, 1988), p. 429.

4. G. Tyler Miller, Jr., *Living in the Environment*, 5th ed. (Belmont, Calif.: Wadsworth, 1988), p. 473.

5. Except where otherwise noted, the material on agenda setting is from Roger Cobb and Charles Elder, *Participation in American Politics* (Boston: Allyn and Bacon, 1972), especially chaps. 5–9.

6. Jack Walker, "Setting the Agenda in the U.S. Senate," *British Journal of Political Science* 7 (October 1977): pp. 423–45.

7. The discussion of legitimation which follows is drawn from Guy Peters, *American Public Policy: Promise and Performance*, 2nd ed. (Chatham, N.J.: Chatham House Publishers, 1986), chap. 4.

8. Ibid., p. 63, notes omitted.

9. This is known as the "delegate" theory of representation: that the elected representatives vote their constituents' wishes. An opposing view is the "trustee" theory of delegation, which assumes that legislators, having access to better information, should vote their own consciences, regardless of the wishes of the folks back home.

10. The discussion which follows on bureaucratic resources and implementation, unless otherwise noted, is drawn from Randall Ripley and Grace Franklin, *Policy Implementation and Bureaucracy*, 2nd ed. (Chicago: Dorsey Press, 1986), especially chaps. 1 and 2.

11. A very clear explanation of the implementation process is found in Daniel Mazmanian and Paul Sabatier, *Implementation and Public Policy* (Glenview, Ill.: Scott, Foresman, 1983), especially p. 22.

12. National Standards Association, *National Directory of State Agencies* (Bethesda, Md.: National Standards Association, 1987), tabulating under natural resources, water resources, health, environmental affairs, water pollution, air pollution, and solid waste.

13. One excellent definition of *sunk costs* is found in NEPA, section 102(C)(v), which refers to "irreversible and irretrievable commitment of resources."

14. This discussion of evaluation is from Peters, *American Public Policy*, chapter 7.

15. This speculation on the motives underlying the moratorium is based on numerous conversations between 1985 and 1988 with resource managers in the Chesapeake Bay and with political analysts interested in Maryland-Virginia conflicts.

Chapter 4

1. A case I find particularly frustrating is *Shaughnessy v. United States* ex rel. *Mezei*, 345 U.S. 246 (1953). Mezei was an alien resident who

remained abroad for nineteen months and, upon attempting to return to the United States, was excluded for overstaying. He had gone to Europe to visit his sick mother and been caught by World War II. No other country would receive him, on the logical grounds that if the United States wouldn't let him in, there must be a good reason; and he was confined to Ellis Island for twenty-one months. I have been unable to find out what happened to poor Mezei. Was he ever allowed to return to his home of twenty-five years? Or did he go back to Europe?

2. In common law, if a property owner allows his land to be used by the public or by another property owner for a certain period of time and without objection, he has in law granted an easement to the users. For example, footpaths criss-cross the English countryside, and property owners may not barricade them no matter how inconvenient the path has become. An easement becomes part of the property description and accompanies property transfers.

3. Among the acts providing for citizen suits are the Toxic Substances Control Act of 1972, the Endangered Species Act of 1973, the Marine Protection, Research, and Sanctuaries Act of 1972, the Federal Water Pollution Control Act Amendments of 1972, the Deepwater Port Act of 1974, the Safe Drinking Water Act of 1974, the Clean Air Amendments of 1970, the Noise Control Act of 1972, the Energy Policy and Conservation Act of 1975, and the Resource Conservation and Recovery Act of 1976.

4. William H. Rodgers, Jr., *Handbook on Environmental Law* (St. Paul: West, 1977), p. 80, n. 34, quoting the Endangered Species Act, 16 U.S.C. § 1540[g][1][B].

5. *Data Processing*, 397 U.S. 150, at 153.

6. It is important to emphasize that this holding would not have affected *Fontainebleau* because in that case there was no question of an improper administrative action. The old standard was still good because it was a suit between two private parties, not between an aggrieved party and the government.

7. John Naff responded to Douglas's dissent:

If Justice Douglas has his way—
  O Come not that dreadful day—
We'll be sued by lakes and hills
  Seeking a redress of ills.
Great mountain peaks of name prestigious
  Will suddenly become litigious.
Our brooks will babble in the courts,
  Seeking damages for torts.
How can I rest beneath a tree
  If it may soon be suing me?
Or enjoy the playful porpoise

While it's seeking habeas corpus?
Every beast within its paws
Will clutch an order to show cause.
The courts, besieged on every hand,
Will crowd with suits by chunks of land.
Ah! But vengeance will be sweet
Since this must be a two-way street.
I'll promptly sue my neighbor's tree
*   For shedding all its leaves on me.*

John Naff, *Journal of the American Bar Association* 58 (1972): p. 820, quoted in Christopher Stone's *Earth and Other Ethics* (New York: Harper and Row, 1987), p. 5.

8. I can't locate a source for the story that this case began as a law-school class assignment; but true or not, it's a lovely story.

9. The Court had lifted the absolute bar against taxpayer suits in *Flast v. Cohen*, 392 U.S. 83 (1968), replacing it with a stringent test of whether there is a constitutional link between the taxpayer's harm and the government action. *Flast* challenged the 1965 Elementary and Secondary Education Act, which provided public funds to religious schools; it was alleged that the act violated the constitutionally mandated separation of church and state.

10. In England, where the right to fish a particular part of a stream is a property right that may be bought and sold, the doctrine of nuisance has been used to force up-stream industrial polluters to stop their activities. Since the anglers' associations have property rights in the fishing, the pollution that impairs the fishing is actionable for monetary damages, and the prospect of having to reimburse a group of trout fishermen often leads to prompt remedial action by the polluters.

11. Unless otherwise noted, the discussion on property is from Robert R. Wright and Susan Webber Wright's *Land Use in a Nutshell* (St. Paul: West, 1985).

12. See Susan Jane Buck Cox, "No Tragedy on the Commons," *Environmental Ethics* 7 (Spring 1985): pp. 49–61, for a more detailed discussion of the medieval commons and the reasons for the success of enclosure.

13. W. O. Ault, *Open-field Farming in Medieval England* (London: Allen and Unwin, 1972), p. 17.

14. E. C. K. Gonner, *Common Land and Inclosure*, 2nd ed. (London: Cass, 1966), p. 306.

15. Notably *Bi-Metallic Investment Co. v. State Board of Equalization*, 239 U.S. 441 (1915), in which the city had increased the valuation of all taxable property without affording individual property owners the right to a hearing. The Court ruled that when a taxing action applied to all taxpayers (rather than a definite subset as in *Londoner*), no hearing was required. This is not a surprising decision in light of the absolute bar to taxpayer suits that was the rule until *Flast* (see note 9 above).

16. Florence Heffron and Neil McFeeley, *The Administrative Regulatory Process* (New York: Longman, 1983), p. 268.

17. *Nebbia v. New York*, 291 U.S. 502 (1934).

18. William B. Lockhart, Yale Kamisar, and Jesse Choper, *The American Constitution: Cases–Comments–Questions* (St. Paul: West, 1970), p. 332.

19. Unless otherwise noted, the discussion of zoning is drawn from Wright and Wright, *Land Use in a Nutshell*, especially chap. 6.

20. Unless otherwise noted, this discussion is drawn from Rodgers, *Handbook*, pp. 170–86.

21. Joseph Sax, "Public Trust Doctrine in Natural Resource Law: Effective Judicial Intervention," *Michigan Law Review* 68 (No. 3, January 1970): p. 490.

22. Charles Wilkinson, "Public Trust Doctrine in Public Land Law," in *The Public Trust Doctrine in Natural Resources Law and Management*, ed. Harrison Dunning (Davis: University of California, 1981), p. 169.

23. Marianne K. Smythe, "Environmental Law: Expanding the Definition of Public Trust Uses," *North Carolina Law Review* 51 (1972): p. 322.

24. Rodgers, *Handbook*, pp. 175–76.

25. Joseph Sax, "Introductory Perspectives," in *Public Trust Doctrine*, ed. Dunning, p. 6.

26. James Trout, "A Land Manager's Commentary on the Public Trust Doctrine," in *Public Trust Doctrine*, ed. Dunning, p. 57. At the time of this statement, Mr. Trout was the assistant executive officer for the California State Lands Commission.

27. Rodgers, *Handbook*, p. 172.

28. *City of Milwaukee v. State*, 193 Wis. 423, 214 N.W. 820 (1927), at 830, quoted in Helen Althaus, *Public Trust Rights* (Washington, D.C.: GPO, 1978), p. 157.

29. Unless otherwise noted, this discussion is drawn from Michael J. Bean, *The Evolution of National Wildlife Law* (New York: Praeger, 1983).

30. *Smith v. Maryland*, 59 U.S. 71, at 75.

31. *Manchester v. Massachusetts*, 139 U.S. 240 (1891).

32. *Douglas v. Seacoast Products, Inc.*, 431 U.S. 265, at 284.

33. *Tangier Sound Watermen's Association v. Douglas*, 541 F. Supp. 1287, at 1294.

Chapter 5

1. W. F. Dodd, "Administrative Agencies as Legislators and Judges," *American Bar Association Journal* 25 (November 1939): p. 976.

2. H.R. 986, 76th Cong., 3d Sess. (1940), p. 3.

3. Charles K. Woltz, Preface to *Administrative Procedure in Government Agencies*, a report by the Attorney General's Committee (Charlottesville: University Press of Virginia, 1968). This is a facsimile edition of Senate Document No. 8., 77th Congress, 1st Session (1941).

4. Unless otherwise noted, this material is from Phillip Cooper, *Public Law and Public Administration*, 2nd ed. (Englewood Cliffs, N.J.: Prentice-Hall, 1988), especially chap. 5.
5. Florence Heffron and Neil McFeeley, *The Administrative Regulatory Process* (New York: Longman, 1983), pp. 202–4.
6. Cooper, *Public Law*, p. 121.
7. Heffron and McFeeley, *The Administrative Regulatory Process*, p. 251.
8. Unless otherwise noted, this section is drawn from Heffron and McFeeley, *The Administrative Regulatory Process*, chap. 10.
9. Lisa Heinzerling, "Actionable Inaction: Section 1983 Liability for Failure to Act," *University of Chicago Law Review* 53 (Summer 1986): p. 1063.
10. *Marks v. Whitney*, 6 Cal. 3d 251, 491 P.2d 374, 98 Cal. Rptr. 790, at 797 (1971), quoted in David B. Hunter, "An Ecological Perspective on Property: A Call for Judicial Protection of the Public's Interest in Environmentally Critical Resources," *Harvard Environmental Law Review* 12 (1988): p. 372, n. 288.
11. Unless otherwise noted, this discussion is from Heffron and McFeeley, *The Administrative Regulatory Process*, chap. 11.
12. Ibid., p. 293.
13. Civil Rights Act of 1871, 42 U.S.C. § 1983.
14. G. Tyler Miller, Jr., *Living in the Environment*, 5th ed. (Belmont, Calif.: Wadsworth, 1988), p. 423.
15. Ibid, p. 424.
16. On August 7, 1990, during congressional hearings on the sudden increase in gasoline prices following Iraq's invasion of Kuwait, the head of the American Petroleum Institute charged that prices went up because environmental controls had ruined the free market!
17. Miller, *Living*, p. 451.
18. Janet Hook, "Legislative Summary: 101st Congress Leaves Behind Plenty Laws, Criticism," *Congressional Quarterly Weekly Report* 48 (November 3, 1990): p. 3692.
19. Unless otherwise noted, the material on the 1990 Clean Air Act is from resource materials furnished to accompany *Legal Winds of Change: Business and the New Clean Air Act*, a videoconference on November 28, 1990, presented by the EPA, the PBS Adult Learning Satellite Service, the Public Television Outreach Alliance, and the University of North Carolina at Greensboro.
20. *Legal Winds of Change*, p. 18.
21. This information is drawn from panel remarks by Kathy Bailey, assistant general counsel for the Chemical Manufacturers Association during the *Legal Winds of Change* videoconference.
22. Miller, *Living*, p. 455.
23. Ibid., p. 475.

24. Ibid., p. 456.
25. Ibid., p. 483.
26. Walter A. Rosenbaum, *Environmental Politics and Policy* (Washington, D.C.: Congressional Quarterly, 1985), pp. 154–55.
27. Miller, *Living*, p. 484.
28. Ibid.
29. Ibid.
30. John Hartwick and Nancy Olewiler, *The Economics of Natural Resource Use* (New York: Harper and Row, 1986), p. 387 (notes omitted).
31. J. H. Dales, *Pollution, property & prices: an essay in policy-making and economics* (Toronto: University of Toronto Press, 1968).
32. Ibid., pp. 107–8.
33. The discussion which follows is from Hartwick and Olewiler, *Economics of Natural Resource Use*, pp. 443–45.
34. Roger Findley and Daniel Farber, *Environmental Law* (St. Paul, MN: West, 1988), p. 93.
35. Environmental Protection Agency, *Environmental Progress and Challenges: An EPA Perspective*, CPM-222 (Washington, D.C.: Office of Management Systems and Evaluation, 1984), pp. 95 and 82.
36. Findley and Farber, p. 136.
37. Ibid., p. 137.
38. Ibid., p. 117.
39. Hook, "Legislative Summary," p. 3692.
40. Bureau of National Affairs, *U.S. Environmental Laws, 1988 Edition* (Washington, D.C.: Bureau of National Affairs, 1988), p. 145.
41. United States Environmental Protection Agency, *Environmental Monitoring at Love Canal* (Washington, D.C.: USEPA, 1982).
42. See Jonathan Lash, Katherine Gillman, and David Sheridan, *A Season of Spoils: The Reagan Administration's Attack on the Environment* (New York: Pantheon, 1984), especially chap. 2. See also Steven Cohen, "Defusing the Toxic Time Bomb: Federal Hazardous Waste Programs," in *Environmental Policy in the 1980s: Reagan's New Agenda*, ed. Norman Vig and Michael Kraft (Washington, D.C.: Congressional Quarterly, 1984), pp. 273–91.
43. Alyson Pytte, "Superfund Stowaway," *Congressional Quarterly Weekly Report* 48 (November 3, 1990): p. 3717.
44. For a more complete discussion of English environmental policy see Susan Buck, "Environmental Policy in the United Kingdom," in *Education and Environment*, vol. 2 of *International Public Policy Sourcebook*, ed. Frederick Bolotin, (New York: Greenwood Press, 1989), pp. 310–33.
45. Eric Ashby and Mary Anderson, *Politics of Clean Air* (Oxford: Clarendon, 1981) pp. 1–2.
46. Cynthia Enloe, *Politics of Pollution in a Comparative Perspective* (New York: David McKay, 1975), p. 268.

47. Timothy O'Riordan, "Culture and the Environment in Britain," *Environmental Management* 9 (1985): p. 115.

48. David Vogel, *National Styles of Regulation: Environmental Policy in Great Britain and the United States* (Ithaca, N.Y.: Cornell University Press, 1986), p. 43.

49. Central Directorate of Environmental Protection, *Pollution Control in England* (London: Department of the Environment, 1984), p. 1.

50. David Vogel, *National Styles*, pp. 22, 153, 157.

51. Ibid., p. 242.

Chapter 6

1. Michael J. Bean, *The Evolution of National Wildlife Law* (New York: Praeger, 1983).

2. The preceding discussion is drawn from the National Audubon Society's *Audubon Wildlife Report, 1985* (New York: National Audubon Society, 1985) and the 1986 and 1987 reports.

3. National Audubon Society, 1986 report, p. 15.

4. National Audubon Society, 1987 report, p. 15.

5. Bean, *Evolution*, p. 105.

6. Ibid., p. 108.

7. Ibid., p. 125.

8. National Audubon Society, 1985 report, p. 307.

9. Ibid., p. 311.

10. 16 U.S.C § 670(a) (1976), quoted in Bean, *Evolution*, p. 176.

11. Walter J. Mead, Asbjorn Moseidjord, Dennis Muraoka, and Phillip Sorensen, *Offshore Lands: Oil and Gas Leasing and Conservation on the Outer Continental Shelf* (San Francisco: Pacific Institute for Public Policy Research, 1985), p. 7.

12. Texas and the west coast of Florida have state control for 3 marine leagues or 10.4 miles. These states are entitled to the wider boundary because they held it at the time of their admission as states.

13. Bean, *Evolution*, p. 177.

14. 43 U.S.C. § 1346(a)(1)(Supp. IV 1980) and § 1346(a)(3), quoted in Bean, *Evolution*, pp. 177–78.

15. Ibid., pp. 281–82.

16. Ibid., pp. 282–83 (notes omitted).

17. Ibid., p. 285.

18. 16 U.S.C. § 1371(a)(3)(A)(1976), quoted in Bean, *Evolution*, p. 296.

19. Bean, *Evolution*, p. 297.

20. National Audubon Society, 1985 report, p. 187.

21. Bean, *Evolution*, p. 321.

22. Edward Wolf, "Avoiding a Mass Extinction of Species," in *State of the World 1988*, project directed by Lester Brown (New York: Norton, 1988), pp. 103–4.

23. William Mansfield, quoted in "Species Dying Daily, Conservation Group Warns Toxic World," *New York Times* (International Edition), November 29, 1990, p. A9.

24. National Audubon Society, 1985 report, p. 77.

25. Unless otherwise noted, this material is from Marion Clawson, *The Federal Lands Revisited* (Baltimore: Johns Hopkins University Press for Resources and the Future, 1983), especially chaps. 1 and 2.

26. Clawson, *Federal Lands*, p. 11.

27. Ibid., p. 17.

28. Ibid., p. 4.

29. Ibid., p. 25.

30. Although Yellowstone National Park was established in 1872, Clawson (*Federal Lands*, p. 28) notes that this was an isolated instance of reserving land not otherwise in demand. He quotes John Ise, *Our National Park Policy* (Baltimore: Johns Hopkins University Press for Resources for the Future, 1961), pp. 17–18:

> The establishment of Yellowstone was, of course, due partly to the efforts of [a] few of these idealists, several of them men of influence. Reservation was possible because most private interests were not looking so far west at this early date, for there were no railroads within hundreds of miles of Yellowstone. Lumbermen had moved into the Lake States and were too busy slashing the pine forests there to reach out for timber lands in this inaccessible region; the hunters and trappers were here, but were not an important political force; the cattlemen, who have been in recent years so powerful an influence against some conservation legislation, were not yet invading the Far West in large numbers; the water-power interests that have been among the most serious threats to a few later national parks were not interested here. With Indians still a lurking danger, the "poor settlers" had not ventured into this region in great numbers and were not calling for Congressional consideration.

31. Tom Arrandale, *The Battle for Natural Resources* (Washington, D.C.: Congressional Quarterly, 1983), p. 41, citing *United States v. Midwest Oil Company*, 236 U.S. 459 (1915).

32. Gifford Pinchot, *The Fight for Conservation* (Garden City, N.Y.: Harcourt, Brace, 1919), quoted in Roderick Nash, *American Environmentalism: Readings in Conservation History*, 3rd ed. (New York: McGraw-Hill, 1990), pp. 76–78.

33. Ronald A. Foresta, *America's National Parks and Their Keepers* (Baltimore: Johns Hopkins University Press, 1984), pp. 45–46.

34. Ibid., p. 54.

35. Clawson, *Federal Lands*, pp. 37–38.

36. See, for example, Perri Knize, "Chainsaw Environmentalism," *Backpacker* (November 1987): pp. 55–59. The title tells it all.

37. Quoted in Foresta, *America's National Parks*, p. 79.

38. Michael Kraft and Norman Vig, "Environmental Policy from the Seventies to the Nineties: Continuity and Change," in *Environmental Policy in the 1990s*, ed. Norman Vig and Michael Kraft (Washington, D.C.: Congressional Quarterly, 1990), p. 23.

39. This material comes from Jonathan Lash, Katherine Gillman, and David Sheridan, *A Season of Spoils: The Reagan Administration's Attack on the Environment* (New York: Pantheon, 1984), especially pp. 215–24. This is a superb book, but it does have a bias, which I may be exaggerating by putting a more explicit interpretation on the facts they present. The reader should view the case presented in the text as speculation—but informative speculation.

40. Bob Burnett, quoted in Lash, Gillman, and Sheridan, *Season of Spoils*, p. 223.

41. Quoted in ibid., pp. 223–24.

42. Letter dated October 25, 1982, from Alexander Good, associate solicitor for Energy and Resources, Department of the Interior; quoted in Lash, Gillman, and Sheridan, *Season of Spoils*, p. 220.

43. Ibid., p. 221.

44. At the time the Lash book was written, the final resolution of Yates's conflicts with the U.S. Fish and Wildlife Service was not settled; observers expected a similar out-of-court agreement to be reached. Yates's payments to the BLM totaled $537.50 (ibid., p. 221).

Chapter 7

1. National Audubon Society, *Audubon Wildlife Report, 1985* (New York: National Audubon Society, 1985), p. 182.

2. G. Tyler Miller, Jr., *Living in the Environment*, 5th ed. (Belmont, Calif.: Wadsworth, 1988), p. 311.

3. Lynton Caldwell, *International Environmental Policy* (Durham, N.C.: Duke University Press, 1984), p. 32 (notes omitted).

4. Miller, *Living*, p. 311.

5. *American Cetacean Society v. Baldridge*, 604 F. Supp. 1398 (D.C. 1985).

6. National Audubon Society, *Audubon Wildlife Report, 1987* (Washington, D.C.: National Audubon Society, 1987), p. 166.

7. Caldwell, *International*, p. 33.

8. Caldwell, *International*, p. 21.

9. Jean Dorst, *Before Nature Dies*, trans. Constance D. Sherman (Boston: Houghton Mifflin, 1970); Rolf Edberg, *On the Shred of a Cloud*, trans. Sven jAham (Montgomery: University of Alabama Press, 1969).

10. Caldwell, *International*, p. 53.

11. See Peter H. Sand, *Lessons Learned in Global Environmental Governance* (Washington, D.C.: World Resources Institute, 1990), especially pp. 14–18.

12. Lynton Caldwell, "International Environmental Politics: America's Response to Global Imperatives," in *Environmental Policy in the 1980s: Reagan's New Agenda*, ed. Norman Vig and Michael Kraft (Washington, D.C.: Congressional Quarterly, 1984), p. 308.

13. Walter Rosenbaum, *Energy, Politics, and Public Policy*, 2nd ed. (Washington, D.C.: Congressional Quarterly, 1987), p. 117.

14. *New York Times*, June 28, 1983, quoted by Walter Rosenbaum in *Environmental Politics and Policy* (Washington, D.C.: Congressional Quarterly, 1985), p. 135.

15. Orval Nangle, "Stratospheric Ozone: United States Regulation of Chlorofluorocarbons," *Environmental Affairs* 16 (1989): p. 544.

16. Ibid., p. 546.

17. James Koehler and Scott Hajost, "1989: Advent of a New Era for EPA's International Activities," *Colorado Journal of International Environmental Law and Policy* 1 (Summer 1990): p. 183.

18. Nangle, "Stratospheric," p. 578.

19. David Vogel, *National Styles of Regulation: Environmental Policy in Great Britain and the United States* (Ithaca, N.Y.: Cornell University Press, 1986), p. 102; quoted in David Vogel, "Environmental Policy in Europe and Japan," in *Environmental Policy*, ed. Vig and Kraft, p. 272.

20. Vogel, "Environmental Policy," p. 273.

21. Margaret Thatcher, quoted in British Information Services, "The London Conference on Substances that Deplete the Ozone Layer" (New York: British Consulate General, June 28, 1990), p. 1.

22. Richard Elliot Benedick, "Protecting the Ozone Layer: New Directions in Diplomacy," in *Preserving the Global Environment: The Challenge of Shared Leadership*, ed. Jessica Tuchman Mathews (New York: Norton, 1991), pp. 113–53, especially pp. 143–49.

23. Ibid., p. 149.

24. Caldwell, *International*, p. 254.

25. Ibid.

26. The seven states asserting territorial claims at the time the treaty went into force were Great Britain, France, Norway, Chile, Argentina, Australia, and New Zealand.

27. Michael J. Bean, *The Evolution of National Wildlife Laws* (New York: Praeger, 1983), p. 269.

28. Caldwell, *International*, p. 257.

Afterword

1. For a fuller discussion of cultural theory and western cattle ranchers, see Susan J. Buck, "Cultural Theory and Management of Common Property Resources," *Human Ecology* 17 (March 1989): pp. 101–16.
2. Michael Thompson, "The Cultural Construction of Nature and the Natural Destruction of Culture" (Working paper for the International Institute for Applied Systems Analysis, Laxenberg, Austria, 1984).

Acronyms

ABA	American Bar Association
APA	Administrative Procedure Act
ASPA	American Society for Public Administration
BAT	best available technology
BLM	Bureau of Land Management
BNA	Bureau of National Affairs
CEQ	Council on Environmental Quality
CERCLA	Comprehensive Environmental Response, Compensation, and Liability Act
CFC	chlorofluorocarbon
CITES	Convention on International Trade in Endangered Species of Wild Fauna and Flora
DEQ	Department of Environmental Quality
EC	European Community (see EEC)
EEC	European Economic Community (see EC)
EIS	environmental impact statement
EPA	Environmental Protection Agency
FAO	Food and Agricultural Organization (United Nations)
FCC	Federal Communications Commission
FDA	Food and Drug Administration
FIFRA	Federal Insecticide, Fungicide, and Rodenticide Act
FLPMA	Federal Land Policy and Management Act
FTC	Federal Trade Commission
FWPCA	Federal Water Pollution Control Act
FWS	Fish and Wildlife Service
GAO	Government Accounting Office
GOO	Get Oil Out
GPO	Government Printing Office

ICC   Interstate Commerce Commission
IWC   International Whaling Commission

MMPA   Marine Mammal Protection Act

NAAQS   National Ambient Air Quality Standards
NCP   National Contingency Plan
NEPA   National Environmental Policy Act
NOAA   National Oceanic and Atmospheric Administration
NPL   National Priority List (Superfund)
NPS   National Park Service

OCS   outer continental shelf
OMB   Office of Management and Budget
OPEC   Organization of Petroleum Exporting Countries
OTA   Office of Technology Assessment

PRP   potentially responsible parties

RCRA   Resource Conservation and Recovery Act
RPA   Forest and Rangeland Renewable Resource Planning Act

SARA   Superfund Amendment and Reauthorization Act
SCRAP   Students Challenging Regulatory Agency Procedures
SIP   state implementation plan
SPM   suspended particulate matter

TMI   Three Mile Island
TSCA   Toxic Substances Control Act
TVA   Tennessee Valley Authority

UNEP   United Nations Environmental Programme
UNESCO   United Nations Educational, Scientific, and Cultural
            Organization
USDA   United States Department of Agriculture
USGS   United States Geological Survey
UST   underground storage tank

GLOSSARY

acid deposition   Droplets of sulfuric acid and nitric acid dissolved in rain, snow, or other forms of precipitation. Formed when sulfur dioxide and nitrogen oxides combine with water vapor.

acid rain   See *acid deposition*.

action forcing   Characteristic of environmental legislation that requires agencies and businesses to take positive action rather than simply to avoid harmful actions.

administrative law judges (ALJs)   Hearing examiners established under the Administrative Procedure Act. They are specialists in their substantive fields and are appointed to conduct administrative hearings. They are protected under the civil service system but lack the extensive constitutional protections enjoyed by judges of Article III courts.

agenda   Issues that have been identified as meriting public attention. The *systemic agenda* consists of all items perceived by the general public as meriting attention and falling within governmental authority. The *institutional agenda* consists of items up for the active consideration of political decision makers.

alienation   The transfer of public property from public ownership into private ownership or private legal control. Also the transfer of private property to another private owner (or to public ownership).

ancient lights   The doctrine that, if a building's windows have existed for at least twenty years, the light going into those windows may not be blocked by a neighboring structure.

Article I court   An administrative court established by the executive branch of the federal government, which is itself established by article I of the Constitution. Examples are Tax Courts and Admiralty Courts.

Article III court   A judicial court established under article III of the Constitution. The Supreme Court of the United States is an article III court.

attention group   Citizens who are concerned about specific issues but are not concerned about public issues in general. This is the first level of the public to which an issue is expanded.

attentive public   The group of citizens that are generally informed and interested in public issues of all sorts. An issue is expanded to this group after reaching the attention group.

beneficent degradation   The economically desirable level of pollution in a body of water.

best practicable environmental option   In British environmental policy, the notion that regulatory authorities should select the option for disposal of pollution that provides the least harm, given present scientific, technical, practical, economic, and geographic factors.

best practicable means   In British environmental policy, the concept that pollution control must employ the most efficient and reasonable technology currently available, subject to scientific, technical, and economic consideration.

biosphere   The notion that the entire planet is ecologically interrelated.

black letter law   The written law found in constitutions, statutes, administrative regulations, executive orders, treaties, and appellate court decisions.

bubble policy   Concept under the Clean Air Act that sets air quality standards for an imaginary enclosed area or "bubble," within which area plants may adjust emission levels as long as the overall air quality within the bubble does not deteriorate. See *emissions offset policy*.

captured agency   An agency that identifies so closely with the interests of the regulated industry that it forgets its responsibilities to society.

cetaceans   Animals belonging to the order Cetacea, which includes fishlike aquatic mammals such as the whale and porpoise.

circumstantial reactors   Initiators who take advantage of unanticipated "trigger events" to create or to magnify issues.

civil law   A legal system in which legal decisions are based on statutes rather than on previous cases.

coming to the nuisance   Building or developing property near a previously existing nuisance.

commons   Property to which a class of individuals has access and from which no one in the class may be excluded; for example, the public grazing lands in medieval English villages.

common law   A legal system relying on custom and on the development of precedent derived from court decisions. Contrast with *civil law*.

competitive regulatory policy   A type of public policy which limits the provision of specific goods and services to a few who are chosen from a group of competitors, the selected companies then being regulated; for example, the allocation of routes to the airline industry prior to deregulation.

Congressional Record   The daily publication of the U.S. Congress which carries the official account of congressional proceedings.

covenant   An agreed restriction on the uses of real property, such as the banning of children from a retirement community.

discretion   The power of administrators to make substantive or procedural decisions they deem advisable as long as they do not act in an arbitrary or capricious manner.

distributive policy   A type of public policy which supports private activities that are beneficial to society as a whole but that would not usually be undertaken by the private sector; for example, grazing subsidies.

do-gooders   In the context of the public policy process, initiators who use events to publicize issues but who gain no personal benefit from the issue.

due process   The constitutional obligation of government to follow existing rules and fair procedures when taking action to deprive any persons of "life, liberty, or property."

due process explosion   A marked increase in the judicial extension of due process protections for entitlements as well as for tangible property, signaled by the Supreme Court's decision in *Goldberg v. Kelly* (1970).

easement   The right to make limited use of another's property, such as a right-of-way.

eminent domain   The right of the sovereign or state to take private property for public purposes. In the United States, the Fifth and Fourteenth amendments to the Constitution provide that citizens are entitled to just compensation when eminent domain is exercised by the national or state governments.

emissions offset policy   Under the Clean Air Act, a policy which allows a new firm to enter an area and to pollute if an established firm will agree to reduce its emissions to match. See *bubble policy*.

endangered species   Any species which is in danger of extinction throughout all or a significant portion of its range, other than an insect species which presents a risk to humans. See *threatened species*.

environmental impact statement   Under the National Environmental Policy Act, any major federal project and its alternatives, including a "no action" alternative, must be evaluated in terms of its potential impact on the natural and human environment.

evaluation   Comparing the desired outcomes of a policy with the actual outcomes. *Formative evaluation* occurs while the policy is being formulated and implemented; it allows midcourse corrections. *Summative evaluation* is used when a program is completed; it measures how closely the goals of a program were achieved.

executive order   A formal presidential mandate or directive having the force of law.

exploiters   In the context of the public policy process, initiators who manufacture issues for their own gain.

federalism   A form of government in which power is shared between the central or national government and the states.

Federal Register   Government publication that prints presidential proclamations, reorganization plans, executive orders, notices of proposed and final rules and regulations, and administrative orders.

groundwater   Water that sinks into the soil, where it may be stored in aquifers.

hearing examiner   See *administrative law judge*.

identification group   The narrowest kind of public, consisting of people with a detailed awareness of specific issues.

initiators   People who use situations to place issues on the public policy agenda.

iron triangle   See *subgovernment*.

judicial review   The power of a court to determine the legality and constitutionality of an action of a government official, agency, or legislative body.

legislative history   The formal record of all legislative hearings, testimonies, debates, and votes preceding the enactment of a statute.

mass public   The general public; the portion of the population that is less active, less interested, and less informed than any smaller group of citizens. The last group to which an issue is expanded.

nonattainment region   Under the Clean Air Act, any area that did not achieve primary ambient air quality standards by 1982. These regions then faced restrictions on new plant construction and on plant expansions until emission standards were met.

non-point-source pollution   Pollution without readily identified egress points, such as agricultural runoff.

nuisance   An action by one property owner that impairs the legal rights of another property owner. A *private nuisance* is an unreasonable interference with the use or enjoyment of another individual's land. A *public nuisance* is an activity that adversely affects the health, morals, safety, welfare, comfort, or convenience of the public in general.

outer continental shelf (OCS)   The submerged and relatively accessible land adjacent to the coastline. The federal government claims jurisdiction from the three-mile state territorial limit to an outer ten-mile limit.

ozone layer   A layer of gaseous ozone in the upper atmosphere that protects living organisms by filtering ultraviolet radiation.

pelagic   Occurring in open oceans or seas rather than inland waters or adjacent to coastal lands.

pinnipedian   Animals belonging to the order Pinnipedia; aquatic mammals including seals, walruses, and similar animals having finlike flippers as organs of locomotion.

point source pollution   Pollution with a readily isolated egress point such as a sewer treatment plant or an oil tanker.

police power   The power of the government to protect public health, safety, and morals. In the American federal system, this power is reserved to the states.

polluter pays   In British environmental policy, the concept that whoever generated the pollution must bear the costs of removing it and remedying its bad effects.

pollution rights   Legal permission to discharge a given amount of pollution. These rights may be transferred.

precedent   A legal judgment enunciated in the resolution of a case that is used as a standard in subsequent, similar cases.

primary air pollutants   Air pollutants that are harmful as soon as they enter the atmosphere, such as carbon monoxide.

procedural due process   The forms and procedures that government must follow when exercising its legitimate functions.

property   Any tangible item to which the owner has an enforceable right of use, or an intangible right, the removal of which requires due process.

protective regulatory policy   A type of public policy that regulates the conditions under which private activities may occur, such as setting emission standards for coal-fired plants.

public-trust doctrine   The common-law concept that the tidelands, the navigable waters, and the wildlife found in them are held by the sovereign in trust for the people.

ratcheting   The practice of administrative regulatory agencies frequently increasing pollution control standards imposed on industries which have already spent resources to comply with earlier standards. This increases compliance costs and frustrates cooperative agencies.

readjustors   Policy initiators who perceive a real imbalance or inequity and strive to correct it.

redistributive policy   A type of public policy that changes the allocation of valued goods and services such as money, property, or rights among different groups; an example is the distribution of welfare.

rule   An agency statement of general or particular applicability and future effect designed to implement, interpret, or prescribe law or policy. *Substantive rules* implement or prescribe law or policy, for example, safety requirements for nuclear power plants. *Procedural rules* describe the organization, procedure, or practice requirements of an agency, for example, defining who may intervene in an agency adjudication. *Interpretive rules* are statements issued by agencies that present the agency's understanding of the meaning of the language in its regulations or the statutes it administers.

rule making   The process of promulgating rules. *Informal rule making* follows section 553 of the Administrative Procedure Act (APA) and requires notice and comment. *Formal rule making* follows sections 556 and 557 of the APA and requires a full administrative hearing. *Hybrid rule making* combines features of both informal and formal rule making; its key requirement is the creation of a formal record.

Sagebrush Rebellion   A movement in the early 1980s by some western states to regain control of the federal lands within their boundaries.

scope of review   The extent to which a court examines questions of law, interprets constitutional and statutory provisions, and determines the meaning or applicability of the terms of an agency action.

secondary air pollutants   Pollutants that are formed from the chemical reaction of several air components, such as *acid deposition*.

snail darter   A species of minnow which was declared endangered, halting the construction of the Tellico Dam.

standing   The legal right to have a case heard, defined in common law as having suffered an actual injury to a legally protected right.

state ownership doctrine   In American wildlife law, the doctrine that the wildlife found within a state's borders is the property of the state rather than of the individual on whose property the wildlife is found. This doctrine had been substantially modified in favor of federal control of wildlife.

subgovernment   A coalition of interest groups, relevant agencies in the executive branch, and the appropriate congressional committee or subcommittee that is concerned with a given policy area. Also known as an *iron triangle*.

substantial evidence   The amount of evidence—more than a mere token but less than a preponderance (which would outweight the evidence presented by opposition)—that an agency must present to a reviewing judge in order to justify its decisions.

substantive due process   The constitutional doctrine that all government action must be fair and reasonable and must fall within a sphere of activity that is a legitimate government concern.

sunk costs   Resource expended on a project prior to its completion.

surface water   Water that does not penetrate the ground or return to the atmosphere, for example, lakes, rivers, streams, ponds, and wetlands.

technology forcing   Legislation that requires businesses to develop new technology in order to meet statutory and regulatory standards on pollution control.

threatened species   Any species which is likely to become an *endangered species* within the foreseeable future throughout all or a significant portion of its range.

trigger event   An unexpected occurrence that provides an opportunity for an issue to be expanded to larger publics.

waste   Acts commmitted upon the land that are harmful to the rights of the owner, such as a tenant cutting down all of the landlord's trees.

zoning   Dividing a community into districts which are then subject to regulation concerning permissible uses and buildings.

CASES

American Cetacean Society v. Baldridge, 604 F. Supp. 1398 (D.C., 1985).

American Textile Manufacturers Institute v. Donovan, 452 U.S. 490 (1981).

Association of Data Processing Service Organizations v. Camp, 397 U.S. 150 (1970).

Bi-Metallic Investment Co. v. State Board of Equalization, 239 U.S. 441 (1915).

Bivens v. Six Unknown, Named Agents of the Federal Bureau of Narcotics, 403 U.S. 388 (1971).

Board of Regents v. Roth, 408 U.S. 564 (1972).

Boomer v. Atlantic Cement Co., 26 N.Y. 2d 219, 309 N.Y.S. 2d 312, 257 N.E. 2d 870 (1970).

Boyce Motor Lines v. United States, 342 U.S. 337 (1952).

Calvert Cliffs Coordinating Committee, Inc. v. United States Atomic Energy Commission, 449 F.2d 1109 (1971).

City of Milwaukee v. State, 193 Wis. 423, 214 N.W. 820 (1927).

Dalehite v. United States, 346 U.S. 15 (1953).

Dooley v. Town Plan and Zoning Commission of Fairfield, 197 A.2d 770 (1964).

Douglas v. Seacoast Products, Inc., 431 U.S. 265 (1977).

Duke Power Co. v. Carolina Environmental Study Group, Inc., 438 U.S. 59 (1978).

Euclid v. Ambler Realty Co., 272 U.S. 365 (1926).

First English Evangelical Lutheran Church of Glendale v. City of Los Angeles, 487 U.S. 1211 (1987).

Flast v. Cohen, 392 U.S. 83 (1968).

Fontainebleau Hotel Corp. v. Forty-Five Twenty-Five, Inc., 114 So. 2d 357 (Fla. App.) (1959).

Foster-Fountain Packing Co. v. Haydel, 278 U.S. 1 (1926).

Geer v. Connecticut, 161 U.S. 519 (1896).

Sierra Club v. Morton, 405 U.S. 727 (1972).

Smith v. Maryland, 59 U.S. (18 How.) 71 (1855).

Spur Industries v. Del Webb Development, 108 Ariz. 178, 494 P.2d 700 (1972).

Tangier Sound Waterman's Association v. Douglas, E.D. Virginia, 541 F. Supp. 1287 (1982).

Tennessee Valley Authority v. Hill, 437 U.S. 153 (1978).

The Abbey Dodge, 223 U.S. 188 (1912).

United States v. Midwest Oil Company, 236 U.S. 459 (1915).

United States v. Students Challenging Regulatory Agency Procedures, 412 U.S. 669 (1973).

STATUTES

Administrative Procedure Act of 1946.
U.S. Code 1982 Title 5, §§ 551 et seq., 701 et seq.

Air Quality Act of 1967.
U.S. Code 1982 Title 42, § 7401 et seq.

Alaska Native Claims Settlement Act of 1971.
U.S. Code 1982 Title 42, § 1601 et seq.

Bald Eagle Protection Act of 1940.
U.S. Code 1982 Title 16, § 668 et seq.

Black Bass Act of 1926.
U.S. Code 1982 Title 16, § 851 et seq.

Civil Rights Act of 1871.
U.S. Code 1982 Title 18, §§ 241 et seq., 372, 2384;
U.S. Code 1982 Title 28, §§ 1343, 1443, 1446;
U.S. Code 1982 Title 42, § 1981 et seq.

Clean Air Act of 1955.
U.S. Code 1982 Title 42, § 7401 et seq.

Clean Air Act Amendment of 1970 (an amendment to the Clean Air Act of 1955).
U.S. Code 1982 Title 42, § 7403 et seq.

Clean Air Act Amendment of 1990 (an amendment to the Clean Air Act of 1955).
November 15, 1990, P.L. 101-549, 104 Stat. 2399.

Clean Water Act of 1977.
U.S. Code 1982 Title 33, § 1251 et seq.

Coastal Zone Management Act of 1972.
U.S. Code 1982 Title 16, § 1451 et seq.

Comprehensive Environmental Response, Compensation, and Liability Act of 1980 (Superfund).
U.S. Code 1982 Title 26, § 4611 et seq.
U.S. Code 1982 Title 42, § 9601 et seq.

Deepwater Port Act of 1974.
U.S. Code 1982 Title 33, § 1501 et seq.

Desert Land Act of 1877 (an amendment to the Homestead Act of 1862).

Duck Stamp Act of 1934, *see* **Migratory Bird Hunting Stamp Act.**

Endangered Species Act of 1973.
U.S. Code 1982 Title 16, § 1531 et seq.

Endangered Species Conservation Act of 1969.
U.S. Code 1982 Title 16, § 668aa et seq.

Endangered Species Preservation Act of 1966.
U.S. Code 1982 Title 16, § 668aa et seq.

Energy Policy and Conservation Act of 1975.
U.S. Code 1982 Title 42, § 6201 et seq.

Federal Environmental Pesticide Control Act of 1972.
U.S. Code 1982 Title 7, § 136 et seq.

Federal Insecticide, Fungicide, and Rodenticide Act of 1947.
U.S. Code 1982 Title 7, § 136 et seq.

Federal Land Policy and Management Act of 1976.
U.S. Code 1988 Title 43, § 1701 et seq.

Federal Property and Administrative Services Act of 1949.
U.S., June 30, 1949, c. 288, 63 Stat. 377.

Federal Register Act of 1935.
U.S. Code 1982 Title 44, § 1501 et seq.

Federal Water Pollution Control Act of 1972.
U.S. Code 1982 Title 33, § 1251 et seq.

Fish and Wildlife Coordination Act of 1934.
U.S. Code 1982 Title 16, § 661 et seq.

Fishermen's Protective Act of 1967.
U.S. Code 1982 Title 22, § 1971 et seq.

Fishery Conservation and Management Act of 1976.
U.S. Code 1982 Title 16, §§ 971, 1362, 1801, 1802, 1811 to 1813,
1821 to 1825, 1851 to 1861, 1881;
U.S. Code 1982 Title 22, §§ 1972, 1973.

Forest and Rangeland Renewable Resources Planning Act of 1974.
U.S. Code 1982 Title 16, § 1600 et seq.

Forest Management Act of 1897 (*see* National Forest Management Act of
1976 which supersedes this act).

Forest Management Act of 1976 (*see* National Forest Management Act of
1976).

Forest Reserve Act of 1891.
U.S. Code 1982 Title 16, § 471a et seq.

**Freedom of Information Act of 1966 (an amendment to the Administrative
Procedure Act of 1946).**
U.S. Code 1982 Title 5, § 552.

**Government in the Sunshine Act of 1976 (an amendment to the
Administrative Procedure Act of 1946).**
U.S. Code 1982 Title 5, § 552b.

Homestead Act of 1862.
U.S. Code 1982 Title 43, §§ 161 et seq., 890 to 892.
Repealed in 1976.

Insecticide Act of 1910.
U.S. Code 1982 Title 7, § 136 et seq.

Knutson-Vandenburg Act of 1930.
U.S. Code 1988 Title 16, §§ 576 to 576b.

Lacey Act of 1900.
U.S. Code 1982 Title 16, § 701.

Lacey Act Amendments of 1981.
U.S. Code 1982 Title 16, §§ 1540, 3371 et seq.;
U.S. Code 1982 Title 18, § 42.

Land and Water Conservation Act of 1964.
U.S. Code 1982 Title 16, §§ 460d, 4601-4 et seq.

Lea Act of 1948.
U.S. Code 1982 Title 16, § 695 et seq.

Marine Mammal Protection Act of 1972.
U.S. Code 1982 Title 16, § 1361 et seq.

Marine Protection, Research, and Sanctuaries Act of 1972.
U.S. Code 1982 Title 33, § 1401 et seq.

Migratory Bird Act of 1913.
Mar. 4, 1913, c. 145, 37 Stat. 828.
Repealed in 1918.

Migratory Bird Conservation Act of 1929.
U.S. Code 1982 Title 16, § 715 et seq.

Migratory Bird Hunting Stamp Act of 1934 (the Duck Stamp Act).
U.S. Code 1982 Title 16, §§ 718 to 718h.

Migratory Bird Treaty Act of 1918.
U.S. Code 1982 Title 16, §§ 703 to 711;
U.S. Code 1982 Title 18, § 43.

Multiple-Use Sustained-Yield Act of 1960.
U.S. Code 1982 Title 16, § 528 et seq.

National Environmental Policy Act of 1969.
U.S. Code 1982 Title 42, § 4321 et seq.

National Forest Management Act of 1976.
U.S. Code 1982 Title 16, § 1600 et seq.

National Park Service Organic Act of 1916.
U.S. Code 1988 Title 16, § 1 et seq.

National Wildlife Refuge System Administration Act of 1966.
U.S. Code 1982 Title 16, §§ 668dd, 668ee.

Noise Control Act of 1972.
U.S. Code 1982 Title 42, § 4901 et seq.
U.S. Code 1982 Title 49, Appendix, § 1431.

Ocean Dumping Act of 1972.
U.S. Code 1982 Title 33, § 1401 et seq.

Outer Continental Oil Shelf Lands Act of 1953.
U.S. Code 1982 Title 43, § 1331 et seq.

Park, Parkway and Recreation Area Study Act of 1936.
June 23, 1936, c. 735, 49 Stat. 1894.

Price-Anderson Act of 1957.
U.S. Code 1982 Title 42, § 2210.

Privacy Act of 1974 (an amendment to the Administrative Procedure Act of 1946).
U.S. Code 1982 Title 5, § 552a.

Resource Conservation and Recovery Act of 1976.
U.S. Code 1982 Title 42, § 6901 et seq.

Resource Recovery Act of 1970.
U.S. Code 1970 Title 42, § 3251 et seq.

River and Harbor Act of 1899.
U.S. Code 1982 Title 16, §§ 460d, 492;
U.S. Code 1982 Title 22, § 275a;
U.S. Code 1976 Title 31, § 680;
U.S. Code 1982 Title 33;
U.S. Code 1982 Title 48, § 1399.

Safe Drinking Water Act of 1974.
U.S. Code 1982 Title 42, §§ 300f to 300j-9.

Sikes Act of 1960.
U.S. Code 1982 Title 16, § 670a et seq.

Stock-Raising Homestead Act of 1916.
U.S. Code 1982 Title 43, § 291 et seq.

Submerged Lands Act of 1953.
U.S. Code 1982 Title 43, § 1301 et seq.

Superfund, see Comprehensive Environmental Response, Compensation, and Liability Act of 1980.

Superfund Amendment and Reauthorization Act of 1986.
Oct. 17, 1986, P.L. 99-499, 100 Stat. 1613.

Surplus Grain for Wildlife Act of 1961.
Aug. 17, 1961, P.L. 87-152, 75 Stat. 389.
(U.S. Code citation not given in U.S. Statutes at Large.)

Swamp Land Acts of 1849, 1850, and 1860.
U.S. Code 1982 Title 43, § 981 et seq.

Tariff Act of 1930.
U.S. Code 1958 Title 19, § 1001 et seq.

Taylor Act of 1934.
U.S. Code 1982 Title 43, § 315 et seq.

Timber and Stone Act of 1878 (an amendment to the Homestead Act of 1862).

Timber Culture Act of 1873 (an amendment to the Homestead Act of 1862).

Toxic Substances Control Act of 1976.
U.S. Code 1982 Title 15, § 2601 et seq.

Water Bank Act of 1970.
U.S. Code 1982 Title 16, § 1301 et seq.

Waterfowl Depredations Act of 1956.
July 3, 1956, P.L. 654, c. 512, 70 Stat. 492.
(U.S. Code citation not given in U.S. Statutes at Large.)

Weeks Act of 1911.
U.S. Code 1982 Title 16, §§ 480, 500, 515 to 519, 521, 552, 563.

Wetlands Act of 1961.
U.S. Code 1982 Title 16, § 715k-3 et seq.

Wilderness Act of 1964.
U.S. Code 1982 Title 16, § 1131 et seq.

Wild Free-Roaming Horses and Burros Act of 1971.
U.S. Code 1982 Title 16, § 1331.

BIBLIOGRAPHY

Althaus, Helen. *Public Trust Rights*. Washington, D.C.: GPO, 1978.

Arrandale, Tom. *The Battle for Natural Resources*. Washington, D.C.: Congressional Quarterly, 1983.

Ashby, Eric, and Mary Anderson. *Politics of Clean Air*. Oxford: Clarendon Press, 1981.

Attorney General's Committee. *Administrative Procedure in Government Agencies*. Preface by Charles K. Woltz. Charlottesville: University Press of Virginia, 1968.

Ault, W. O. *Open-Field Farming in Medieval England*. London: Allen and Unwin, 1972.

Battle, Jackson. *Environmental Law*. Vols. 1 and 2. Cincinnati: Anderson Publishing Co., 1986.

Bean, Michael J. *The Evolution of National Wildlife Law*. New York: Praeger, 1983.

Benedick, Richard Elliot. "Protecting the Ozone Layer: New Directions in Diplomacy." In *Preserving the Global Environment: The Challenge of Shared Leadership*, edited by Jessica Tuchman Mathews. New York: Norton, 1991.

Bolotin, Fredric. *International Public Policy Sourcebook*. vol. 2, *Education and Environment*. New York: Greenwood Press, 1989.

British Information Services. "The London Conference on Substances That Deplete the Ozone Layer." New York: British Consulate General, June 28, 1990.

Buck, Susan J. "Cultural Theory and Management of Common Property Resources." *Human Ecology* 17 (March 1989): pp. 101–16.

———. "Environmental Policy in the United Kingdom." In *International Public Policy Sourcebook*, vol. 2, *Education and Environment*, edited by Fredric Bolotin. New York: Greenwood Press, 1989.

Buck, Susan J., and Edward Hathaway. "Designating State Natural Resource Trustees Under SARA." In *Regulatory Federalism, Natural Resources and Environmental Management*, edited by Michael Hamilton, pp. 83–94. Washington, D.C.: ASPA, 1990.

Bureau of National Affairs. *U.S. Environmental Laws, 1988 Edition*. Washington, D.C.: Bureau of National Affairs, 1988.

Caldwell, Lynton. *International Environmental Policy.* Durham, N.C.: Duke University Press, 1984.

———. "International Environmental Politics: America's Response to Global Imperatives." In *Environmental Policies in the 1980s: Reagan's New Agenda,* edited by Norman Vig and Michael Kraft. Washington, D.C.: Congressional Quarterly, 1984.

Central Directorate of Environmental Protection. *Pollution Control in England.* London: Department of the Environment, 1984.

Clawson, Marion. *The Federal Lands Revisited.* Baltimore: Johns Hopkins University Press for Resources for the Future, 1983.

Cobb, Roger, and Charles Elder. *Participation in American Politics.* Boston: Allyn and Bacon, 1972.

Cohen, Steven. "Defusing the Toxic Time Bomb: Federal Hazardous Waste Programs." In *Environmental Policies in the 1980s: Reagan's New Agenda,* edited by Norman Vig and Michael Kraft. Washington, D.C.: Congressional Quarterly, 1984.

Cooper, Phillip. *Public Law and Public Administration.* 2nd ed. Englewood Cliffs, N.J.: Prentice-Hall, 1988.

Cox, Susan Jane Buck. "No Tragedy on the Commons." *Environmental Ethics* 7 (Spring 1985): pp. 49–61.

Dales, J. H. *Pollution, property, & prices: An Essay in Policy-making and Economics.* Toronto: University of Toronto Press, 1968.

Dodd, W. F. "Administrative Agencies as Legislator and Judges." *American Bar Association Journal* 25 (November 1939): p. 976.

Dorst, Jean. *Before Nature Dies.* Translated by Constance D. Sherman. Preface by Prince Bernard. Boston: Houghton Mifflin, 1970.

Dunning, Harrison, ed. *The Public Trust Doctrine in Natural Resources Law and Management.* Davis: University of California, 1981.

Edberg, Rolf. *On the Shred of a Cloud.* Translated by Sven jAham. Montgomery: University of Alabama Press, 1969.

Enloe, Cynthia. *Politics of Pollution in a Comparative Perspective.* New York: David McKay, 1975.

Environmental Protection Agency. *Environmental Progress and Challenges: An EPA Perspective.* CPM-222. Washington, D.C.: Office of Management Systems and Evaluation, 1984.

Environmental Protection Agency, PBS Adult Learning Satellite Service, Public Television Outreach Alliance, and the University of North

Carolina at Greensboro. *Legal Winds of Change: Business and the New Clean Air Act.* Videoconference resource materials, presented at the University of North Carolina at Greensboro, November 28, 1990.

Findley, Roger and Daniel Farber. *Environmental Law.* St. Paul: West, 1983.

Foresta, Ronald A. *America's National Parks and Their Keepers.* Baltimore: Johns Hopkins University Press for Resources for the Future, 1984.

Gonner, E. C. K. *Common Land and Inclosure.* 2nd ed. London: Cass, 1966.

Hamilton, Michael, ed. *Regulatory Federalism, Natural Resources and Environmental Management.* Washington, D.C.: ASPA, 1990.

Hartwick, John, and Nancy Olewiler. *The Economics of Natural Resource Use.* New York: Harper and Row, 1986.

Heffron, Florence, and Neil McFeeley. *The Administrative Regulatory Process.* New York: Longman, 1983.

Heinzerling, Lisa. "Actionable Inaction: Section 1983 Liability for Failure to Act." *University of Chicago Law Review* 53 (Summer 1986): pp. 1047-73.

Hook, Janet. "Legislative Summary: 101st Congress Leaves Behind Plenty Laws, Criticism." *Congressional Quarterly Weekly Report* 48 (November 3, 1990): pp. 3683-710.

Hunter, David B. "An Ecological Perspective on Property: A Call for Judicial Protection of the Public's Interest in Environmentally Critical Resources." *Harvard Environmental Law Review* 12 (1988): pp. 311-83.

Ise, John. *Our National Park Policy.* Baltimore: Johns Hopkins University Press, 1961.

Keefe, William, Henry Abraham, William Flanigan, Charles O. Jones, Morris Ogul, and John Spanier. *American Democracy: Institutions, Politics, and Policies.* Homewood, Ill.: Dorsey Press, 1983.

Knize, Perri. "Chainsaw Environmentalism." *Backpacker* (November 1987): pp. 55-59.

Koehler, James, and Scott Hajost. "1989: Advent of a New Era for EPA's International Activities." *Colorado Journal of International Environmental Law and Policy* 1 (Summer 1990): pp. 181-87.

Lash, Jonathan, Katherine Gillman, and David Sheridan. *A Season of Spoils: The Reagan Administration's Attack on the Environment.* New York: Pantheon, 1984.

Lockhart, William B., Yale Kamisar, and Jesse Choper. *The American Constitution: Cases–Comments–Questions*. St. Paul: West, 1970.

Mazmanian, Daniel, and Paul Sabatier. *Implementation and Public Policy*. Glenview, Ill.: Scott, Foresman, 1983.

Mead, Walter J., Asbjorn Moseidjord, Dennis Muraoka, and Philip Sorensen. *Offshore Lands: Oil and Gas Leasing and Conservation on the Outer Continental Shelf*. San Francisco: Pacific Institute for Public Policy Research, 1985.

Meier, Kenneth J. *Regulation: Politics, Bureaucracy, and Economics*. New York: St. Martin's Press, 1985.

Miller, G. Tyler, Jr. *Living in the Environment*. 5th ed. Belmont, Calif.: Wadsworth, 1988.

Naff, John. "If Justice Douglas has his way—." (Poem.) *Journal of the American Bar Association* 58 (1972): p. 820. Quoted in *Earth and Other Ethics*, by Christopher Stone, p. 5. New York: Harper and Row, 1987.

Nangle, Orval. "Stratospheric Ozone: United States Regulation of Chlorofluorocarbons." *Environmental Affairs* 16 (1989): pp. 531–80.

Nash, Roderick. *American Environmentalism: Readings in Conservation History*. 3rd ed. New York: McGraw-Hill, 1990.

National Audubon Society. *Audubon Wildlife Report*. New York: National Audubon Society, 1985, 1986, and 1987.

National Standards Association. *National Directory of State Agencies*. Bethesda, Md.: National Standards Association, 1987.

O'Riordan, Timothy. "Culture and the Environment in Britain." *Environmental Management* 9 (1985): pp. 113–20.

Peters, Guy. *American Public Policy: Promise and Performance*. 2nd ed. Chatham, N.J.: Chatham House Publishers, 1986.

Pinchot, Gifford. *The Fight for Conservation*. Garden City, N.Y.: Harcourt, Brace, 1919.

Pytte, Alyson. "Superfund Stowaway." *Congressional Quarterly Weekly Report* 48 (November 3, 1990): p. 3717.

ReVelle, Penelope, and Charles ReVelle. *The Environment: Issues and Choices for Society*. Boston: Jones and Bartlett Publishers, 1988.

Ripley, Randall, and Grace Franklin. *Congress, the Bureaucracy, and Public Policy*. Homewood, Ill.: Dorsey Press, 1984.

——. *Policy Implementation and Bureaucracy.* 2nd ed. Chicago: Dorsey Press, 1986.

Rodgers, William H., Jr. *Handbook on Environmental Law.* St. Paul: West, 1977.

Rosenbaum, Walter. *Energy, Politics, and Public Policy.* 2nd ed. Washington, D.C.: Congressional Quarterly, 1985.

——. *Environmental Politics and Policy.* Washington, D.C.: Congressional Quarterly, 1987.

Sax, Joseph. "Public Trust Doctrine in Natural Resource Law: Effective Judicial Intervention." *Michigan Law Review* 68 (January 1970): p. 490.

——. "Introductory Perspectives." In *The Public Trust Doctrine in Natural Resources Law and Management,* edited by Harrison Dunning. Davis: University of California, 1981.

Schoenbaum, Thomas. *Environmental Policy Law.* Mineola, N.Y.: Foundation Press, 1985.

Smythe, Marianne K. "Environmental Law: Expanding the Definition of Public Trust Uses." *North Carolina Law Review* 51 (1972): pp. 316–25.

Squillace, Mark. *Environmental Law.* Vol. 3. Cincinnati, Ohio: Anderson Publishing Co., 1988.

Stone, Christopher. *Earth and Other Ethics.* New York: Harper and Row, 1987.

Thompson, Michael. "The Cultural Construction of Nature and the Natural Destruction of Culture." Working paper for the International Institute for Applied Systems Analysis, Laxenberg, Austria, 1984.

Trout, James. "A Land Manager's Commentary on the Public Trust Doctrine." In *The Public Trust Doctrine in Natural Resources Law and Management,* edited by Harrison Dunning. Davis: University of California, 1981.

United States Environmental Protection Agency. *Environmental Monitoring at Love Canal.* Washington, D.C.: USEPA, 1982.

Vig, Norman, and Michael Kraft, eds. *Environmental Policy in the 1980s: Reagan's New Agenda.* Washington, D.C.: Congressional Quarterly, 1984.

——. *Environmental Policy in the 1990s.* Washington, D.C.: Congressional Quarterly, 1990.

Vogel, David. "Environmental Policy in Europe and Japan." In *Environmental Policies in the 1980s: Reagan's New Agenda,* edited by Norman Vig and Michael Kraft. Washington, D.C.: Congressional Quarterly, 1984.

———. *National Styles of Regulation: Environmental Policy in Great Britain and the United States.* Ithaca, N.Y.: Cornell University Press, 1986.

Walker, Jack. "Setting the Agenda in the U.S. Senate." *British Journal of Political Science* 7 (October 1977): pp. 423-45.

Wilkinson, Charles. "Public Trust Doctrine in Public Land Law." In *The Public Trust Doctrine in Natural Resources Law and Management,* edited by Harrison Dunning. Davis: University of California, 1981.

Wolf, Edward. "Avoiding a Mass Extinction of Species." In *State of the World 1988,* project directed by Lester Brown, New York: Norton, 1988, pp. 101-17.

Wright, Robert R., and Susan Webber Wright. *Land Use in a Nutshell.* St. Paul: West, 1985.

ABOUT THE AUTHOR

Susan Buck is Assistant Professor of Political Science at the University of North Carolina at Greensboro. Before earning her Ph.D. in public administration at Virginia Tech, she supervised the Wetlands Research Laboratory at the Virginia Institute of Marine Science. She has contributed several articles and book chapters on environmental policy and law. She is currently working on a book on the legal history of the global commons. Dr. Buck lives in Greensboro, North Carolina.

INDEX

ABA (American Bar Association), 81
The Abbey Dodge, 78
Acid deposition (acid rain), 96-97, 144-145
Acquisition, 127
Adjudication, 83-84, 89-91
Administrative hearing, 60
Administrative officials, liability of, 93-94
Administrative Procedure Act of 1946, 61, 80-83
    administrative adjudication, 89-91
    definition of terms, 83
    fair information practices, 83
    Freedom of Information Act of 1966 amendment, 83
    judicial review, 91-93
    Privacy Act of 1974 amendment, 83
    rule making, 7, 42, 83-89
Adversarial hearing, 69, 123
Agendas, public
    institutional, 35
    reasons for, 34-35
    systemic, 35
Airlines companies, deregulation of, 30
Air pollution control, 94-98
    acid deposition, 96-97, 144-145
    economic approaches, 101-103
    in Great Britain, 109-112
    transboundary air issues, 143-147
Air Quality Act of 1967, 104
Air toxics, 96-97
Alaska Native Claims Settlement Act of 1971, 24
Alienation, 75
Alkali Act of 1863 (Great Britain), 110
Alkali Inspectorate, 109
American Bar Association (ABA), 81
American Textile Manufacturers v. Donovan, 7
"Ancient Lights" doctrine, 57, 59
Antarctica, controlling development in, 147-149
Antarctic Treaty, 148
APA. *See* Administrative Procedure Act of 1946
Arizona Department of Environmental Quality, 90-91

Association of Data Processing Service Organizations v. Camp (1970), 59
Attention groups, 36
Attentive public, 36

Bakewell, Robert, 65
Balancing of hardships doctrine (balancing of equities), 63
Bald Eagle Protection Act of 1940, 115
Bargaining strategies, for policy formulation, 40-41
BAT (best available technology), 106
Best available technology (BAT), 106
Best practicable environmental option concept, 111
Best practicable means concept, 111
Biosphere protection, 141-143
Bitter Lake National Wildlife Refuge (New Mexico), 132
Bivens tort, 93
Bivens v. Six Unknown, Named Agents of the Federal Bureau of Narcotics, 93
Black, Hugo, 10
Black Bass Act of 1926, 116-117
BLM. *See* Bureau of Land Management
Board of Regents v. Roth (1972), 89
Boomer v. Atlantic Cement Co., 63
Bork, Robert, 85
Boyce Motor Lines v. United States, 53-55
Briefing a case, 55-57
Britain's Clean Air Act of 1956, 109
Broadcasting companies, 30
Bubble policy, 102
Bureaucracy, policy formulation and, 38
Bureaucratic resources, 43-45
Bureau of Biological Survey, 114
Bureau of Land Management (BLM), 6, 11, 113
    discretionary powers of, 131
    National Wildlife Refuge System and, 118
    oil and gas leasing and, 33, 133-134
    protection of wildlife under multiple-land use concept, 119-120

United Nations Educational, Scientific,
   and Cultural Organization
   (UNESCO), 142
United Nations Environment Programme
   (UNEP), 24, 142-143
United States Geological Survey (USGS),
   33, 121
United States v. Midwest Oil Company (1915),
   128
*United States v. Students Challenging
   Regulatory Agency Procedures* (1973),
   60
Urban renewal, 32

Virginia, 11, 13-15, 21

Walter-Logan Bill, 81
Waste, 66
Water Bank Act of 1980, 118
Watergate investigation, 85
Water pollutants, types of, 99
Water pollution control, 98-100
   economic approaches, 101-103
   in Great Britain, 109-112
Water Pollution Control Act of 1972, 99
Water systems, 90-91
Waterworks Clauses Act of 1847 and 1863
   (Great Britain), 109
Watt, James, 25, 130, 133
Wetlands, 72-73, 118-119
Wetlands Act of 1961, 118
Whale taking, regulation of, 135-140
White, Justice Edward, 78
Wilderness Act of 1964, 18, 120, 130, 132
Wild Free-Roaming Horses and Burros Act
   of 1971, 115-116
Wildlife management, 113
   conservation of endangered species,
      124-125
   federal regulation and, 78-79
   habitat, acquisition and management
      of, 117-121
   protection of marine mammals,
      122-123
   regulation of commerce in wildlife,
      116-117
   regulation of taking of wildlife, 114-116
   state ownership and, 77-78

Wirth, Conrad, 129

Yates Petroleum Corporation, 132-134

Zoning, 70-71

ALSO AVAILABLE FROM ISLAND PRESS

Ancient Forests of the Pacific Northwest
By Elliott A. Norse

Balancing on the Brink of Extinction: The Endangered Species Act and Lessons for the Future
Edited by Kathryn A. Kohm

Better Trout Habitat: A Guide to Stream Restoration and Management
By Christopher J. Hunter

Beyond 40 Percent: Record-Setting Recycling and Composting Programs
The Institute for Local Self-Reliance

The Challenge of Global Warming
Edited by Dean Edwin Abrahamson

Coastal Alert: Ecosystems, Energy, and Offshore Oil Drilling
By Dwight Holing

The Complete Guide to Environmental Careers
The CEIP Fund

Economics of Protected Areas
By John A. Dixon and Paul B. Sherman

Environmental Agenda for the Future
Edited by Robert Cahn

Environmental Disputes: Community Involvement in Conflict Resolution
By James E. Crowfoot and Julia M. Wondolleck

Forests and Forestry in China: Changing Patterns of Resource Development
By S.D. Richardson

The Global Citizen
By Donella Meadows

Hazardous Waste from Small Quantity Generators
By Seymour I. Schwartz and Wendy B. Pratt

Holistic Resource Management Workbook
By Allan Savory

In Praise of Nature
Edited and with essays by Stephanie Mills

The Living Ocean: Understanding and Protecting Marine Biodiversity
By Boyce Thorne-Miller and John G. Catena

Natural Resources for the 21st Century
Edited by R. Neil Sampson and Dwight Hair

The New York Environment Book
By Eric A. Goldstein and Mark A. Izeman

Overtapped Oasis: Reform or Revolution for Western Water
By Marc Reisner and Sarah Bates

Permaculture: A Practical Guide for a Sustainable Future
By Bill Mollison

Plastics: America's Packaging Dilemma
By Nancy Wolf and Ellen Feldman

The Poisoned Well: New Strategies for Groundwater Protection
Edited by Eric Jorgensen

Race to Save the Tropics: Ecology and Economics for a Sustainable Future
Edited by Robert Goodland

Recycling and Incineration: Evaluating the Choices
By Richard A. Denison and John Ruston

Reforming the Forest Service
By Randal O'Toole

The Rising Tide: Global Warming and World Sea Levels
By Lynne T. Edgerton

Saving the Tropical Forests
By Judith Gradwohl and Russell Greenberg

Trees, Why Do You Wait?: America's Changing Rural Culture
By Richard Critchfield

War on Waste: Can America Win Its Battle With Garbage?
By Louis Blumberg and Robert Gottlieb

Western Water Made Simple
From High Country News

Wetland Creation and Restoration: The Status of the Science
Edited by Jon A. Kusler and Mary E. Kentula

Wildlife and Habitats in Managed Landscapes
Edited by Jon E. Rodiek and Eric G. Bolen

*For a complete catalog of Island Press publications, please write:
Island Press, Box 7, Covelo, CA 95428, or call: 1-800-828-1302*